To our husbands, families, co-contributors, friends and colleagues for their support and tolerance

Organizational
STRESS

Jane Cranwell-Ward
and Alyssa Abbey

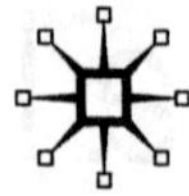

First published 2005 by
PALGRAVE MACMILLAN
Houndmills, Basingstoke, Hampshire RG21 6XS and
175 Fifth Avenue, New York, N.Y. 10010
Companies and representatives throughout the world

PALGRAVE MACMILLAN is the global academic imprint of the Palgrave Macmillan division of St. Martin's Press, LLC and of Palgrave Macmillan Ltd. Macmillan® is a registered trademark in the United States, United Kingdom and other countries. Palgrave is a registered trademark in the European Union and other countries.

ISBN-13: 978 1–4039–4501–3
ISBN-10: 1–4039–4501–2

This book is printed on paper suitable for recycling and made from fully managed and sustained forest sources.

A catalogue record for this book is available from the British Library.

A catalog record for this book is available from the Library of Congress.

10 9 8 7 6 5 4 3 2 1
14 13 12 11 10 09 08 07 06 05

Printed and bound in Great Britain by
Creative Print & Design (Wales), Ebbw Vale

Contents

List of Figures

Foreword
Constant Change and the Disposable Workforce

The old adage that "change is here to stay" epitomizes the workplace over the past two decades. In the developed world, the 1980s were described as the decade of the "enterprise culture," with people working longer and harder to achieve individual success and material rewards. We had globalization, privatization, process reengineering, mergers/acquisitions/joint ventures, strategic alliances, and the like transforming UK plc into a hot-house, free-market environment. In the short term, this entrepreneurial period improved economic competitiveness in the countries that embraced it. But as the strains began to appear, the concepts of stress, burnout, downshifting, and work–life balance became part of our modern business vocabulary. Then we had the 1990s, where a major restructuring of the workplace took center stage, which would have significant consequences for the health and well-being of people at work. This took the form of substantial outsourcing, delayering, downsizing, and the like. Now many organizations are smaller, with fewer people doing more and feeling much less secure. New technology has added the burden of information overload as well as accelerating the pace of work and immediacy of expectations regarding the delivery of work. All this has continued into the new millennium, but with the added undermining of the psychological contract between employee and employer. Jobs are no longer for life or secure, and increasingly people are being perceived as part of a "disposable workforce" but expected to be committed and deliver all their energies to the bottom line of the enterprise without any commitment from the organization itself. These developments have led to individuals feeling more pressure, with less support and more vulnerable to the whims of managers, the organization, and the marketplace. Organizational stress is now high on the agenda of senior and top managers because of the increasing sickness absence days, premature retirement due to stress, litigation, and lack of added value to products and services due to excessive pressure. This book comes at a timely moment during this process, and should be welcomed by HR professionals and senior managers in their efforts to cope with the pressures on employees during these changing times. It is up to HR managers to explore the causes and possible interventions that may help them deal with "their" people problems today and in the next few years – this book will go a long way in helping them.

Professor Cary L. Cooper, CBE
Professor of Organizational Psychology and Health
Lancaster University Management School

Acknowledgements

The authors would like to thank the following:

The numerous organizations that contributed to shaping the thinking of the authors across a broad context and provided best practice examples, including BT, BUPA Wellness, London Borough of Havering, Microsoft, West Dorset Health Authority and Xerox.

The Henley Stress Best Practice Group:
Mike Wagland, BT; Tony Urwin, BUPA Psychological Services; Su Alexander, Marks & Spencer; Andrea Knight, Microsoft; and Carol Cook and Vicky Smith, Xerox for their participation in the group and their contribution to the book.

The Henley Stress Special Interest Group:
Guillermo Casado, Christophe Desplace, Janette Durbin, John Francis, Clare Harvey, Catherine Keeling, Alex Kotsos, John Metherell, Nicola Partridge, Janet Peel, Chris Pond, Robin Roy, Katie Sherlock and Sheila Stork for their active debate and discussion, and for allowing us to use the material generated in the book.

Geoffrey Bignell of Just Employment Solicitors for his sharp attention to legal detail.

Dr. Jenny Leeser of BUPA Wellness and Tony Urwin of BUPA Psychological Services for their valuable advice and professional views.

Sue Gover for her tireless effort, encouragement, and support, and her constant vigilance and attention to detail. The authors were delighted that she agreed to be part of the team.

John Metherell and Nicola Partridge for their contribution to the research and writing of the book and their support throughout the project.

June Sebley, Tereena Hartin and Melanie Thomas of Henley Management College for their help and support with running the Best Practice and Special Interest Groups.

Personnel Today for giving permission to include adapted or paraphrased material from both the magazine and online.

Every effort has been made to trace all the copyright holders but if any have been inadvertently overlooked, the publishers will be pleased to make the necessary arrangements at the first opportunity.

PART I

Overview of the Book and Business Context

1 Overview of the Book

Introduction

This book has been written to share the experience of the two authors who both consult with organizations and managers on the topics of stress, health, vitality management, and well-being at work. Both believe passionately that, with the right guidance and adequate attention, organizations and managers can greatly enhance the well-being of staff and keep stress at acceptable levels. Prevention of excessive stress is much better than helping people to cope once they are already suffering.

The authors are aware that whilst people understand the importance of managing stress in organizations, many still fail to take steps to deal with it. This is partly because people lack the knowledge, skills, and confidence to handle stress. A few still think that stress is a sign of weakness and the macho cultures within organizations prevent appropriate policies and procedures from being implemented.

Many see stress as negative and something that should be avoided at all costs. The authors feel much can be learnt from sportspeople who know the value of channeling energy in a positive way to achieve peak performance. Those able to adopt a positive approach to stress thrive under pressure, whilst others suffer the negative effects that can become life threatening if ignored.

How to Use the Book

The book has been written to enable different readers to use the knowledge and lessons learnt, drawing on:

- The expertise of the practitioners attending the Stress Best Practice and Stress Special Interest Groups at Henley Management College
- Consultation with a range of organizations
- Extensive internet research and reading appropriate journals and books
- The experience of authors running workshops and talking with managers
- Discussions with a range of experts
- First-hand experience!

It is not expected that readers will read the book from cover to cover. Instead the chapters are stand-alone and readers can focus on those that are most relevant for them. The table at the end of this chapter has been designed to help the reader to select the sections that will be most relevant for them. Different parts of the book have been written with different readers in mind. The summaries at the end of each chapter will also give the reader an overview of that chapter and the important lessons for that topic area.

The book is divided into six parts and the topics covered in each are now discussed.

PART I – OVERVIEW OF THE BOOK AND BUSINESS CONTEXT

All readers should read this first part of the book. It has been written to position stress within a broader business framework. This chapter provides an overview of the book, and will help to direct the readers to the most relevant parts of the book with the help of the table. Chapter 2 will help readers to understand the changes taking place in business and organizations and why the management of stress is moving up the agenda alongside the overall well-being of employees. It will be helpful for those required to make a decision on whether to invest in stress management initiatives within their own organizations.

PART II – WHAT IS STRESS? BACKGROUND AND IMPORTANCE

The most important first step for all readers is to understand the nature of stress. It has become an umbrella term meaning different things for different people and is a complex concept. Chapter 3 will help everyone be much clearer about the elements of stress, including why people react differently to similar situations and the nature of those reactions. It will also help readers to understand the difference between stress and pressure, two words that are often used interchangeably.

Human resource (HR) advisers and health and safety experts who may be required to take responsibility for stress risk assessment will find this chapter will provide a useful starting point for later parts of the book. Occupational health experts are likely to be familiar with the concept and will understand the approach taken by the authors having read this chapter. Managers will find dealing with the stress of others, and their own stress, easier, having reached a greater understanding of stress.

Chapter 4 is written for all readers to make them realize that they cannot ignore the stress issue. It will be particularly useful for those having to decide to invest time and money in stress initiatives and will help all readers to appreciate the business gains that can be achieved and the seriousness of the situation if stress is ignored.

PART III – STRESS: AN ORGANIZATIONAL PERSPECTIVE

Part III provides the essential building blocks for those wishing to manage stress. It is written from an organizational perspective and takes the view that understanding the sources of stress is the best place to start in any stress initiative. Readers are alerted to those jobs that expose people to higher levels of pressure and gives advice on steps that can be taken to reduce the risks of stress for people in those jobs. Chapter 8 draws heavily on the advice of the Health and Safety Executive (HSE) in the UK, helping the readers to assess stress levels within their own organizations. The following chapters address the questions of what can be done to manage the stress, how to meet the legal requirements, and how to develop a stress policy. Towards the end of Part III, chapters are devoted to discussing the positive nature of stress and ways to create a culture and climate to develop a resilient workforce.

HR, health and safety, and occupational health specialists will benefit from reading Part III. It will also be helpful for consultants and trainers. Organizational leaders and line managers should skim through this part as they will benefit from understanding what is involved in effectively managing stress from an organizational perspective.

PART IV – MANAGING THE STRESS OF OTHERS

The purpose of Part IV is to help line managers to increase their confidence to manage stress. Firstly, it will make clear their legal responsibility and moral obligation to take care of the health and well-being of their staff. This part goes on to give practical help and advice on managing the stress of teams. This includes policies and procedures related to stress-related illness, individual risk assessment, managing absence, and critical incident management. This part will help managers to become aware of the stress levels of their staff and will help them to intervene much earlier before individuals are experiencing excessively high levels of stress. Managers will find Chapter 19 particularly helpful when they need to talk with team members about stress. Managers often fail to act because they lack the skills to handle the situation. Chapter 19, and Part IV as a whole, will help them to overcome their nervousness.

Line managers should read this part of the book in depth to help them to manage the stress of others with greater confidence. All those who manage stress from an organizational perspective should also read this part, so that they can understand the vital role that managers play in stress reduction. It builds on the chapters in Parts II and III, and will enable HR and occupational health specialists, and trainers to support line managers even more effectively.

PART V – UNDERSTANDING AND DEALING WITH STRESS: AN INDIVIDUAL PERSPECTIVE

This part has been written to help individual readers manage their own stress, and with this enhanced understanding they will, in turn, be in a better position to manage the stress of others. Readers should remember that everyone has a responsibility to manage his/her own stress and make others aware if their stress levels are unacceptably high. Chapter 22 will make it much easier for individuals to spot the warning signs of excessive stress in themselves and others by explaining some physiology behind these symptoms. Readers can take advantage of questionnaires to help them to assess the signs that they may typically exhibit when stress levels rise. As with many things, awareness is the first step to making improvements. Chapter 23 gives advice on how to feel "in control" and Chapter 24 discusses the management of emotions – an area of life so closely linked to stress. Chapter 25 will give readers a wide range of helpful coping strategies. The authors, however, know that even when people know what they need to do, they do not always do it. Chapter 26 will remind people of some of the blocks to action and will provide advice on how to maintain positive coping strategies.

All readers will benefit from reading Part V. Managers will be more able to act as role models in managing their own stress and will be equipped with strategies to help others. For HR, trainers, and consultants this part will be of personal interest but will also provide useful content for advice and the development of training programs.

PART VI – CONCLUSIONS

This final part of the book brings together the key lessons for the readers. Written in four sections, it will help HR, leaders, occupational health, and managers shape their own agenda for managing stress for the rest of this decade. All readers must play their part and accept responsibility for managing stress within their organizations. Further reading and websites that may be of interest to readers are included in this final part. We hope that this book will help readers to become as passionate as the authors in taking care of the well-being of others.

Below we indicate the priorities of the book's parts for categories of readers: X indicates that the part is a high priority.

Part of book	HR	Manager	Occupational health	Health and safety	Trainer/ consultant	Decision maker
I Overview of the Book and Business Context	X	X	X	X	X	X
II What is Stress?	X	X	X	X	X	X
III Stress: an Organizational Perspective	X		X	X	X	
IV Managing the Stress of Others	X	X	X	X	X	
V Understanding and Dealing with Stress: an Individual Perspective	X	X			X	
VI Conclusions	X	X	X	X	X	X

2 The Business Context and Organizational Drivers for Managing Stress

Introduction

All those concerned with the well-being and mental health of people need to be aware of the broader business environment and the changes taking place that are likely to put additional pressure on people. This chapter will help to explain why the management of stress has had to move higher up the priority list of most organizations. Occupational health, training, and personnel specialists will all benefit from understanding the business context. It will also provide a useful introduction for managers seeking to manage the stress of others.

The context and changes can be divided into external and internal factors. These are summarized in Figure 2.1 and further discussion of selected factors will follow.

External factors	Internal factors
Globalization	Cost of stress and stress-related illness
Competition and drive for profit	Organizational change
Economic environment	Company culture: values, work ethic and work style
Technological change	Relocation
The media	Working environment
Expectations of customers, stockholders, and the public	Leadership styles
Restructuring of organizations	Downsizing and workloads
Work–life balance	Silo mentality: team versus individual
Changing demographics in the workforce	Teamwork and remote teams
Changing structure of the family	Increased violence and bullying at work
Diversity	
Changing psychological contract	
New ways of working	
Legislation/Health & Safety Executive	

Figure 2.1 **External and internal drivers for managing stress**

External Factors

GLOBALIZATION AND CROSS-CULTURAL WORKING

This is becoming a big issue for organizations today as they increasingly have to compete in a global marketplace. This gives people particular challenges that are likely to add to pressure and increase levels of stress. Particular pressures include:

- A requirement to increase skills and capability to compete as a global player
- Coming to terms with the different management style of the parent company, for example Orange managed by its French owner and Wyeth driven from the US
- Increased travel around the world
- Working in dispersed teams
- Working across different time zones that sometimes increase the working day.

International working creates big challenges for managers required to work overseas. This might mean relocation, impacting on both the manager and his or her family. Alternative forms of working overseas are used to get around the problem of relocation, either by shorter term assignments when the manager might go alone, or by making frequent trips. This creates the problem of working long hours, fatigue with frequent travel, and difficulty with maintaining a satisfactory work–life balance.

ECONOMIC ENVIRONMENT

In tough economic times there is an expectation on staff to achieve greater productivity with fewer resources. This increases the pressure that individuals experience. Pollock (1998) reported that the economic turmoil overseas had impacted on employees in the US: a financial adviser reported the tensions he was experiencing; a banker had been skipping his lunch; and others had been compulsive about checking the share price of the company. In one bank stress levels were rising even though no layoffs had been announced.

Hymowitz and Silverman (2001) stated that employees reported more stress-related illnesses in an economic downturn than in booms. In 1998, a boom year for the US, the Bureau of Labour Statistics reported 53 percent fewer stress-related cases than in 1993 when the job market was weaker and corporate layoffs rife. Stress, however, still took its toll on productivity. The median job absence for stress-related conditions was 15 days in 1998. By 2001, people were reporting additional stress in a weakening economy, particularly as the crisis was beginning to develop in both the US and the UK, with a falling stock market and the impact this was having on pensions.

The situation became worse post 9/11 and the Gulf War of 2003. Trigaux (2002) wrote that whilst national leaders were still insisting that the US economy was steady, insecure workers sensed that the US was right on the edge of another recession. Most employees were reporting higher levels of stress than a year previously. This rise was partly caused by rising unemployment, corporate scandals, the ongoing threat of terrorism, and, at this stage, the threat of war with Iraq. As the stock market was less buoyant, many of the large corporates were into cost-cutting mode.

Trigaux reported a surge in the number of people out of work and having a tough time finding comparable jobs. Many had moved to an area in more prosperous years to take technology jobs that they have since lost in cutbacks. Any openings were flooded with applicants and organizations were paying less than in previous years. In Chicago an employee assistance provider had experienced a 35 percent increase in calls from employees citing financial issues as a source of stress.

With rising productivity, employees must be working harder, thus adding to stress levels. In the US at this time, more employees were phoning in sick or taking longer vacation time than they were really allowed.

TECHNOLOGICAL CHANGE

The last decade has shown unprecedented developments in the technology used by organizations. Cooper (2001), commenting on this growth, referred to a survey that found:

- 78 percent of managers said the desktop PC was completely or somewhat integral to their jobs
- 89 percent said email was integral to their jobs
- 64 percent said the mobile phone was integral to their jobs
- 69 percent said the internet was integral to their jobs
- 51 percent said the laptop was integral to their jobs.

Whilst most managers would find these technological advances helpful, there is a downside: they are inundated with emails such that work comes in on a 24/7 basis. Clearly managers have a choice about when they respond to emails, but many are aware of the quick response time that people expect today. The growth of email has also cut back on the amount of personal contact and, together with more remote working, this can make work socially isolating and increase stress levels.

What are the positive aspects of changing technology? These can be summarised as follows:

- Speed of contact and reply to a large number of people
- People can deal with work when they want to, thus avoiding interruptions
- Ease of access for those working remotely, and those working at different geographical locations
- The range of technology including mobile phones and remote access to email means the capability to work anytime, anywhere. This increases the opportunity to work in a flexible and more productive way, cutting downtime, for example waiting at airports, on train journeys, and spare time between meetings away from an office environment

- Accessibility of information via the Internet or company intranet
- Greater scope for sharing information in a way that can be managed via electronic transfer.

Despite these advantages there is a downside creating increased stress levels. The negative aspects of changing technology include:

- Constant interruptions to leisure time through the 24/7 accessibility
- The problem of information overload from others and through use of the internet
- Contact using email extensively can be impersonal, reducing the amount of direct contact. This can be particularly isolating for those working remotely
- The volume of junk email can result in individuals facing large quantities of emails to deal with on a day-to-day basis
- Breakdowns in technology result in frustration and wasted time and effort, particularly when networks crash or work is lost through computer viruses and corrupted files
- The volume of work now conducted using computers can create physical and mental strain for individuals, particularly those working from home who lack ergonomically designed office furniture.

Technological developments go hand in hand with organizations becoming leaner and more competitive, with fewer people doing more work. The trend is for more people to work remotely, on a contract, or as part of an outsourced operation.

There are several inherent stresses associated with technological change. Firstly, technology can create fear with some users and adequate training must be given. Technology also needs to be as user-friendly as possible, and organizations must pick software that is easy to operate and meets the needs of the organization. Stress is much greater when people are working remotely and do not have technological support close at hand. Finally, with the flexibility offered by technology, organizations must ensure that the work–life balance is not eroded. Technology can easily take over, particularly when managers are working across different time zones.

RESTRUCTURING OF ORGANIZATIONS

In the past 20 years organizations have undergone a dramatic transformation from rigid and hierarchical to more flexible, flatter structures. This change has come about in response to global competition, a tougher economic environment, and the need to be flexible and lean, to help drive down costs. In addition, as a result of changing technology, information is available much faster and organizations need to be more innovative to stay ahead. Certain changes experienced in organizations are summarized in Figure 2.2.

Old style organization (1980s)	New style organization (2000s)
Hierarchical – many layers	Flatter structures
Working in functional silos	Working in cross-functional teams
Command and control management style	Shared leadership
Clear boundaries	Boundaryless
Majority of staff are permanent employees	Increase in contract and outsourced staff

Figure 2.2 **Changes experienced in organizations**

Reorganizations are necessary for companies to adapt to changing business environments and market conditions and have become a normal part of life. However, reorganizations have become goals in themselves: new management feel obliged to initiate their own restructuring and can lose sight of the vision, strategic direction, and goals of the organization, with the result that staff cannot always understand the reasons for the restructure.

How do these changes impact people? New style organizations can create insecurity and uncertainty and greater flexibility is required. Some people feel positive challenge and stimulation by this new way of working, others who like certainty and security experience greater levels of stress.

Schabracq and Cooper (2000) predicted a number of potential stressors for full-time staff in new style organizations:

- Too many hours, unsocial hours, across different time zones
- Ambiguous and unclear goals, priorities, and procedures
- Tasks becoming too difficult and complex, requiring instant creativity when staff are too tired
- Having to take too many decisions – often with insufficient information
- Risk of making mistakes, with serious consequences
- Working in different configurations of diverse people frequently from different cultures
- Exposure to "contagiously" stressful colleagues
- Exposure to frequent changes in tasks, technical equipment, managers, colleagues, working arrangements, production processes, and jobs, as well as changes stemming from mergers, outsourcing, layoffs, and job mobility between organizations
- Spill over to other life domains and the risk of adverse effects.

However, as Schabracq and Cooper pointed out, whilst the restructuring of organizations has brought with it a host of potential stresses, there is the other side of the equation to be considered. The new style organizations offer well-paid jobs; people can have more control over their life; they are motivated by their work and can experience greater pleasure and meaning in it. They also have the opportunity to develop themselves and actualize their personal motives in their work.

WORK–LIFE BALANCE

All work and no play makes Jack a dull boy

In the 21st century both men and women are struggling to achieve the right balance between their professional and personal lives. From the mid-1990s onwards this issue has become more important for employers, staff, and the economy at large. Kodz et al. (2002) stated that work should be healthy and leave time and energy to pursue interests outside work. Individuals with responsibilities for childcare and care for the elderly have particular needs. However, work flexibility should be available to all employees, not just those with care responsibilities, and should apply to men as well as women.

Keogh (2003) expressed the view that managing the work–life balance is not something that, once achieved, stays static. Circumstances are constantly changing and therefore it requires vigilance to achieve a good work–life balance. Those who achieve this are more likely to be physically healthy, emotionally happy and well balanced, and, overall, feel in control of their lives. In contrast, many struggle to achieve an acceptable balance; they feel constantly tired, if they have children they feel guilty and life seems an uphill struggle.

Employers need to encourage their staff to maintain a good balance between home and work. In France the government has cut the working week, and companies and their senior executives can be prosecuted if their staff work more than 35 hours. Some French companies are using security guards to encourage staff to leave the buildings at the end of the working day. Experience has shown that staff waste less time dealing with trivia and attending long meetings. Employees in France, however, want to work longer hours.

It was not until *Management Today* (2002) ran a survey in 1998 that realization came about that the work–life balance was such a critical issue. The survey revealed resentment, anger, and misery amongst workers at the demands of the job and the lack of time for family and private lives, with the knock-on effect on health, relationships, children, and performance at work. In 2002 *Management Today* reported on research on the work–life balance from the Department of Trade and Industry (DTI), which looked at issues of job satisfaction, stress, balance, and attitude in five different sectors: accountancy, media, voluntary, manufacturing, and retail. It revealed that the work–life balance cannot be bought with money or granted by HR departments alone, no matter how enlightened. It is a complicated jigsaw in which business buy-in, intelligent policies, and quality management are fitted around a great central foundation: our own personality and attitude not just to our jobs, but also to the role of work in our lives.

Looking across the sectors, men still get more balance than women and are more likely to have outside interests such as sport, committees, and charity work, while women use more of their spare time for domestic work and childcare. Men are more likely to put work before their personal lives; women are more likely to take their stress home with them. Accountants were the most stressed of the five sectors, despite having the greatest access to flexible working options. Their stress came from long commutes, a strong culture of presenteeism (being at work although ill), and from a sense of pride and responsibility about their work. They are the sector most likely to put work first and find it harder to switch off when they leave the office. Asked for the biggest cause of stress, they cited the worsening economic situation.

In summary, the work–life balance is a complex subject, which means different things to different people. Job satisfaction, coupled with a supportive working structure that acknowledges life outside work, leads to lower stress and a happier workplace in general. However, the business case reasons for helping people to achieve a better balance cannot be achieved just through increased flexibility. The authors will return to this issue in Chapter 13 when the issue of creating a culture and climate to build a resilient workforce will be addressed.

CHANGING DEMOGRAPHICS IN THE WORKFORCE

In the UK, the working population is getting older, as life expectancy increases and the birth rate declines. This trend is likely to increase as employees choose to work after the normal retirement age to avoid an impoverished old age. This is happening for several reasons:

- Life expectancy is increasing
- Uncertainty regarding pensions grows as the stock market underperforms
- More older people are still funding mortgages, as endowment mortgages fail to perform.

Extending the working life is of benefit to employees, customers, and the organization itself. From an organizational perspective, an older employee can fill the gaps left by certain skill sets in short supply. Tesco introduced a flexible policy about ten years ago: they found they could retain staff who really knew the business and had a rapport with customers. Nationwide introduced a flexible retirement option in 2001 and also reported widespread benefits.

Trapp (2004) reported on the "four pillars project" on work and retirement run by the Geneva Association Research Centre that has identified similar pressures across Europe. Its view is that society needs to respond to demographic and economic change by taking a more flexible view of the whole of an individual's working life.

Trapp also referred to research conducted by Reed Consulting and Age Concern, which found that 48 percent of people aged 50 or over intended to work beyond the state pension age, and this included 23 percent who stated they would work until forced to stop.

However, as employees' ages increase, organizations need to show greater vigilance in terms of the physical and mental health of their staff. This will involve more one-to-one meetings to assess the well-being of the person, and intervention if the person appears to be failing to cope. The older person is likely to have less physical stamina and the pressure of working at this stage in his or her life may mean extra mental pressure too.

CHANGING STRUCTURE OF THE FAMILY

> *The family trend of our time is the de-institutionalization of marriage and the steady disintegration of the mother–father child raising unit. This trend of family fragmentation is reflected primarily in the high rate of divorce among parents and the growing prevalence of parents who do not marry.* Skolnik (2004)

Demands from the workplace spill over into family life and, in turn, family demands spill into the workplace. This might not be just for people who find themselves raising children in a one- or two-parent family, but for people who are primary carers for older members of the family. The demographic changes, that have seen the rise of an aging population and an increase in the number of women delaying childbirth until later in their careers, mean that increasing numbers of employees are becoming carers to their parents whilst raising a young family at the same time.

There are more single parents within the workforce than ever before – these are usually mothers, but a significant number are fathers. Studies in Canada in the late 1990s found that women reported high levels of stress because of demands upon their time; but between 1992 and 1998, the number of men reporting this kind of stress increased. Women aged 25–44 holding full-time jobs and raising children were the most likely to be severely stressed over a period of time.

In America, about 20 percent of children nationwide live in single-parent households and a recent study concluded that long hours at work increase work–family conflict which, in turn, is related to depression and other stress-related health problems. The findings of the Canadian studies indicated that employees took an average of 13.2 days off to deal with family-related problems, compared with 5.9 days by those who reported low levels of work–family conflict. Healthcare costs arising from this stress amounted to roughly $425 million annually for extra trips to the doctor. Family-related absences from work alone were estimated to cost employers at least $2.7 billion per year.

In two-thirds of UK families, both parents work outside the home, with a growing number working "atypical" hours, that is, the traditional 9–5 day is no longer the norm and families are obliged to adapt accordingly.

The impact of the modern family structure on employers is primarily focused on how they manage the support given to employees, the flexibility they can offer, and how they manage individual expectations. Without a degree of flexibility and support, stress levels are likely to become unacceptably high.

DIVERSITY

Employers almost universally agree that diversity is something they are unquestionably in favor of, but when it comes to actually making things happen, they seem to move incredibly slowly.

Companies are beginning to see the benefits of appealing to the wider population for a number of reasons, for example enabling their customers to identify more closely with a company and more realistically reflecting the areas and markets within which they work. In turn, organizations benefit from having recruitment and retention policies which take account of diversity issues, meaning there is a wider pool of talent to recruit from and a higher retention level.

Caulkin (2003) cited a Conference Board study in the US in 2001, which highlighted hard economic reasons for making diversity work. It has been estimated that women have a buying power of $1 trillion; African Americans $550 billion, Hispanic Americans $360 billion, and disabled Americans $460 million. Of the new entrants into the US labor market, 80 percent were other than white males and similar considerations apply to the UK.

Caulkin (2003) also cited a report by Rajan (2003), in which 40 percent of the 500 companies surveyed stated that productivity had increased as a direct result of diversity initiatives, with similar numbers reporting increased customer satisfaction and retention, a wider spread of customers across different markets, and higher sales. An even higher percentage claimed that diversity had increased innovation, now that more diverse teams, in terms of mixed ethnic backgrounds, gender, and age, had become commonplace.

Managing and promoting diversity can require significant change depending on an organization's starting point. In order to attract more women to some City traders, for example, organizations would have to consider abolishing the perceived male-dominated, macho cultures and work out how they could provide options for flexible working, which fit in with the staff they are trying to recruit and retain.

The consequences of not dealing effectively with organizational cultures that do not support diversity are also plain. Where people are being bullied, harassed or discriminated against within an organization because of their gender, sexual orientation, religious beliefs, or ethnic background, employers have to be seen to take action and mean what they say. The Health and Safety Executive (HSE) says that bullying should be treated like any other workplace hazard, which means that employers should assess the risks of staff being bullied and take steps to prevent it, thus removing a major source of stress.

According to a survey undertaken by Helge Hoel and Professor Cary Cooper of UMIST (2000), one in four people said they had been bullied at work in the last five years and that victims of bullying are more likely to suffer ill health. People who are not treated fairly are far more likely to be prone to stress and, again, become absent from work.

Effective diversity management means that employers are able to tap into the wide potential of both the employment and commercial markets, whilst employees can benefit from employers who provide opportunities for them to work in a fair, equitable, and supportive environment, where differences are worked with and not against. It does, however, need to be carefully managed if stress of individuals is to be avoided.

THE CHANGING PSYCHOLOGICAL CONTRACT

A CIPD Fact Sheet (2003) stresses the importance of employees as a key driver in the success of a business. The psychological contract offers a framework for understanding the attitudes and expectations of work. Employers now recognize the importance of creating an "employer brand" that is a statement of the psychological contract and helps the recruitment of staff, gaining and sustaining their commitment and talent retention.

The term "psychological contract" was first adopted in the 1960s, but became a more popular focus of attention following the recession of the 1990s. As talent has become scarcer, power has shifted from employer to employee and employers have recognized the importance of understanding the expectations of staff.

In the 1960s and 1970s people joined organizations with an expectation of a job for life, career progression, and reward for service. Employees, in return, were loyal to the organization and had a strong work ethic. Those born between 1965 and 1980 (Generation X) grew up with a very different attachment to work, as prevailing economic and social forces shaped their attitudes. The previous generation (the baby boomers) had grown up in the post-war era, a time of great economic hardship, which placed emphasis on job security and the importance of loyalty. The Generation X group are more independent, self-reliant, and have grown up with choice; if they are unhappy in a job, they will leave. A comparison between the old psychological contract and the new deal is summarized in Figure 2.3.

Those born after 1980 are referred to as Generation Y. Verret (2000) referred to Eric Chester, the first to use the term Generation Y, as commenting on the fact that Generation Y has never known unemployment. They value education and are focused on achieving personal goals. They are technologically able, fast paced, like teamwork and are good at multitasking. Managing through the use of intimidation and threats will not work for Generation Y: they need praise, can handle the truth, however tough it may be, and need to know the reasons for doing things if they are to be committed. This generation needs to be inspired and given the opportunity to have fun. When organizations fail to meet the needs and expectations of employees, stress levels will rise.

Old psychological contract – the baby boomers	**The new deal – Generation X**
The employee offers: Loyalty Commitment Trust Know-how	*The employee offers:* Conditional loyalty Conditional commitment Performance Willingness to develop
The employer offers: Security of employment Career progression Rewards for service Care	*The employer offers:* Fair pay and treatment Opportunities Rewards for performance More accountability/responsibility

Figure 2.3 **A comparison of the old psychological contract and the new deal**

THE GOVERNMENT, LEGISLATION, AND ITS ASSOCIATED COSTS

The HSE has brought in tough rules that require employers to monitor and tackle stress at work. If organizations fail to meet the requirements, they will face harsh financial penalties. This has received strong government backing, faced with the level of stress in the workplace. Wigham (2003a) quoted Des Browne, minister for work and pensions, as saying "the move would help employers face up to the issue." He said that stress was costing society £3.7 billion every year. The cost of stress will be discussed further in Chapter 4 when the business case for managing employee stress will be discussed more fully. Chapter 10 will focus on the legal perspective.

Internal Factors

COST OF STRESS AND STRESS-RELATED ILLNESS

In a UK survey conducted jointly by *Personnel Today* and the HSE (2003), four out of five employers believed that stress had a negative impact on productivity and half believed that stress had an adverse effect on the organization's ability to retain staff. The survey also found the larger the organization, the greater the impact. Statistics for the UK included:

- 1,554,256 working days lost to stress
- Absence costs employers £1.24 billion a year
- 11 percent of absence is caused by stress
- 83 percent believed stress harms productivity.

The cost of stress will be explored further in Chapter 4.

ORGANIZATIONAL CHANGE

Change is one of the big certainties within organizations today. Markets, products, and technology are constantly changing and, during periods of rapid change, people experience high levels of pressure and many experience excessive stress. Those organizations that take care of their staff are more likely to protect themselves from loss of performance. Change is a known source of stress and will be discussed fully in Chapter 6.

COMPANY CULTURE: VALUES, WORK ETHIC, AND COMPANY STYLE

Hours worked by staff is a factor influenced by the culture of the organization. It is evidence of the extent that the organization values and supports the work–life balance and well-being of its staff. Rubens (2004) referred to companies establishing a long hours culture by making jokes when people leave early, or by providing staff with mobile phones or fax machines in their homes, effectively putting them on call 24 hours a day. There is evidence that this way of working is widespread. Royal Mail conducted a survey recently and found 65 percent of UK workers have been contacted about a work-related issue during weekends and 48 percent by a colleague during a bank holiday weekend.

How do working hours vary around the world? Kodz et al. (2003) compared the working hours in the UK with EU and other developed countries to show the UK workforce has some of the longest working hours in Europe. Working more than 48 hours a week was defined by Kodz et al. as working long hours. Full-time male managers work the longest hours in the UK and across the EU member states as a whole. In the USA, 25 percent of men and 10 percent of women work more than a 48-hour week. In Australia, approximately 33 percent of men now work long hours compared with 20 percent in 1984; 15 percent of women worked more than 48 hours a week.

However, working long hours does not equate to productivity in the UK and productivity is lower than that in other European countries. The effects of excessive stress may well explain part of the gap. This is discussed further in Chapter 4.

COMMUNICATION

Communication processes form one of the biggest causes of stress within organizations. Technology has changed the whole dynamic of communication in the workplace: email has replaced the paper mountain that arrived on people's desks, although some still like the security of a hard copy filed away.

Email itself has resulted in people becoming inundated with communication. Many adopt the practice of copying to everyone they can; as a result, people have excessive numbers of email, as well as junk mail, to deal with. This new technology has speeded up communication, but also puts added pressure on people to stay on top of their workloads. The increased use of mobile phones keeps people accessible 24/7. Whilst the technology aids remote and flexible working, it can put additional strains on people.

Reade (2004) referred to recent research, conducted by the Digital World Research Centre and the University of Surrey, that found that technology is causing stress, anger, and distraction amongst office workers, and an underlying resentment of communication intrusion. Office workers are frustrated when they cannot reach someone but, at the same time, resent the distractions caused by communication interrupting their own work or meetings.

Communication is particularly important during times of change and uncertainty. It helps to stop the spread of rumors and people can adapt more readily to change if they understand why change is happening.

RELOCATION

Moving house is placed reasonably high on the "change" items that can lead to stress-related illnesses on the Holmes and Rahe scale (see Chapter 6 for further information). In the UK a trend has developed to relocate offices away from Central London, which usually means that staff affected by the relocation may have to move house or face redundancy. Examples of this include:

- The move of the government's Communication Headquarters (GCHQ) was one of the biggest IT relocations in recent years in Europe, according to Wray (2004). Four thousand staff and a host of IT systems from two sites had to be relocated to one high-tech site costing £337 million. GCHQ had to continue normal working throughout the move, just at a time of an increased workload post-September 11, 2001. GCHQ also wanted to achieve a more flexible and open culture as part of the relocation.
- National Air Traffic Services managed an equally complex relocation. A new system for air traffic control was developed and simulations were built to enable the systems to be thoroughly tested and staff trained on the new technology. The air traffic control services were relocated to Swanick (near Southampton) from a site quite close to London's Heathrow Airport, which meant that the majority of staff had to move house in order to work at the new site.

WORKING ENVIRONMENT

The working environment can have a huge impact on the way people feel at work. In the last few years the buildings of many organizations have undergone facelifts, refurbishments, or been replaced by purpose-built sites. Organizations such as British Airways, Visa, Canon UK, Diageo GB, and National Air Traffic Services have all relocated to purpose-built accommodation. Woolnough (2004) reported that companies are making these moves because of a growing realization that pleasant, well-designed offices can boost productivity and morale, as well as improve corporate identity, image, recruitment, and retention and absentee rates.

An important trend in office design is towards the open-plan office. This helps communication, knowledge sharing, teamwork, creates a more informal working environment, and breaks down hierarchical barriers. Organizations found that less use was made of email and more face-to-face conversations took place. Open plan also takes up less space, meaning that, in some cases, employees could all be located in a single building instead of being spread over several sites.

Several of the purpose-built sites include facilities for staff. Some have incorporated "streets" that accommodate coffee shops where meetings can take place in an informal atmosphere. They also offer shopping facilities and dry cleaning services to make the working lives of employees easier. Gyms are also provided.

LEADERSHIP STYLES

> *If you find your boss inspirational, the chances are you will be far happier and more productive at work.* **Collins (2004)**

The 20,000 UK workers who took part in the *Sunday Times* survey (2004) listed inspirational leadership (including qualities of energy and inspiration) as the major factor in making a company a great place to work. This survey will be discussed fully in Chapter 13. The managing director of Beaverbrooks, a UK retail jewelry chain, ensures that employees live the core values of the business, and thus 82 percent of staff feel inspired by him and 91 percent have a great deal of faith in him. Staff feel valued and respected by their managers who regularly express appreciation for good work.

According to Weymes (2003), in the traditional hierarchical organization, with functional silos, communication was inhibited, information protected, and success defined as the ability of one silo to outperform another. Once an organization rejects the silos, a complex set of relationships emerges. It is now recognized that innovation and inspiration are the key to knowledge creation and a successful organization. Very different leadership styles are required where trust and integrity are encouraged. Management by fear may produce results in the short term, but to achieve long-term sustainability, leaders must be sensitive to the emotions of others and convey passion and a sense of purpose and direction for others to follow.

DOWNSIZING AND WORKLOADS

Most organizations have been forced to downsize, faced with increasing competition, demanding targets, and turbulent and changing environments. In many cases this has resulted in increased workloads for people, with more work to be done and fewer people employed to do the work. In the UK this has affected both the private and public sector. The most dramatic example was one organization that employed 45 people to deliver a service that was downsized to 9. The customers still expected the same level of services but, given staffing levels, this was impossible to achieve and the remaining staff reported high levels of stress.

Sutherland and Cooper (2000) described the negative impact in one hospital environment. It was suggested that there were too many patients and too few nurses and this led to high levels of stress amongst hospital and community mental health nurses. The nurses were struggling to maintain patient care standards in an environment of constant change. They reported lack of resources, high workload, lack of time for planning and evaluating treatment, understaffing, a dangerous working environment, and the awareness that patients were suffering as a result of inadequate services. One mental health trust had to settle a widow's stress suicide claim. The employee concerned had taken a job as a manager, having been a nurse on a ward that was closed down. He was unqualified and untrained for the managerial job, quickly felt unable to cope and received no support from his line manager. In desperation and faced with a ruthless and macho style of management, he killed himself.

When people have to be made redundant, the focus of attention is mainly on the leavers who often welcome the redundancy package and the chance to make a new and different start. In contrast, little attention is given to those who remain and who have to cope with increased workloads, the loss of colleagues, and sometimes the guilt of keeping their jobs. In difficult economic times, the morale in the organization often suffers.

Those who are made redundant are often the older people, with long service and a wealth of knowledge. The stayers not only undergo a loss of stability, but have lost access to the experience of the people made redundant. In the UK in the 1990s, many organizations brought people back on a consultancy basis, having previously given them early retirement. The organizations had difficulty operating with the loss of years of expertise and know-how.

Some organizations appoint consultants to conduct a strategic review that often results in structural changes. The organization may shift the blame for restructuring on the consultants impacting on morale and trust. Once trust is lost, it takes a long time to rebuild.

INCREASED VIOLENCE AND BULLYING AT WORK

Staff in frontline jobs are increasingly experiencing violence and aggression from their customers. Kent (2004) refers to comments by Jo Ricke from the Institute of Employment Studies (IES) that organizations have become better at telling their customers what constitutes unacceptable behavior. The IES has carried out studies for the HSE researching ways of handling traumas that are useful for organizations with staff that are exposed to violent behavior.

The International Labour Organization (ILO) produced a draft code of practice on violence and stress at work (2003). It had become aware of the growing importance of violence and stress at work as an issue affecting millions of workers around the world in the public and private sectors. The problem is particularly acute in service sectors because of the direct contact between workers and their customers/clients or the general public. Most working environments are exposed to these problems, but sectors such as education, health, hotels, and transport and certain occupational groups such as nurses, teachers, and emergency services are particularly under threat. Violence and stress impact on the quality of service and costs, disrupt workplaces and relationships and trust between work colleagues.

The ILO (2003) defined workplace violence as:

> *Any action, incident or behaviour in which a person is assaulted, threatened, harmed, injured or humiliated in the course of, or as a result of, his or her work because of the action of another person.*

Types of behavior departing from reasonable conduct include physical violence, verbal abuse, aggressive body language, harassment, bullying, and threatening behavior.

The ILO stated that violence and stress can reinforce one another and are often interrelated but there is no automatic connection between the two – although harassment is a form of stress and violence. Organizations that tackle stress and violence by adopting a broader approach embracing the health and safety and well-being of their staff have been largely successful. The draft code of practice was developed to provide guidance to those addressing violence and stress around the world, including the following key areas:

- Developing a process of risk assessment
- Steps to prevent violence and stress
- Reduction of violence and stress
- Management and coping strategies
- Development of a policy for violence and stress.

Ballard (2003), director general of the British Safety Council, stated that bullying is greatest in jobs that have high demands and a low degree of individual control, such as broking. He commented on a case brought against Cantor Fitzgerald for constructive dismissal by a broker for a bullying and abusive culture. Ballard commented that early action should be taken against a destructive work environment. Organizations should be aware of the huge costs associated with workplace bullying and the stress that accompanies it.

Summary

The main reasons why stress has moved further up the priority list for organizations are summarized below:

- Globalization has brought with it a range of challenges that put people under added pressure. Those involved have to come to terms with working cross-culturally, responding to different management styles, and often increasing the working day working across different time zones. Employers can help by providing adequate training and adopting a flexible approach to working hours to accommodate the different time zones.
- In tough economic times, there is an expectation of staff achieving more productivity with fewer resources. Expectations of staff should be realistic to avoid excessive overload and staff should be encouraged to prioritize and drop anything that has a low priority.
- Recent years have seen unprecedented technological change. Whilst some of this change is positive, a negative impact has been identified, resulting from constant access to mobile phones and the internet, making work possible seven days a week. Employers should ensure that this does not become the cultural norm within their organizations by encouraging senior managers to act as role models for a satisfactory work–life balance.
- In the past 20 years organizations have been dramatically transformed from rigid to more flexible structures and ways of working, often down-

sizing at the same time. The changes, whilst welcomed by many, can create insecurity, uncertainty, and the associated stress. If, despite these changes, there is still a macho culture, stress levels can become extremely high. What is needed for the new style organizations is a different approach to leadership and management that is far more sensitive and in tune with people's emotions.

- Faced with the pressures of work and family, many struggle to achieve and retain an appropriate life balance. It is a complex issue and means different things to different people. Successful organizations allow for flexibility and are rewarded by having a happy and motivated workforce.
- Changing demographics resulting in an aging workforce and women rearing children as well as caring for elderly relatives require a flexible approach to staff to ensure home and work demands can both be met.
- In the UK, the government, through the HSE, has brought in tougher measures to ensure that employers monitor and address workplace stress. Failure to do so will result in tough financial penalties.
- The culture of an organization can have a dramatic affect on stress levels. The long hours culture and an associated macho approach to people management will result in increased stress. Changing the culture of organizations requires good role models at the top and awareness that leadership style is important at all levels within organizations.
- A growing trend within the UK is for organizations to relocate offices away from central London, often requiring people to move or face redundancy. Many have taken the opportunity provided to build state-of-the-art office accommodation, often improving communication amongst the workforce. Employers need to aware that the working environment has a huge impact on the way people feel and, with the right facilities on site (such as shops, coffee bars, and ATMs), can greatly increase well-being.
- There is increased awareness of the problem of workplace bullying and harassment. This not only increases the stress of those who are victims, but can result in costly claims for discrimination or the cost of absence through stress-related illness.

PART II

What is Stress?

Background and Importance

3 What is Stress?

Introduction

Stress is not a new issue but the past few years have seen an unprecedented growth in stress awareness, making the problem of stress appear greater than it was ten years ago. Today there is a general acceptance of stress as a problem that needs to be tackled urgently. Although the exact link between stress and illness is not fully understood, there is a wide acceptance of a connection between the two.

The term "stress" is often misused and has become an umbrella term. When people refer to stress, they have their own understanding of the term and it becomes confusing and difficult to understand statements such as: "I am stressed," or "The situation is stressful." There is a tendency for people to want simple solutions to a complex problem. Part of this complexity lies in the fact that people react to situations very differently and, therefore, what can be a source of stress and a negative experience to one person can be a very positive experience to someone else.

The first step in stress management is to understand what is meant by the term "stress." Distinguishing between the elements of stress helps to demystify the term and give greater clarity to the concept. The purpose of this chapter is to increase understanding of the term. The relationship between stress, pressure and performance will be discussed, followed by the reactions that people have when they feel threatened. People react to pressure in very different ways. Some of the factors that determine the way people respond to pressure will be outlined and the impact that this pressure can have individually and organizationally.

This chapter provides a foundation for later parts of the book. HR, health and safety, and occupational health professionals as well as consultants and managers should, therefore, read it. It will help people to understand their own reactions and the impact of stress on others, as well as organizationally.

How People View Stress

A survey of managers who were asked how they viewed stress made the following comments:

> The experience of stress is very personal.
> When I think about stress I think of times when I felt unable to cope.

realize the extent to which stress is self-generated.
Stress can be associated with situations where I felt out of control.
Stress can be viewed as positive and a stimulant.

The authors believe:

- Stress management is integral to good management practice
- Stress is both positive and negative
- It is the interpretation of demands, constraints, and support that determines the stress response
- Stress arises from the interplay between demands, constraints, and the individual's ability to cope
- We manage stress by maintaining a balance between demands, constraints, and coping mechanisms
- We need to understand the demands, spot the signs that demands are excessive, and be prepared with the right coping mechanisms
- Many associate stress with situations where they feel out of control.

Definitions of Stress

Various definitions are used and the one adopted by the Health and Safety Executive (HSE) is shown in Figure 3.1, together with the definition that is favored by the authors.

Stress can be viewed as a reaction by the individual to pressure; both external pressure and any internal pressure that is self-imposed and gives rise to physiological, psychological, and behavioral changes.

The authors' definition recognizes the interaction between people weighing up the situation, assessing the demands, and their perception of their ability to meet these demands on this particular occasion. This appraisal happens without people being consciously aware of what is happening and results in various changes that are described in the case study of three administrators in Figure 3.2.

Depending on the level of pressure, stress can be described in different ways:

- *Hypo-stress* – too little pressure or boredom can be a source of stress, often taking the form of pent-up emotion, frustration, or apathy and depression.

HSE definition

The adverse reaction people have to excessive pressures or other types of demand placed upon them

The authors' definition

Stress occurs when there is a perceived imbalance between pressure and coping resources for a particular situation

Figure 3.1 **Definitions of stress**

Margaret, Jill, and Fiona were three administrators who were fulfilling similar roles but reacted to excessive pressure for quite different reasons. Once an imbalance occurred between pressure and coping resources, they experienced a high level of stress. Margaret was very capable and seemed to thrive on stress. The pressure she experienced was matched by her coping skills. She provided administrative support for several managers and could always be relied on to meet tight deadlines.

However, when Margaret was asked to provide support for two additional managers, the extra demands were such that she suddenly lacked the coping skills to deliver. Her work output dropped dramatically and she started to miss deadlines. Some of her workload had to be reallocated to overcome the problem.

Jill was different from Margaret. She was a lively person who had been appointed more for her personality than her administrative skills. When her manager gave her clear instructions Jill was able to deal with pressure well. However, without this clear direction Jill experienced excessive stress. This was a reflection of Jill's perception of her capability to do the job rather than an excessive workload.

Finally, Fiona, like Margaret, was able to meet the normal demands of her job but she regularly suffered ill health. On these occasions, her stress levels rose and she had difficulty achieving what was expected of her. In this case the imbalance arose from a lack of stamina, causing her increased pressure that resulted in excessive stress.

Figure 3.2 **Three administrators and their approaches to stress**

- *Eu-stress* – at optimum pressure, the individual thrives and maximizes performance. This is the stimulating side of stress, sometimes referred to as "stress arousal;" it enables people to access hidden mental and physical abilities.
- *Hyper-stress* – once pressure becomes excessive, the individual experiences hyper-stress. The moment when stimulation becomes hyper-stress will vary from person to person and, even for the same person, from situation to situation. At this stage, the person is likely to feel out of control or in a panic and unable to cope as well.
- *Distress* – after prolonged stress, the individual experiences distress. This results in costs to both the individual and the organization. The individual is likely to suffer from health problems and a desire to escape from the situation and may well be signed off long term with a stress-related illness.

Thus, managing stress is a delicate balancing act to keep pressure at the optimum level. Stress management requires the level of arousal to be maintained at the right level to enable personal, professional, and organizational goals to be achieved. When pressure is at the optimum, people tend to view stress as positive; when pressure is too low or too high, stress is seen negatively.

Elements of Stress

Figure 3.3 demonstrates the elements of the stress process and the interaction between:

1. *The person* – the way the situation is perceived, influenced by his/her personality, thought processes, and state of well-being/resilience

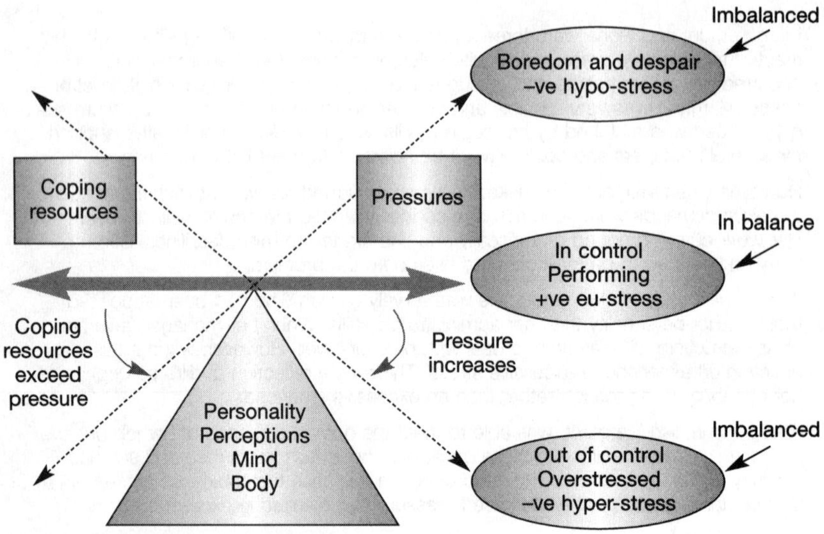

Figure 3.3 **The elements of stress**

2. *The situation* that provides the context that is perceived by the individual as more or less stressful
3. *The stressors/pressure* – the pressure generated both externally and internally
4. *The reaction* of the person to the perceived pressures he/she is experiencing
5. *The strategies* used by the person to deal with the situation.

As a result of the interaction between these five elements, the level of stress and performance will vary considerably. Each of these elements will now be discussed.

THE PERSON

The factors that will influence the way the person reacts to a situation are summarized in Figure 3.4.

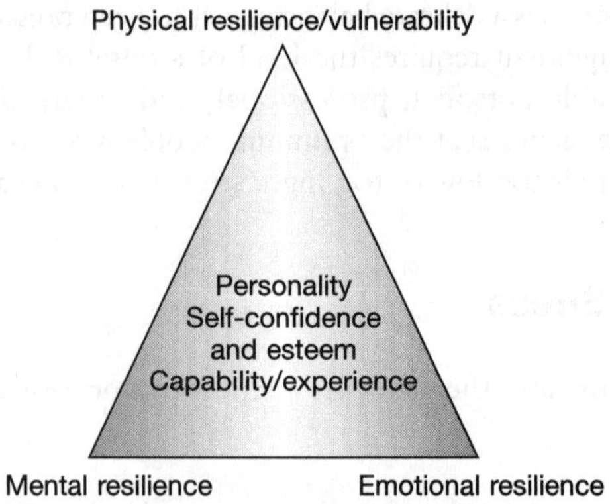

Figure 3.4 **Factors influencing the way a person reacts to a situation**

The personality of the person is an important determinant of the way he or she will react to pressure. Friedman and Ulmer (1985) in the US differentiated between two different types:

> *Type A – those people who are ambitious, live life in the fast lane, are always in a hurry and are pushing themselves to achieve deadlines.*
>
> *Type B – in contrast are much more relaxed, pace themselves carefully and set realistic expectations.*

The research found that whilst both were likely to be successful in organizations, Type A people were far more likely to suffer a heart attack.

Conscientiousness is an important factor, making this type of person far more likely to worry about achieving what is expected, not being late for deadlines, and doing work to the best of his or her ability. The more relaxed type of person puts himself or herself under less pressure than the person who is conscientious.

The anxious person is likely to spend a great deal of time worrying about what has happened or what could go wrong. The past and the future are difficult to control so this approach puts the person under a great deal of pressure. Many people are anxious to meet the needs of others and satisfy others at great personal cost. Often people will agree to do things, putting themselves under tremendous pressure to achieve within the timescales set by others.

Self-confidence and self-esteem are critical ingredients of successful stress management. Often when pressure becomes unacceptably high or low, people will become far less confident and lose their self-esteem, and the level of stress the person experiences rises.

Personality has an important relationship with the amount of internal pressure that people experience. Personality characteristics related to internal pressure include:

- ▶ *Perfectionism* – a particular issue in today's world of increasing workloads
- ▶ *Desire to please others* – making it difficult for the person to say no
- ▶ *Anxiousness* – causing the person to think about what has happened or might happen
- ▶ *Insecurity* – a particular problem with the level of change in organizations and in life generally
- ▶ *Lack of flexibility* – again changing situations require people to adapt and change
- ▶ *Defeatist attitude* – an overall negative outlook tends to reduce the person's ability to think of solutions or utilize various coping strategies
- ▶ *Desire for control* – this type of personality becomes exceedingly frustrated by an inability to control events, and does not distinguish well between things inside and outside of his/her control
- ▶ *Fear of failure* – an extreme worry about the consequences of failure raises stress levels greatly
- ▶ *Inability to ask for help* – some individuals value independence so much, or worry about troubling others, such that they take everything on their own shoulders, resulting in excessive pressure.

A person's physical, mental, and emotional resilience are also important:

- *Physical resilience* – an important determinant of the person's capability to deal with pressure. In particular, people need a healthy diet, to take exercise, and have adequate rest and relaxation to be physically fit. This is dealt with more fully in Chapter 25.
- *Mental resilience* – provides people with the mental energy to think clearly, solve problems, and perform at their best. Being well organized helps to keep the mind uncluttered and give the feeling of being in control. Thought processes have an important bearing on the pressure that is generated by people. It is the way people think about a situation that can give rise to stress. This is often based on past experience. When a person experiences stress in one situation, when faced with a similar situation, they are far more likely to perceive it as stressful. Changing their thought processes is a way of reducing the stress they will experience. This is discussed further in Chapters 23 and 25.
- *Emotional resilience* – people need to have the capacity to perform consistently even when under excessive pressure. This means keeping control of the emotions. In the fight or flight response, the person not only responds physically but also emotionally (discussed later in this chapter and in Chapter 24).

THE SITUATION

Examples of the factors within the situation that will impact on stress are shown in Figure 3.5. The factors within the situation represent the potential sources of stress or stressors. Clearly, the way the situation is perceived relates closely to the personality of the person. The causes of stress are discussed in greater detail in Chapter 6.

New	Familiar
Changing	Stable
Low support	High support
High pressure	Low pressure
Ambiguous	Unambiguous

Figure 3.5 **Examples of factors within a situation impacting on stress**

THE STRESSORS/PRESSURE

The relationship between pressure stress and performance is shown in Figure 3.6.

At low levels of pressure, stress levels can often run high, particularly when

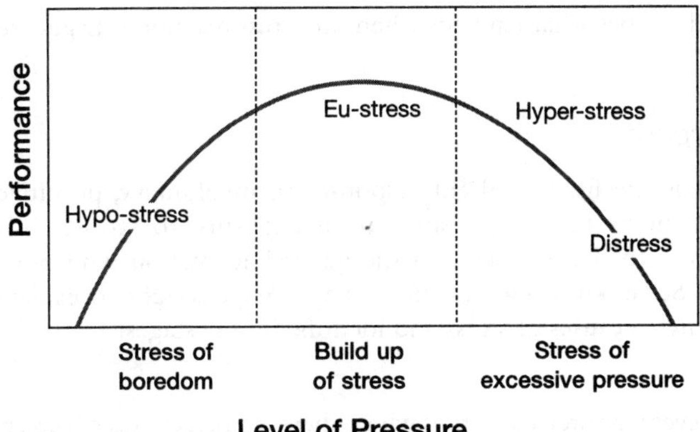

Figure 3.6 **Relationship between performance and pressure**
Source: Adapted from Melhuish (1978)

people experience frustration from the lack of challenge and being required to do mundane or repetitive work.

As pressure increases and performance levels increase, people often experience the stimulation of positive stress. This needs to be carefully monitored to ensure that positive stress does not turn to negative stress. The best way to manage pressure is to address it in two ways:

1. Increase the person's resistance to pressure by building their resilience – discussed in Chapter 25.
2. Reduce the amount of pressure – discussed in Chapter 8.

THE REACTION TO PRESSURE

People do respond differently to pressure. Key factors that impact on the response include:

- Level of pressure which is acceptable to the individual
- The internal state of mind of the person
- The personality of the person
- Extent to which the person needs to feel in control
- Whether change is viewed as stimulating or a threat
- Perceived need for security
- Need to consistently achieve a high standard, verging on perfectionism
- Level of experience and expertise
- Motivation of the individual
- Perceived support available.

This places emphasis on the need to treat people differently and the types of strategy and the culture and climate needed if an organization is to manage stress successfully.

The following describes what happens when the stress reaction is triggered in people.

Fight or flight response

The basic reaction is the fight or flight response, an involuntary, primitive mechanism, which helps to explain short-term exposure to stress. This response is equivalent to the first stage of the general adaptation syndrome, identified by Hans Selye, known as the alarm stage. Selye sought to explain longer term exposure to causes of stress and identified three stages.

Alarm phase

This happens whenever we enter a situation where there is a perception of threat. The basic purpose of this stage is to prepare the body for immediate action: energy is mobilized to cope with the emergency, real or imagined, and physical capabilities are heightened for speed or power. Specifically, within the body:

- The hypothalamus and pituitary gland initiate the stress reaction
- The adrenal glands produce epinephrine (adrenaline) and norepinephrine (noradrenaline) associated with fight or flight.

These are released into the bloodstream, leading to:

- Raised heartbeat by as much as 100 percent
- Widening airways in the lungs
- Constricting blood vessels supplying skin and intestines
- Eyes stare, pupils dilate
- Salivary glands close down and mouth becomes dry
- Breathing becomes faster to increase oxygen intake
- Sugar is released from the liver for instant energy
- Fat in the form of cholesterol is released from the liver for energy
- Digestion stops so that blood is available to carry energy to the muscles
- Muscles tense ready for action and release lactic acid into the bloodstream
- The body begins to sweat to cool down
- The immune system is inhibited.

The stress reaction is summarized in Figure 3.7. This string of reactions happens very quickly and effectively to prepare people to deal with life-threatening situations. Normally, if no physical activity takes place, the level of arousal will gradually fall back to its previous level. However, in today's world, people are likely to encounter another situation before they have returned to the lower level of arousal and the fight or flight reaction is again triggered. Problems occur not only because the reaction is being triggered inappropriately but also because the reaction is prolonged.

Goleman (1996) described how in some situations, particularly when people feel threatened, signals from the eyes and ears to the thalamus in the brain are routed to the amygdalae – two almond-shaped structures on either side of the brain that respond quickly in an emergency. It sets in train the fight or flight response and is the emotional storehouse, a part of the brain's limbic

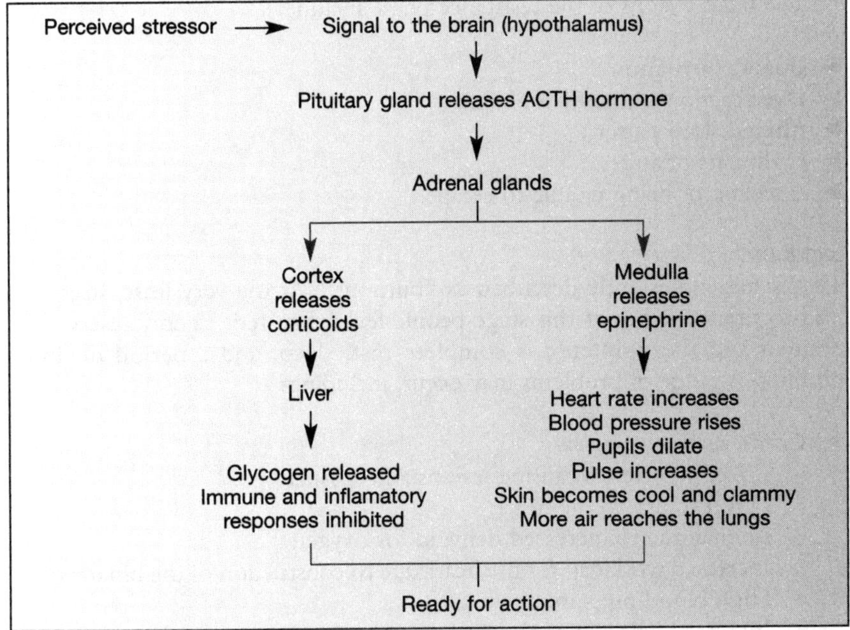

Figure 3.7 **The stress reaction**

system, overriding the thinking part of the brain, the neocortex. Thus, people can have the feeling of being swamped by emotion and unable to think straight unless the neocortex can come in to function. Figure 3.8 gives an example of an amygdala highjack.

Resistance phase

This is the second stage of the stress response. It is known as the "plateau of resistance." During this phase people can perform at a high level of activity for a long period of time. At this stage the body seems to move into top gear, drawing on energy reserves quite heavily. People can move from challenge to challenge with no rest; epinephrine masks the feelings of tiredness and the problems of underlying illness. This reaction is again a lifesaver. However, towards the end of this phase, the person becomes mentally and physically weaker.

Richard, a test pilot, was testing a small aircraft with just an instructor on board. He had put the plane through its paces and was making one last difficult turn before returning to the airfield. At this moment the engine stalled and the aircraft started to lose height rapidly. Richard described his reaction as one of "freezing." Fear had completely immobilized him and he was unable to think straight. He sat in his seat feeling blind panic. He then realized that to stay alive he had to act quickly: he collected himself together and was able to land the aircraft safely. The instructor later trained him to manage the excessive pressure to prevent a reoccurrence.

Figure 3.8 **A case of experiencing an amygdala highjack**

The danger signs of the resistance phase include:

- Bouts of irritation
- Overreaction to minor problems
- Altered sleep pattern
- Outbursts of anger
- A feeling of being unable to escape.

Exhaustion phase

This is sometimes aptly described as "burnout." At the very least, stress can lead to tiredness, but at this stage people feel exhausted. Energy reserves are drained and the only cure is complete rest, sleep, and a period of doing nothing. A range of problems may occur, including:

- *Cardiovascular problems:*
  - Effect on arteries causing lesions and spasms
  - Direct injury to the heart
  - Angina due to increased demand for oxygen
  - Increased workload for the heart due to constriction of the blood vessels
  - High blood pressure
  - Increased levels of cholesterol
- *Respiratory problems*
- *Digestive problems*
- *Skin problems*
- *Muscular problems*
- *Immune system impairment:*
  - Prone to illness
  - Cancer
  - Prone to allergies.

The stress response and the nervous system

The nervous system is divided into the central nervous system (CNS) and the peripheral nervous system (PNS). The PNS is further divided into the somatic nervous system and the autonomic nervous system (ANS). The somatic system deals with voluntary action, and the ANS deals with involuntary action, including the stress response, switching it on and off. When a threat is perceived, and the body needs to react, one part of the ANS (the sympathetic nervous system) is activated. This triggers a chain of reactions needed to fight or flee.

The other side of the ANS is the parasympathetic nervous system, which calms the body by reversing the effects of the sympathetic nervous system. It conserves and restores energy, and reduces the stress response by bringing about a reduction in heart rate and blood pressure. It also looks after maintenance aspects of the body such as cell repair, digestion, the immune system and sexual function (see Figure 3.9).

The two sides of the nervous system act like a seesaw. When one side is in operation, the other side is dormant. When the sympathetic system is activated

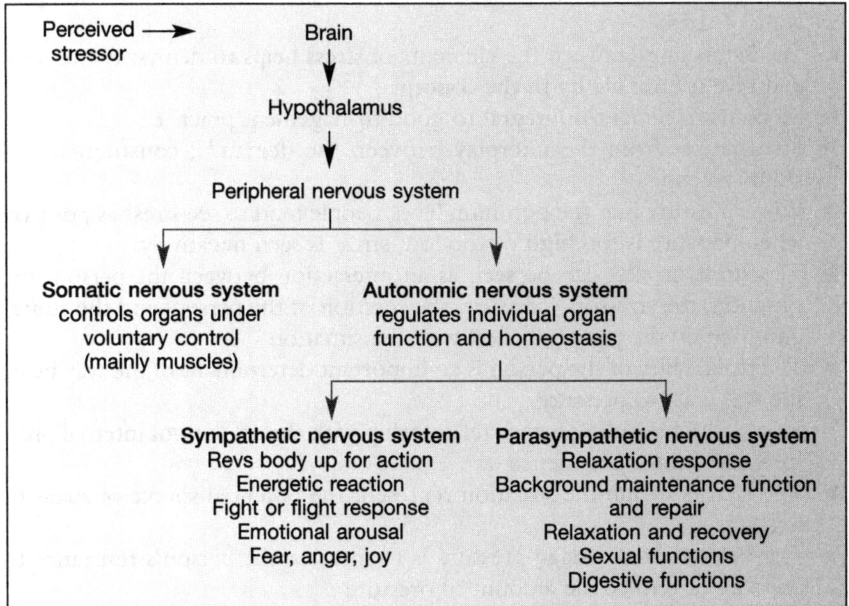

Figure 3.9 **The stress response and the nervous system**

for too long, people lose the ability and opportunity to activate the parasympathetic nervous system, resulting in a wide range of conditions and illnesses as described above.

People often experience a difficulty in relaxing through this failure of the parasympathetic nervous system to be activated.

THE STRATEGIES TO DEAL WITH THE SITUATION

The final element refers to the attempts people make to deal with the situation, either consciously or unconsciously. The strategies may be effective or ineffective in reducing stress levels. The ineffective strategies are often adopted unconsciously and are ineffective because they fail to deal with the cause of stress, tending to be props. The effective strategies are all likely to increase the individual's resilience in one way or another. The strategies will be discussed further in Chapters 9 and 25.

Summary

To manage stress successfully people need to remember the following:

- Although the exact link between stress and illness is not fully understood, there is a wide acceptance of a connection between the two

- There is a tendency for people to want simple solutions to the complex issue of stress
- Distinguishing between the elements of stress helps to demystify the term and give greater clarity to the concept
- Stress management is integral to good management practice
- Stress arises from the interplay between the demands, constraints, and ability to cope
- When pressure is at the optimum level, people tend to see stress as positive; when pressure is too high or too low, stress is seen negatively
- The stress process can be seen as an interaction between the person, the situation, the stressors/pressure, the reaction of the person, and the strategies used by the person to deal with the situation
- The personality of the person is an important determinant of the way he or she will react to pressure
- Personality has an important relationship with the amount of internal pressure that people experience
- The factors within the situation represent the potential source of stress or stressors
- The best way to manage pressure is to increase the person's resistance to pressure or reduce the amount of pressure
- People respond differently to pressure, placing emphasis on the need to treat people differently and the types of strategy, culture, and climate needed if an organization is to manage stress successfully
- The basic reaction to stress is the fight or flight response, preparing the body for immediate action. In today's world, problems occur not only because the reaction is triggered inappropriately, but also because the reaction is prolonged
- The strategies people adopt to deal with stress may be effective or ineffective to reduce the stress levels. Those that are ineffective usually fail to address the situation.

4 Why do Organizations Need to Act Now?

Introduction

Until recently stress was viewed as a sign of weakness and few people would admit to their employers if they were suffering from excessive stress. Fortunately, the more enlightened organizations in the UK have left behind the macho view that stress is for wimps, taking the lead from the US who, for some time, has been taking the situation more seriously.

It is known that stress can cause damage to people physically and psychologically. In the previous chapter the stress reaction was described in detail. Physically stress can be life threatening as a result of heart attacks and strokes. Mental illness and ultimately a nervous breakdown can also result from prolonged exposure to pressure and the resulting stress.

This chapter presents the business case for taking stress management seriously. The dysfunctional effects of stress from an individual and an organizational perspective are evaluated. The indicators of stress that can be used are discussed, including the more direct costs such as absence, labor turnover, and litigation, and the hidden costs such as poor customer service, mistakes, lack of creativity and innovation, and decreased performance, some of which are more difficult to quantify.

This chapter has been included for HR, health and safety, and occupational health specialists who have to make the business case for addressing stress management. Managers should also take note of this chapter to make themselves more aware of the costs associated with ignoring the issue of stress.

Stress is Dysfunctional for the Individual

What are the statistics telling employers? A recent survey conducted jointly by *Personnel Today* and the Health and Safety Executive (2003) revealed the statistics given below.

1,554,256 working days were lost to stress in the UK

11 percent of absence is caused by stress

Melissa had joined a large HR department on completion of her graduate program. Following a number of performance and development reviews, she quickly became identified as a potential "star" within the business. Not only did Melissa have considerable competence, she was extremely efficient and organized in her work. Her manager relied on her to provide all the relevant data and reports that she needed when meeting with senior people in the business, which meant Melissa was frequently required to work longer hours and even postponed holidays to complete work for her boss.

After a couple of years working within the same specialism and feeling somewhat taken for granted, Melissa requested a move to another part of HR. This was refused. Melissa began to openly discuss with colleagues how depressed she felt with her current situation and how stressed she was beginning to feel at the start of each working day. She was unable to sleep and often became impatient and terse with customers and during business meetings, as well as frequently breaking down in tears in the office. Her workload continued to increase and her manager – despite being told very clearly of Melissa's deteriorating health and dissatisfaction by both Melissa and other team members – appeared to ignore the situation completely.

In desperation, Melissa requested a meeting with the head of the department and again asked to be moved, citing the fact that she was unable to cope and her workload was taking its toll on her health. Her problems at work were also affecting life at home, with Melissa's husband becoming increasingly frustrated at his wife's continual emotional outbursts and inability to sleep or rest. In spite of this, Melissa was again refused a move, as the department felt her expertise could not be lost. They did offer to see what work could be allocated elsewhere, but Melissa felt guilty that her colleagues who were also under pressure from her manager should be put in the same position as her.

Inevitably, the situation deteriorated to the point where Melissa was signed off sick because she was no longer able to cope. This in itself led to her becoming further depressed and feeling under even more pressure because she was worried that her absence would define her as being "weak" and unable to deal with high-profile work and deadlines. She refused contact with her line manager, dealing only with the departmental head and after a period of several months' absence, has recently started to return to work.

The organization, despite restructuring the department, has again refused a request for Melissa to move teams, stating that she is not well enough to be considered for a move. She has been told only to come into work when she feels well enough and to work only on supporting projects or back-room work, rather than on the front line. Her manager has recently begun reissuing work to Melissa and little seems to have changed. Melissa has had some relief from the levels of stress she was previously experiencing, but frequently has to leave the office early or not come in at all, as she feels unable to face her work or deal with her manager.

Figure 4.1 **The case of Melissa and the stress that was badly managed**

All sectors were represented, including the public and private sector and small to large organizations; 680 HR professionals participated in the UK-based survey. Seventy percent of respondents said that business pressures were the main barrier to reducing stress.

Business pressures are felt strongly in Japan, where the strong work ethic means that people work excessively long hours and, in extreme cases, even sleep in the office. What is the price in human terms? In Japan they have a word, ***karoshi***, that means death through overwork. A study conducted by the University of Tsukuba reported by Warner (2002) found that of 73,000 men and women aged 49–79, nearly 9000 women and 7000 men reported high mental stress. Highly stressed women were also more likely than their relaxed colleagues to have a history of high blood pressure and diabetes.

We can see that when stress is ignored, the result can be life threatening or, at the very least, will be responsible for great human misery that is likely to permeate people's lives at home – as the example in Figure 4.1 demonstrates. Sadly, this case is common in organizations today. The authors believe that far too many people are left to suffer for a number of different reasons:

- Managers lack an understanding of the nature of stress
- Managers lack the skills to deal with the situation
- The situation requires expert help that is not always available to managers
- Managers are unsympathetic towards those suffering from stress
- Managers are experiencing increased business pressures
- A lack of good performance management systems.

Left ignored, people ultimately become ill and take time off work. The latest figures from the TUC, reported by Jaggi (2004), reinforce this view, stating that up to 13 million working days are lost as a result of stress-related illness.

It was evident from the last chapter that stress can be associated with life-threatening illnesses as well as mental health problems that can have extremely serious consequences for the individual. Organizations cannot afford to be complacent. In one organization it was only after a member of staff had a nervous breakdown that they started to take the situation seriously. Sometimes the situation is far more serious, as Figure 4.2 illustrates.

In the early 1990s the UK, like other parts of the world, was undergoing a recession. This was affecting the construction industry particularly badly. One organization within this sector became aware that managers were experiencing high levels of stress, but took the view that any intervention to try and reduce the stress levels would impact on the bottom line, so nothing was done.

One evening a director of the organization felt ill while driving home from the office and stopped in a lay-by. He had a massive heart attack and died shortly afterwards. The organization instantly set up training courses for all managers to help them understand stress, be able to spot the signs of excessive stress and develop strategies for dealing with it. Despite a tough, male-dominated, macho culture, all managers attended and worked hard to implement strategies and change their lifestyles to help to reduce the harmful effects of stress. Sadly the intervention was too late for one individual.

Figure 4.2 **Company case illustrating the business case for an intervention**

Stress can be Dysfunctional for the Organization

Statistics again reveal problems for employers at a time when productivity is critical. Statistics from the *Personnel Today* and HSE survey (2003) are shown below.

> **Absence costs employers £1.24 billion a year**
>
> **83 percent of the organizations in the survey believe that stress harms productivity**

Stress can cost an individual employer over £1 million a year. Stress has wider implications for employers. Sutherland and Cooper (2000) summarized a range of behaviors displayed by people who are experiencing excessive stress:

- Arrive to work late and/or leave early
- Take extended breaks
- Make more errors as a result of impaired judgment, poor decision making or poor concentration
- Have more rejects in quality inspections
- Miss deadlines
- Have accidents at work and more work-related travel accidents
- Engage in petty theft
- Interpersonal conflict with colleagues at work
- Be more likely to be moved as a result of departmental transfers
- Be less innovative and creative.

One could add to this list:

- Work very long hours and become fatigued
- Are absent from work more frequently
- Communicate less and make little contribution.

All these behaviors will not only impact on the productivity of the people who are experiencing excessive stress, but also on colleagues whose stress levels are likely to be affected.

Costs that can be Monitored to Make the Business Case

DIRECT COSTS

Absence monitoring

Most organizations implementing a stress management program can monitor the impact that any intervention has on sickness absence, providing they have a tracking process. Most would agree that results are encouraging, particularly when accompanied by a return to work process for addressing the problem of long-term absence. In this way the cost of any stress management intervention can be quickly recovered. The authors firmly believe that cost should not be a deterrent to mounting a stress management initiative – it does not have to be expensive.

Litigation

One of the most commonly cited cases is the *Walker* v. *Northumberland County Council* case that will be discussed in Chapter 10. The total cost of this case was likely to be in the region of £400,000, including:

- Damages of £175,000
- The cost of the trial and associated staff costs
- Sick pay
- Ill health pension.

Litigation is expensive and should be assessed not just from the perspective of the damages awarded. Consideration should also be given to the cost of preparing the defence, legal fees, and the damage to the company, its brand, and the impact it will have on attracting and retaining staff.

Labor turnover

When stress levels become unacceptably high, one course of action for people is to leave the organization. People are more likely to stay in jobs if the level of pressure is under control. Once people experience hyper-stress or distress they may go off long-term sick or just leave.

When adding up the costs of labor turnover, not only should the costs of recruitment and training of replacements be taken into account, but also the issue of intellectual capital – particularly for more senior jobs or where people have been doing the job for a long time.

HIDDEN COSTS

The impact of stress on performance

There has been a growing awareness of a phenomenon known as "presenteeism" which means that people go to work even though they feel too unwell to work. This is a critical cost associated with stress and has a great impact on performance. Clive Pinder, CEO of Vielife, referred to research conducted by Burton et al. (1999) which reported that fit and healthy staff are as much as 20 percent more productive than their ill or unhealthy colleagues. The research found a productivity gap between "poor" and "good" health of seven hours, which is equivalent to losing one working day a week. Previous studies conducted in the US also suggested an important link between health and well-being, and productivity. When people are experiencing hyper-stress and distress, not only will the volume of work suffer but also the quality of the work undertaken.

Poor customer service

With increasing competition, particularly in the service industry, customer satisfaction and retention is a critical issue. Early signs of hyper-stress in people are irritability and the desire to withdraw from situations. Consequently, these people are less likely to interact as effectively as their less stressed colleagues. The effects are particularly important in call centers where good customer relations are extremely important. It is far easier to retain a customer than to attract a new one.

Mistakes

Stress is likely to have an impact on people's thought processes, leading to a lack of clear thinking, poor concentration and attention to detail, and, in turn, people are more likely to make mistakes. Mistakes in themselves can be costly but in addition there is the time taken to put things right. There is clearly an impact on quality and customer satisfaction and it will also impact on relationships with colleagues.

Innovation and creativity

Most organizations today require people to have the capability to think differently, look for new and better ways of doing things, and respond positively to change. The brain functions far more effectively when people experience eustress. In this state people feel stimulated, but have the right degree of calmness to be able to access new thinking. When people reach the state of hyper-stress, they are likely to operate as if on autopilot, doing things the way they have always done, and become much less open to new and different ways of doing things.

Without a degree of creativity and innovation, organizations are likely to fall behind their rivals. Whilst the effects on sectors such as the pharmaceutical and IT industries mean the difference between survival or failure, most sectors – because of the level of competition and the level and quality of service expected by customers – need creativity and innovation to survive and grow.

Summary

When making the business case for stress interventions or taking time to manage the stress of others, remember:

- Stress can cause damage to people both physically and psychologically
- When stress is ignored, the result can be life threatening or will be responsible for great human misery and suffering at work and home
- People are left to suffer because of a lack of understanding of stress, business pressures, managers who do not have the necessary skills to deal with the situation and a lack of expert help

- Productivity of people experiencing excessive stress is likely to suffer, as well as their colleagues
- Costs of mounting a stress initiative should not be a deterrent, it does not have to be expensive and the costs will be recovered
- Fit and healthy staff are as much as 20 percent more productive than their ill or unhealthy colleagues
- People will interact less effectively with others when excessively stressed
- People make more mistakes when stress levels are excessive
- When people experience hyper-stress, they are likely to operate as if on autopilot, doing things the way they have always done, and are less receptive to new and different ways of doing things.

PART III

Stress
An Organizational Perspective

5 Introduction

This section has been written from an organizational perspective, that is, to help the reader to manage stress within the organization. It has been primarily written for HR specialists, health and safety advisers, and occupational health professionals. Consultants advising organizations on managing stress will also find this part useful. Line managers seeking to manage stress within their area of the organization are advised to skim through this part, as most organizations require line managers to take responsibility for stress management. Having read Part III, managers will be more able to take a proactive role and gain the benefits of staff that are able to fulfil their potential. They will receive further help in Parts IV and V of the book.

This section of the book offers answers to the questions posed below.

Why do people experience excessive stress?	(Chapter 6)
Which are the most stressful jobs?	(Chapter 7)
How do we know whether there is a problem associated with stress?	(Chapter 8)
What do we do about it?	(Chapter 9)
What do we legally have to do about it?	(Chapter 10)
Does a stress policy help?	(Chapter 11)
What is the upside of stress?	(Chapter 12)
How can we be proactive?	(Chapter 13)
What are the key learning points?	(Chapter 14)

This part of the book will help readers to address the questions identified. The approach adopted supports the view of the authors that stress management is an integral part of sound management practice. If the stress levels of employees are effectively managed, it will result in a productive, healthy workforce able to fulfil its potential. With the right processes in place, excessive stress will be prevented and the organization will, in turn, meet legislative requirements.

An approach based on a clear understanding of the issues will result in more effective interventions and outcomes and, in the long-term, will help prevent stress from reaching unacceptable levels for people within the organization. Chapter 6 introduces the reader to frameworks for understanding the causes of stress within organizations and likely external pressures. Chapter 7 reviews research into jobs that have the potential to raise stress levels for the jobholders and strategies for keeping stress at more acceptable levels are summarized.

Having identified possible causes, the next stage is to gather data to highlight any problem areas within the organization and develop action plans for dealing with issues. The approach outlined in Chapter 8 draws heavily on the advice given by the Health and Safety Executive in the UK. This stage provides an essential building block for developing sound action plans to cope with and ultimately prevent stress from occurring in the first place.

Chapter 9 outlines the various interventions an organization can make to manage stress. A framework for dealing with the root causes is described, followed by a range of approaches that can be adopted at organizational level. These approaches are described in greater detail in Part V.

Most organizations are concerned with complying with legal requirements. Chapter 10 gives a detailed overview of the relevant UK legislation to raise awareness; it also explains the implications for organizations and managers in managing stress of others. Chapter 11 looks at how organizations can create and introduce a stress policy, with an extensive example from the public sector.

Chapter 12 explains that stress can be positive – eu-stress. In a competitive and changing environment, every effort should be made by organizations to help people to operate at peak performance. It draws on research to help people get "in the flow" and this approach will be built on in Part V when readers will be helped to build and sustain resilience.

Chapter 13 adopts a proactive approach to stress management. It summarizes findings from major research into health and well-being and the initiatives that seek to encourage organizations to create great working environments. Progressive organizations have moved beyond managing stress, to strategies for enhancing health and well-being at work.

Chapter 14 is a summary of the key lessons to be learnt from Part III.

6 Causes of Stress within Organizations

Introduction

The potential causes of stress are many and various and the list grows longer as, for whatever reason, people are forced to change the way they view the world, their work, and the way they see themselves. Change, whether looked for or imposed, leads to expected and unexpected consequences that will affect the pressure people experience and their ability to deal with it.

It is useful to use a framework to categorize the causes of stress, whether considering its risk and impact from an individual or an organizational perspective. Adopting this approach helps to focus attention on where stress is most likely to occur and what the root cause might be. In the UK it is mandatory to conduct a stress risk assessment to identify potential causes of stress (risk assessment is discussed fully in Chapter 8). Conducting a risk assessment helps to identify potential causes of stress either for a job in general, or for a particular individual – depending on whether the risk assessment is specifically focused on the job or on the person doing the job. This, in turn, helps to identify those interventions that will be most appropriate to minimize the risk of stress or deal with its impact. Interventions will be discussed fully in Chapter 9.

This chapter outlines a model for categorizing causes of stress within an organization, and some examples, identified by the Henley Stress Special Interest Group, will be outlined. Those concerned with managing people's stress cannot ignore sources of stress outside the workplace. Major life event changes are outlined, with reference to the Holmes and Rahe scale, as well as some of the everyday occurrences that can contribute to increased levels of stress.

All those with an interest in stress should read this chapter. HR specialists and occupational health experts will find the framework helpful when trying to assess the root cause of stress and planning appropriate interventions. Managers concerned with managing their own and other's stress will be more able to do so having understood the dynamic relationship between a range of factors that can contribute to increased stress levels.

Classifying the Causes of Stress

Figure 6.1 shows a simple model to classify possible causes under three headings. This model is based on the view that whatever a risk analysis indicates in the workplace, and whatever inherent risk there may be in particular jobs, the actual occurrence of negative stress is "person specific." In any given scenario, no individual will react in the same way – one person demonstrating resilience and a potential to deal with far more pressure than another. This is likely to be due to a range of factors, some more and others less apparent, as the example in Figure 6.2 demonstrates.

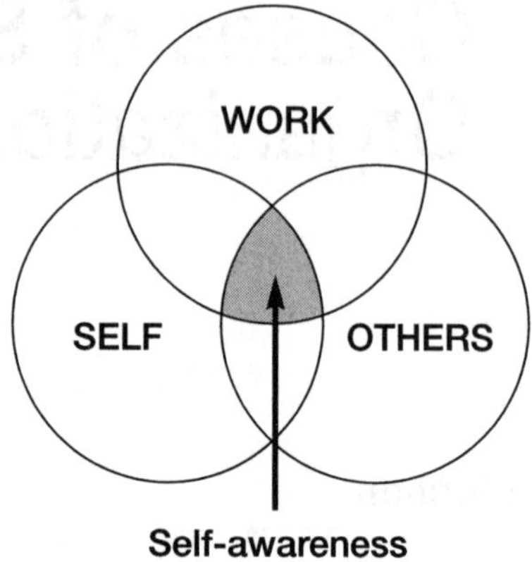

Figure 6.1 **A model to classify the causes of stress**

The occurrence of negative stress is dependent on a number of factors, as outlined in Figure 6.3 and these can be grouped into three categories around the individual's ability to manage:

1. Themselves
2. Their relationship with others
3. Their relationship to work and the workplace.

Showing the model in three interlocking circles recognizes that many single causes will have an impact on more than one of the three categories and may

> **Kevin and Martin were regional sales managers working for a business solutions organization. They had similar experience and length of service and both were doing similar roles, but covering different regions. The company went through a major restructuring program, the regional structure changed quite dramatically and both managers became home-based.**
>
> **Six months later Kevin had adapted well to the changes, but Martin appeared to be struggling and had taken time off sick. This was unusual for him: his manager had a review meeting with him and some of the difficulties started to emerge. Martin was finding it hard to adjust to the new ways of working. He missed the regular contact with the sales team and his restructured region was forcing him to work longer hours. He realized that he was experiencing hyper-stress.**
>
> **Further discussion revealed that he had a young baby, was getting insufficient sleep and the effects of change had made him feel much less confident than usual. His perception of the situation was a critical cause of stress.**
>
> **This example shows that Martin was experiencing stress as a result of factors in all three categories. The manager agreed to reassess the boundaries of Martin's region and organize more regular team meetings to address the work and relationships categories. These, in turn, would reduce some of the pressure and, with appropriate support, Martin would probably regain his self-confidence.**

Figure 6.2 **Responses to a particular situation by different people**

even impact in all three – as was demonstrated in the case study above. A key aspect of an individual's ability to deal with pressure will be self-awareness and this will be true whichever category of cause is being considered. Hence self-awareness has been put in the centre of the model. Self-awareness (or the lack of it) will impact on the person's ability to deal with stress, whatever the cause.

This leads to the conclusion that "my relationship with myself" (the "self" circle) is likely to be the key, even if the apparent cause of the stress is a factor such as work pressure, or a bad relationship with the boss. When considering stress and its causes at an organizational level, remember that any risk of stress will, nevertheless, depend largely on how any given individual perceives and responds to a situation. This was shown in the example in Figure 6.2.

The arrows shown in Figure 6.3 indicate that in assessing the cause of stress and what intervention to use, the assumption should not be made that a work-related issue is the only factor. Tackling a possible cause under the work category may help, but other aspects related to the individual have to be considered to ensure an effective intervention. This is an important consideration when assessing degrees of risk in both the workplace and for any given individual.

Looking at causes of stress in a more holistic way helps to develop awareness that whenever people interventions are made within organizations, they are likely to affect levels of stress, regardless of whether this is the real focus. These will include recruitment and selection techniques, performance and succession management, communication policies, leadership development, and change initiatives. The causes of stress will naturally drive the interventions that an organization will consider to reduce risk and tackle existing stress. This is illustrated in the example in Figure 6.4.

Self	Others	Work
Ways of working	Relationships	Style
Control	Motivation	Mental state
Environment	Flexibility	Attitude
Hours	Style	Personality
Overload	Tone	Preferred style/method
Ethics	Their awareness	Issues e.g. finance worries
Culture	Empathy	Disability
Skill match	Communication	Values
Skill requirements	Stability	Baggage
Politics	Reaction	Flexibility
Support	Boundaries of relationships	Locus of control
Remuneration	Expectations of others	Motivation
Management style		Confidence
Communication		Self-esteem
Expectations		Tolerance of change
Targets		Health
Stability/change		Cultural background
Organizational values		Expectations of job/life
Bureaucracy ➡	➡	Experience

Figure 6.3 **Examples of causes of stress identified by the Henley Stress Special Interest Group**

In one large organization, where high turnover and absence was felt to be a priority issue that needed addressing, not only were the workplace environment and management style felt to be important factors to address, but it was also realized that individual health and fitness and the building of self-awareness, to increase choice and build resilience, should be a critical aspect in any serious initiative.

The organization was about to launch a major leadership program to address key business issues. It incorporated a health and well-being section into the leadership and management training events, thus adopting a more holistic approach to people development. It was felt that a greater, more sustainable impact was achieved as a result of this holistic approach.

Figure 6.4 **An organization's assessment of potential causes**

As we can see from the examples listed in Figure 6.3 the causes of stress are many and various (the list is not meant to be comprehensive, simply illustrative). By categorizing the causes in this simple structure, the authors believe that the importance of tackling the root causes of stress is of critical importance. It is all too easy to focus interventions, be they organizational or at an individual level, at the presenting symptom rather than any deep-rooted causes.

The Health and Safety Executive (HSE) in the UK has identified hazards in its *Management Standards for Tackling Work-related Stress* (2004) in six categories, namely:

1. Demands (for example workload and physical hazards)
2. Control (how much say a person has)
3. Support (encouragement, sponsorship, and resources)
4. Relationships (for example bullying and harassment)
5. Change (the way it is managed and communicated)
6. Role (understanding role and avoiding conflicting roles).

The authors suggest that factors unique to the individual will always have an impact on the likelihood of stress occurring.

In considering possible causes at an organizational level, it is useful to group them in categories. Having identified these, the model helps to clarify why tackling the symptoms, rather than the root causes, may not prove to have a sustainable impact (see Chapter 18). The importance of knowing the individual, and the context in which behaviors indicating stress are exhibiting themselves, now becomes clearer.

Some of the potential causes of stress will now be explored in more detail.

Individuals' Ability to Manage their Relationship with Work and the Workplace

CONTROL

Many people have a need for control, some more than others – depending on their personality type, values, and so on. This often makes itself very clear in the workplace. Control may include the power to make decisions over others or could simply be control over work methods used. Some managers adopt an overcontrolling management style and this, in turn, causes their staff to feel out of control. For some individuals control only becomes an issue at work when they lack control in other parts of their lives.

> *My manager never lets me think for myself. Even the simplest of tasks he explains in great detail and checks my work all the time. I feel so frustrated and disempowered.* **Manager in a local authority**

OVERLOAD

This may be too much work, work that is too demanding, or where there is too much pressure to meet challenging targets, and is regularly quoted as a source of stress. People are tending to work longer hours, either staying at the workplace or taking work home. Many complain of being unable to "switch off" from work during their free time, thus preventing the opportunity to recharge from the pressures of working life. The more enlightened realize that by working shorter hours, productivity rates are likely to improve.

> *Since the last reorganization my workload has increased considerably. I find myself getting to work early and leaving much later in the evening. I have noticed recently that I have become very irritable with people.* **Manager in the service industry**

SKILLS MATCH

The more enlightened organizations endeavor to manage talent in a way that utilizes an individual's strengths to the full; while in other organizations people find themselves moved into work for which they are ill suited, leading to resources being wasted, poor performance, increased levels of stress, and higher turnover levels.

When people find themselves doing work for which they are ill suited in terms of their skills set, stress can occur. This may be for a short period if they are given appropriate skills training that proves successful. Often such training is not forthcoming, or is not entirely successful, resulting in the person being "a square peg in a round hole" and prolonged periods of stress.

> *I had time off work with a stress-related illness. When I returned to work I had an interview with personnel and I moved to a different department and I am coping with my work so much better. The new job is more suitable for me, I feel less pressurized.* **Administrator in a local authority**

MANAGEMENT STYLE

"People don't leave a company, they leave their boss." This is a well-known truism. An employee's relationship with the boss is essential for motivation and high levels of performance. If this relationship is not a positive one, performance and morale may suffer. Some managers have a macho approach to stress, taking the view that "stress is for wimps" and they fail to give the necessary support when a member of the team experiences stress. A critical aspect of the relationship is the management style of the boss.

No boss can be perfect, and no employee really expects him or her to be so. However, the ability to satisfy the needs of an employee by adapting the management style in any given situation will create a positive and motivating relationship. In the absence of such a matching process, the relationship can prove negative and create stress on both sides, but predominantly in the employee. At an organizational level, management style is reflected in the culture/climate of the business and is often set by the senior management team and then cascaded down through the organization.

> *I keep my head down and try to keep out of my boss's way when my stress levels are high. Stress doesn't come up on his radar. He sees stress as a sign of weakness and just doesn't want to know.* **Manager in a utility company**

COMMUNICATION

Part of management style is effective communication, but this also comes into play at an organizational level. Availability of information and regular communication on all issues affecting the work of the individual and the nature of the business is a critical part of morale building; the absence of clear, effective communication will increase uncertainty and possibly cause stress. Information flow is particularly important during times of change when feelings of insecurity make people feel more vulnerable.

Individuals' Ability to Manage their Relationship with Others

MOTIVATION

Motivation in the "others" column (Figure 6.3) indicates that a person's ability to motivate themselves in a team situation and understand what motivates others will have an impact on the likelihood of experiencing stress. Individuals seek to satisfy a range of needs in a team situation, including the need for achievement, the need for affiliation, and the need for power (McClelland, 1961). Relationships are likely to be improved/managed more effectively if needs are met – both in and out of work. Hence, there is less likelihood of stressful situations arising.

BOUNDARIES OF RELATIONSHIPS

Being able to manage others in terms of the nature of differing relationships and the consequent expectations is, again, likely to reduce the occurrence of stress-inducing situations. If the individual is clear about the boundaries of relationships, he or she is less likely to experience stress. This might be the expectation of a boss not calling after work hours or friends not calling at the house on an impulse.

> *I like to keep my work and home life quite separate. I feel additional pressure when my manager expects me to socialize with the team outside office hours. I have a young family and want to spend quality time with them.* **Manager in the IT industry**

EXPECTATIONS

People working together build up expectations of one another in terms of providing support, gaining trust, doing what they say they will do, and generally developing mutual respect. When any of these expectations are unmet, pressure is likely to build.

Individuals' Ability to Manage Themselves

PREFERRED STYLE/METHOD

People have preferred ways of working, being managed, organizing themselves, and dealing with conflict. A variety of diagnostic tools, such as the Occupational Personality Questionnaire and Myers-Briggs Type Indicator, can help us to understand our preferences.

It comes as no surprise that if people find themselves in situations or environments where they have to alter their preferred ways of doing things, particularly if this is for a prolonged period, they run the risk of reacting adversely to this type of pressure.

VALUES

Most of the decisions around how people live their lives can be tracked back to their own personal values. It is common for organizations to articulate and communicate a set of values that provide employees with a context to understand the business in which they are working, how decisions are made in that business, and what is expected of them.

With the best will in the world, it is not always easy for employees to adhere to the espoused values and this can lead to a mismatch between individual expectations and actual outcomes.

At a personal level, individuals may find that their own values do not fit comfortably with those of the organization. This will be true whether they have explicitly defined their own values or not and is likely to be a mismatch with the "real" values represented in the culture of the business – not the espoused values. It is rare that employees find themselves disagreeing with the values listed in the company's internal communications, but they may well be incongruent with the reality.

Individuals may exist happily in the business with this mismatch causing little problem. However, in circumstances where individuals are addressing personal issues that cause them to confront their own behaviors and those of others, this mismatch may be the source of undue pressure and stress. If people are unaware of their own values, there can be a lack of understanding as to why they feel uncomfortable – which, in itself, can further induce stress. If individuals are fully aware of their own values and what these mean in terms of their work life, they are better equipped to deal with the aspects of their work where a confrontation might occur.

> *I have a strong sense of right and wrong and believe in treating people fairly. I am usually very tolerant and always see the good side of people. However, if something happens that I see as morally wrong, I find myself becoming very angry.* **HR manager in the service industry**

SELF-ESTEEM

The authors believe that high self-esteem is likely to lead to a greater resilience to the causes of stress (and even an avoidance of situations that lead to stress), through assertive behavior and the recognition and understanding of situations that might otherwise be damaging to those with a lower self-esteem.

When individuals are exposed to high levels of pressure for prolonged periods, they are likely to experience a loss of self-esteem, which can ultimately lead to high stress levels.

TOLERANCE OF CHANGE

All people experience change at work and in their private lives. Some of this is imposed on them and is out of their control; some they create and drive themselves. A part of resilience is the ability to absorb change whatever its sources, as it is likely to be a buffer against stress.

The emotional cycle of change clearly indicates that during change and prolonged periods of uncertainty, people's needs and emotions alter and if the change is not properly managed, they are likely to experience excessive stress. Figure 6.5 shows the variations that take place in performance and emotional state over a period of time. When change is announced or planned by an organization, individual performance can increase because the period of uncertainty is over and there is a feeling of relief. However, the honeymoon period is often short-lived and people experience a range of negative emotions culminating in depression and despair. Stress levels are high at this stage and can continue for long periods if not properly managed.

However, once people can see a way forward, they can start to take actions that will lead to more positive emotions and increased performance. People's reactions to change situations vary considerably, depending on the size of the change and the level of support available.

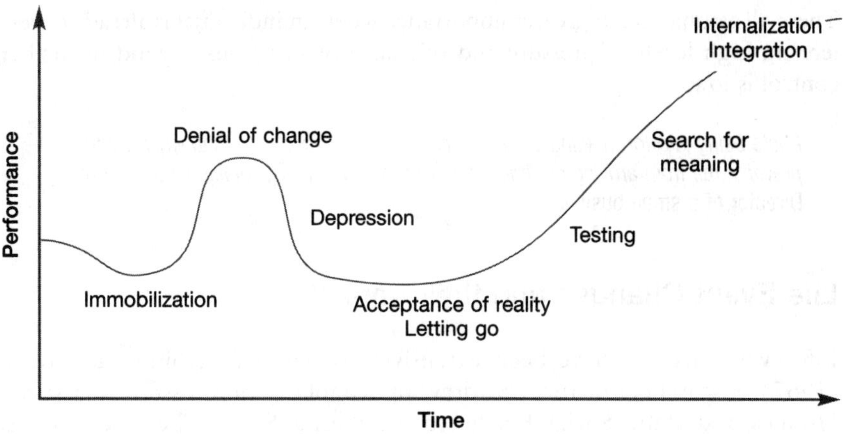

Figure 6.5 **The change curve and its impact on emotions and performance**

HEALTH

Internal pressure can build up when people feel unable to work at their full capacity through ill health. Worry associated with illness can also cause stress. If the illness is sufficiently serious requiring absence from work, people will experience further stress as workloads build up.

Research has shown that much illness is stress-related, setting up a vicious circle. Chapter 25 will help the reader to understand how to build up resilience and stand a better chance of sustaining health and well-being, even when experiencing high levels of pressure.

The Stresses of Everyday Life

There are a number of pressures that occur from situations (usually beyond a person's immediate control) that, by themselves, may appear insignificant but cumulatively can add to stress levels – sometimes the straw that broke the camel's back. These may include:

- Commuting
- Queuing
- Losing items
- Lateness (self or others)
- Computers and email
- Rail strikes
- Difficult neighbours
- Machine breakdown (at home or at work)
- Interruptions
- Jet lag.

These all assume much greater importance when an individual is already experiencing high levels of pressure and tolerance of situations beyond his or her control is low.

> *I hate being late for meetings. There is nothing more frustrating than when traffic prevents me from arriving on time. I get that feeling of being totally out of control.*
> Director of a small business

Life Event Changes and their Impact

Life event changes have been extensively researched. Holmes and Rahe (1967), researchers in the US, drew up a ranking of stressful events: the Holmes and Rahe Social Readjustment Rating Scale. The research was conducted across a range of cultures and findings showed a remarkable similarity in the degree of importance attached to specific life events by different cultural groups. Death of a spouse was viewed as the most stressful, requiring the greatest degree of adjustment and was given a rating of 100. The other 42 events were rated in comparison with this event and are shown in Figure 6.6.

The research found that there was a high correlation between the amount of change people had experienced and their likelihood of becoming ill. Interestingly, the illness sometimes occurred when people had passed the major period of adjustment and were starting to relax a little – rather like getting ill and having headaches at weekends or during holidays when the pressure is off.

To assess the amount of change, people are required to add up their scores for events experienced over the last 12 months. Sometimes it may be necessary to go back as far as 24 months, as stress can be cumulative.

To interpret the scores:

- Less than 150 = moderate chance of developing stress-related illness
- Between 150 and 299 = average risk of developing stress-related illness
- 300 or more = higher than average risk of developing stress-related illness in future.

Summary

LESSONS FOR MANAGERS

- People are unique and causes of stress will vary from individual to individual and situation to situation. Managers need to take a holistic view of the circumstances.
- Good management is good stress management.
- A good manager will know his or her people and will have ensured that they are well matched with their jobs in terms of ability, skill mix, and disposition.
- Manage work allocation to avoid people becoming overloaded.
- When identifying causes of stress, recognize the importance of under-

RANK	LIFE EVENT	MEAN VALUE
1	Death of a spouse	100
2	Divorce	73
3	Marital separation	65
4	Jail term	63
5	Death of close family member	63
6	Personal injury or illness	63
7	Marriage	50
8	Fired at work	47
9	Marital reconciliation	45
10	Retirement	45
11	Change in health of family member	44
12	Pregnancy	40
13	Sex difficulties	39
14	Gain of new family member	39
15	Business readjustment	39
16	Change in financial state	38
17	Death of a close friend	37
18	Change in different line of work	36
19	Change in number of arguments with spouse	35
20	Mortgage over $10,000	31
21	Foreclosure of mortgage or loan	30
22	Change in responsibilities at work	29
23	Son or daughter leaving home	29
24	Trouble with in-laws	29
25	Outstanding achievement	28
26	Spouse begins or stops work	26
27	Begin or end school	26
28	Change in living conditions	25
29	Revision of personal habits	24
30	Trouble with boss	23
31	Change in work hours or conditions	20
32	Change in residence	20
33	Change in schools	20
34	Change in recreation	19
35	Change in church activities	19
36	Change in social activities	18
37	Mortgage or loan less than $10,000	17
38	Change in sleeping habits	16
39	Change in number of family get-togethers	15
40	Change in eating habits	15
41	Vacation	13
42	Christmas	12
43	Minor violations of the law	11
	Total	

Figure 6.6 **Life event changes**

Source: Holmes and Rahe (1967). Reprinted with kind permission of Elsevier Inc.

standing and viewing the person within the context of the team and workplace.
- Understand that the causes of stress may arise from important life event changes. If a person is experiencing several changes in his or her home life, it is likely to lower resistance to stress in the workplace.

LESSONS FOR HR

- It is important to work closely with line managers to select the right people for the jobs.
- Managers need to be trained to understand the importance of diagnosing causes of stress, rather than treating the symptoms.
- Managers need to be skilled up to be effective managers and leaders, who select, train, support, and review the performance of their staff. This is a good strategy for reducing hyper-stress and distress within an organization.
- Understand the importance of helping to ensure that the espoused values of the organization become a reality.

LESSONS FOR OCCUPATIONAL HEALTH AND HEALTH AND SAFETY ADVISERS

- Assess jobs and advise on overload
- Assist HR and line managers in identifying the root causes of stress.

7 The Most Stressful Jobs

Introduction

Stress is self-generated and the extent to which people experience stress varies from person to person, depending on their perception and reaction to the situation. However, certain jobs expose people to higher levels of pressure on a consistent basis. People are put at a greater risk of experiencing stress when the jobs they are performing consistently expose them to high levels of pressure.

This chapter reviews the work of Cooper et al. (1988) and most recently Robertson and Cooper (2004) in identifying jobs that are classified as most stressful and, in contrast, those that are rated least stressful. It includes the discussions held at Henley by the Stress Special Interest Group identifying the jobs that in their experience have proved to be stressful.

Some examples outlining the factors contributing to excessive stress are analysed. This chapter will be useful for those required to recruit and manage staff in particularly stressful jobs, as well as the jobholders. It will also help to alert people towards the potential hot spots in an organization.

The Most Stressful Jobs Survey 1985

The *Sunday Times* commissioned this survey and Cary Cooper worked with six stress researchers. The approach adopted is described in Cooper et al. (1988). They evaluated 100 jobs on a 10-point scale, with 1 being the least stressful and 10 the most stressful. They used their professional judgment based on research findings and available health trend data. Figure 7.1 lists the average rankings of a range of jobs.

This survey was commissioned at the time of the miner's strike in 1985 and

Miner	8.3	Social worker	6.0
Police officer	7.7	Manager	5.8
Airline pilot	7.5	Bus driver	5.4
Prison officer	7.5	Civil servant	4.3
Dentist	7.3	Accountant	4.3
Actor	7.2	Postman	4.0
Politician	7.0	Computer operator	3.7
Doctor	6.8	Occupational therapist	3.5
Nurse/midwife	6.5	Museum worker	2.0
Teacher	6.2	Librarian	2.0

Figure 7.1 **Rankings of a range of jobs**

the job of miner had the highest average ranking. At this time there were threats of closure of mines and job insecurity was running high. Combine this pressure with working in a dangerous and unpleasant environment that is physically demanding and one can understand the high ranking.

An airline pilot was also ranked high. Pilots have responsibility for people's lives and may have to respond quickly and decisively in an emergency. They are also exposed to varying levels of pressure: high activity during takeoff and landing, interspersed with times when pressure is much lower. These variable pressure levels put added strain on the body when compared with more consistent levels.

Occupations such as a museum worker, librarian, and occupational therapist were perceived as less stressful. These jobs were seen to offer greater levels of control and people performing them were perceived as being exposed to lower levels of pressure. However, shortly after the rankings were published in the *Sunday Times,* a library approached one of the authors to run a stress workshop. The librarians' view of the level of stress in the job was very different: one of the pressures was the contact with people who could be rude and aggressive.

The Most Stressful Jobs Survey 1997

Cary Cooper repeated the survey in 1997 assessing 104 jobs. Factors used to make the assessment included hours worked, workload, deadline pressures, and levels of responsibility. Pettit (2003) reported Cooper's findings that 60 percent of jobs assessed by his team showed increased stress levels. Those particularly affected included the armed forces, social workers, teachers, farmers, local government, nurses and the ambulance service. The UK's most and least stressful jobs as identified in the 1997 survey are listed in Figure 7.2.

Cooper was convinced that it was not the jobs themselves that were stressful, but the amount of change the particular profession had undergone. Teachers have seen an enormous increase in paperwork, stressful inspections, assessments, and the introduction of league tables. The civil service has exper-

UK's 10 most stressful jobs	UK's 10 least stressful jobs
Prison officer	Librarian
Police officer	Museum personnel
Social worker	Biologist
Teacher	Nursery nurse
Ambulance service worker	Astronomer
Nurse/midwife	Beauty therapist
Doctor	Linguist
Fireman	Remedial gymnast
Dentist	Speech therapist
Miner	Pharmacist

Figure 7.2 **The UK's 10 most and least stressful jobs**

Source: Adapted from Pettit (2003)

Graham had been a GP for several years when he was interviewed. He said that he had experienced more and more pressure in recent years – firstly dealing with changes in technology requiring him to input data on the computer at each consultation. There had also been changes in funding and he had taken on managerial responsibilities, having become more senior in his practice.

Life has also become more complex for GPs who used only to work alongside other GPs and the receptionists. Today Graham has to work with a variety of other "experts": district nurses, health visitors, physiotherapists, and social workers.

He described the pressures during surgery hours, saying the time allowed for each consultation was much too short to be able to diagnose the underlying causes of many of the symptoms presented to him by his patients. He was also aware of the pressures for making the correct diagnosis – an error of judgment could be life threatening.

In addition to patient care, there is a constant need to keep abreast of changes in the medical field, including knowledge of the latest drugs on the market. Graham also said that the referral process has changed: GPs have always made referrals solely to consultants; today they are also made to osteopaths, physiotherapists, and chiropodists. This, again, adds to the pressure.

Graham was very aware of the excessive pressure he was experiencing, admitting that he often drank too much and was inclined to worry excessively. He was looking forward to taking early retirement as a way of escaping from the pressures of his job.

Figure 7.3 **Stresses experienced by a GP**

ienced similar increases in the volume of paperwork. Change that results in less control makes the job more stressful. One of the most stressful jobs is that of a GP, and some of the reasons for this are shown in Figure 7.3.

In this second survey, airline pilots came out mid-ranking together with air traffic controllers. The job of pilot was high on the list in the first survey, but both pilots and air traffic controllers are very carefully matched to their jobs, according to Cooper (Pettit, 2003). Their training is lengthy and expensive and competition for these jobs is high, enabling recruiters to select those best suited to the jobs. In an earlier study, Sparks and Cooper (1999) identified that air traffic controllers have high levels of control over their job: this factor is important for keeping pressure at acceptable levels.

NURSING STAFF

Woolf (2004) reported that the Health & Safety Executive (HSE) in the UK has found that more than three in ten nurses suffer stress at work. It is likely that workload demands and an increase in violence contribute to this; Unison said that frontline NHS workers were not only suffering from violence, but insults and intimidation from aggressive patients.

Robertson Cooper Survey (2004)

The most recent research identifies the top six most stressful jobs:

- Teachers
- Police officers
- Social care workers
- Emergency paramedics
- Call center staff
- Prison officers.

The least stressful jobs were:

- Private sector executives
- Analysts
- School lunchtime supervisors.

In this latest survey, 26 jobs were evaluated on three stress-related areas: physical health, psychological well-being, and job satisfaction. The most stressful jobs all involved contact with the general public in emotionally intense situations and/or where the working environment was governed by strict rules. The research used a stress evaluation tool – ASSET, which measured a range of stressors and stress outcomes.

Reporting on the research, Millar (2004), stated that ambulance workers: "suffered the most with their physical health. Social services had the worst psychological well being and prison officers got the least job satisfaction." Those in less stressful jobs, such as company directors, have higher levels of job satisfaction and are less likely to be physically injured, or come to psychological harm. They had the lowest level of anxiety and came bottom of the table on all three dimensions. Directors in the public sector also came surprisingly low and reported particularly high levels of job satisfaction. The research found that teachers had a higher level of stress and lower job satisfaction than head teachers and teaching assistants. This is supported by the example of a deputy head teacher outlined in Figure 7.4.

Another problem experienced by professionals, including teachers, prison officers, doctors, and nurses, is workplace bullying, according to Cooper who was interviewed by Pollard (2002). A survey conducted by Cooper and reported by Pollard found that one in four had been bullied at work in the last five years; this grew to one in three in teaching. It is estimated that 30–50 percent of stress is related to bullying. In Cooper's view there are two types of bully:

1. The *psychopathic bully* who has low self-esteem and may not be particularly good at his or her job: they bully others to enhance their own status. This type of person has a personality dysfunction and is less common than the second form of bully.
2. The *overloaded bully* who takes on too much work and then dumps on others. This type of bullying is increasing in organizations as workloads increase generally.

Martin was a deputy head teacher of a junior school when he attended a stress management course for head teachers and their deputies. In discussions during the program, it soon became evident that the deputies were experiencing more stress than the head teachers. Martin explained that deputy heads retained teaching responsibilities, but also had to stand in for head teachers when the latter were off site. This dual role was very stressful.

Martin described how work overload had occurred particularly since the requirement for regular reporting on children came in: the level of paperwork had increased greatly over the last ten years. The national curriculum was introduced in the late 1980s: there are now a set of subjects that have to be taught in a specific way and, combined with SATS and league tables, this has given teachers an even heavier workload.

OFSTED inspections, difficult-to-control children, parents, and the general lack of respect for teachers all raise stress levels considerably.

Figure 7.4 **Stresses experienced by a deputy head teacher**

Those who are repeatedly bullied reported the poorest health, the lowest work motivation, satisfaction, and productivity and the highest absenteeism and intention to leave. Cooper felt that there was a particular problem in the public sector, where a third had experienced or witnessed bullying. The more hierarchical the organization, the more bullying was likely to cascade down.

The *Mail on Sunday* (2004) stated that teachers are claiming more than £50 million a year in compensation for the stress of their jobs – according to insurer Zurich Municipal. Claims have risen 40 percent and a total of 240 percent in five years. Zurich Municipal, which insures local authorities against the cost of legal action by employees, said teachers usually attributed their problems to heavy workloads, badly behaved pupils, or conflicts in the classroom.

CALL CENTER WORKERS

One of the occupations cited in the Robertson Cooper survey was a call center worker. Call centers have grown rapidly in the last 15 years, employing 2–3 percent of the UK working population. Similar numbers also work in call centers in the US, Australia, and other European countries, according to Holman (2003), who has conducted several research studies on call centers.

Holman found that they are not the electronic sweatshops they are reputed to be, nor are call center jobs necessarily stressful. Managers have choices in the way they run such centers and can reduce stress levels. The level of employee well-being in call centers depends on the way jobs are designed, how systems are used for monitoring calls, expectations of performance, the degree of freedom when responding to calls, and how supportive management is. If the right approaches are adopted, stress levels can be dramatically reduced – impacting on the bottom line for organizations.

These findings are particularly important at a time when a number of organizations have relocated their call centers overseas to take advantage of cheap labor. Although it would be difficult to match costs in the UK, experience is showing that customer care and quality of service is more difficult to achieve overseas.

However, in contrast to Holman's findings, Doke (2004) reported a study conducted by the University of Sheffield and UMIST for the HSE, which found that call center work was more stressful than working in other jobs. Occupational health experts who regularly work with call center staff generally agree. A Swedish report found that call center staff in Sweden are similarly affected. In Sweden the focus of attention has been on the repetitive nature of the job and serious discussions are currently taking place to achieve more variety in people's working lives. A plan has been put forward for call center workers to spend half their time working at the call center and the other half taking care of the elderly.

In recent years organizations have been taking steps to act on health issues related to the stress of call center workers. In 2002 Capital One, although ranked one of the top UK employers of choice, had a higher voluntary attrition rate than other employers. It launched a stress audit and proved that stress was affecting employee satisfaction and attrition rates. It took steps to address the issue, including stress management programs and training for managers on conflict, delegation, team development, and counselling; it also introduced chill-out rooms. The actions taken have had positive results.

BT is setting up "next generation" contact centers. Improvements will explore:

- Health and safety
- Welfare
- Branding
- Environment
- Equipment and furniture
- Management.

BT is also launching a large-scale offensive against stress: tested at its call centers, it is now being expanded to the entire BT Group. People complete an online questionnaire aimed at assessing their level of stress and stressors in the workplace (see Chapter 8 for further details).

In summary, managing the stress of call center operators requires sensitive management and effective training and skill development – identified through the monitoring of calls. Targets for call centers need to focus as much on quality of service and customer satisfaction as on productivity and cost efficiency. Finally, attention must be given to the work environment and the well-being of staff, incorporating sufficient rest breaks and a variety of activity where possible.

THE POLICE SERVICE

The police have featured in all stressful job surveys. Wigham (2003b) reported that the Metropolitan Police Service (Met) was about to launch a major stress

Marie talked enthusiastically about her job, having completed eight years of service. She had always wanted to be a policewoman and is currently working on patrol. She described the variety of her work and her desire to serve the community in which she worked – one of the London suburbs. She was, however, well aware of her responsibilities in the police force.

She described how she is constantly called to emergencies, some of which have the potential to be life threatening, others emotionally draining. She is also required to work on shifts that are physically demanding. Marie said she has known colleagues who have had to leave their jobs because they found the pressure was more than they could tolerate.

Figure 7.5 **Stresses experienced by a policewoman**

audit, being aware of the stressful nature of jobs within the force. It aimed to survey 10,000 staff to be clearer about levels of stress and the signs and symptoms of stress; it also planned to investigate sickness levels. The Met viewed the situation as complex and subsequently planned to introduce a variety of interventions to match the range of different jobs within the organization. At the same time, it introduced an extensive health promotion plan to address the well-being of staff, as well as stress. Figure 7.5 explains some of the pressures the police face on a day-to-day basis.

A staff survey at Kent police reported by the BBC (2004) has found many employees are stressed. Phone operators taking calls from the public were found to be particularly at risk, as well as detectives and officers working with prisoners. Staff working in custody suites and specialist units, such as firearms and dog handling, reported concerns over shift patterns and antisocial hours. Some detectives said their workloads were too great, with not enough staff and equipment. At Kent police an average 10–12 working days is lost per employee each year due to sick leave – about three times the rate of the public sector.

Stressful Jobs Identified by the Henley Stress Special Interest Group

The group discussed the concept of stressful jobs and the factors that they considered when identifying a job as being stressful. In common with the authors, they agreed that any job had the potential to be stressful and a person could experience excessive stress because of their own disposition and set of unique circumstances.

They did, however, recognize that certain jobs had higher levels of pressure associated with them. Some of the jobs they identified had been highlighted by earlier research; others based on experience within their own organizations were mentioned for the first time. The jobs identified are summarized in Figure 7.6.

Job	Examples of potential sources of pressure
Police/the armed forces	Jobs with less flexibility Experiencing traumatic situations Adhering to "chain of command" procedures Consequences of mistakes – life or death situations
Football/sports managers	Pressure to achieve high performance through others – the need to achieve winning results Lack of control over the situation
Internal audit staff	Evaluation of performance of others Stress from those being audited
Sales staff	Targets Monthly monitoring against targets Bonus systems
Bailiffs	Repossession of property of others Dealing with the emotions of others (for example angry, or upset) Stress of others
Welfare officers/benefit workers *Social workers*	Exposure to the problems of clients Consequences of mistakes Lack of resources Total absorption in work Stress of others
HR roles/management roles	Frontline management role Influencing change without direct authority Managing in ambiguous situations without sufficient information
Call center staff	Customer-facing Dealing with aggressive people and/or complaints Constant monitoring Reactive work, cannot plan workloads
Information systems delivery staff	Impact of work on others Timescales set by others Dealing with emergencies Working with old/legacy systems due to insufficient investment
Offshore management/staff	Remote working Living away from families Shift patterns

Figure 7.6 **Examples of jobs that may expose people to greater pressure, identified by the Henley Stress Special Interest Group**

Managing those in Stressful Jobs

Employers must be extra vigilant in the management of staff in jobs recognized to put jobholders under higher levels of pressure. Key steps that can help make the difference include:

1. Careful screening at the recruitment and selection stage of employment – this involves ensuring that those selected are well matched in terms of temperament, skills and capabilities, and emotional resilience. It is unwise to put people who have experienced high levels of stress in previous jobs

into new situations that are pressurized. However, it may not be evident to recruiters that a person has a predisposition to suffer from stress.

2. Ensuring that staff have appropriate training to bridge any gaps – staff who receive effective training soon after starting a new job will move up the learning curve more quickly and experience less stress as a result. This includes receiving an adequate induction into the organization.
3. Managing the well-being of staff – call centers offered a good example of stress being kept at appropriate levels when the staff were managed with sensitivity. This included staff being given adequate breaks, ensuring they were kept stimulated by bringing variety into the job and offering them appropriate support when necessary.
4. Monitoring stress levels of staff and conducting a risk assessment, when necessary, for those demonstrating high levels of stress – the use of risk assessment is discussed in Chapter 8. Jobs that expose jobholders to high levels of pressure must be constantly monitored to ensure any problems are picked early before stress has risen to unacceptable levels.
5. Supporting staff who might be vulnerable – this might be at the individual or team level. Having an employee assistance program is advisable for those employing staff in pressurized jobs.

Summary

When recruiting or managing others, remember that:

- Stress is self-generated and the extent to which people experience stress varies from person to person
- People may experience excessive stress because of their own disposition and set of unique circumstances
- People are put at greater risk of experiencing excessive stress when the jobs they are performing consistently expose them to higher levels of pressure
- Pressure on individuals will be high when job insecurity is high, combined with a dangerous or unpleasant working environment and a physically demanding job
- When individuals have to adjust to variable levels of pressure, it puts an added strain on an individual
- When change gives individuals less control over their situation, this makes the job potentially more stressful
- Jobs consistently rated as having high potential for excessive stress involve contact with the general public in emotionally intense situations and/or where jobs are governed by strict rules
- The rising problem of workplace bullying has added to the potential for excessive stress
- There must be extra vigilance given to those people performing jobs that expose them to high levels of pressure
- Care must be given in recruiting the right people, training them well, monitoring for any evidence of excessive stress, and providing appropriate levels of support for those exposed to highly pressurized jobs.

8 The Measurement of Stress

Introduction

Measuring the level of stress in organizations and the potential risks of stress associated with jobs is an important part of preventing and coping with it. An organization needs to know if any of its employees could be vulnerable or at risk. By measuring stress, employers will raise their awareness of its causes and help those suffering from excessive stress by taking action to reduce the causes. It is also important to conduct an assessment once an employee has experienced a stress-related illness: this enables a manager to decide on the best way to manage that individual, thus preventing a recurrence.

Stress is a difficult concept to measure – unlike assessing a physical illness or injury when more objective measurements can be taken. In the UK, prior to the requirement by the Health and Safety Executive (HSE) to conduct a stress risk assessment to measure potential risks, stress audits were conducted by organizations. These were sometimes described as health audits because of the negative connotations associated with the term stress (see Chapter 3). Since 1999 more organizations are conducting stress risk assessments and, once completed, there is now a move towards organizations seeking to integrate stress measurement into broader employee attitude surveys, seeing stress management as part of a broader employee well-being issue.

This chapter gives an overview of ways of measuring stress and their uses, as well as guidance on how to conduct a stress risk assessment following the HSE *Management Standards for Tackling Work-related Stress* launched in November 2004 (see www.hse.gov.uk/stress/standards). There is a case study on BT, outlining the way it has approached risk assessment. The chapter is particularly important for those UK organizations not yet complying with the HSE requirement to conduct risk assessments. It will, therefore, be helpful to HR and health and safety, or occupational health advisers who need to implement stress risk assessment in their own organizations. Managers might like to skim the chapter to understand this element of the stress management process to enable them to take a more proactive role.

The Challenges of Measuring Stress

It is generally accepted that measuring stress is a difficult issue for a number of reasons:

- Any assessment measure only relates to a specific moment in time
- There are doubts about the validity of stress measurements – are they measuring what they are supposed to be measuring?
- Most audits and questionnaires are self-reporting and so rely on people to give assessments that are subjective or may not give the true picture, if the culture of the organization is not supportive of people being stressed; alternatively, people may be unable to assess their own stress levels.

Ways of Measuring Stress

There are a number of ways of measuring stress:

1. Stress audits
2. Stress risk assessments
3. Focus groups
4. One-to-one interviews
5. Stress logs recording critical incidents
6. Data from absence records
7. Accident rates
8. Labor turnover
9. Number of people taking advantage of counselling services
10. The cost of litigation.

Audits and questionnaires provide more extensive data about the people, the likely causes of stress, and the ways people have developed of managing stress. Focus groups can help to expand on the data collected via audits and questionnaires and can facilitate the understanding of variations in different parts of the organization. Other measures such as accident rates, labor turnover, and sickness rates give a broader way of monitoring trends.

Advantages of Stress Audits and Risk Assessments

Despite the above reservations, there are a number of benefits (particularly when an organization is first developing a stress policy) to embarking on some form of audit. These include:

- Providing greater clarity of hot spots for stress by comparing one part of an organization with another
- Identifying the main causes of stress and taking appropriate action
- Raising the profile of stress as an issue that is acceptable and regarded as an important element of the well-being of staff

- Demonstrating that the organization is serious about preventing and dealing with stress
- Helping to identify the most appropriate interventions for dealing with excessive stress
- Providing baseline data to help evaluate future interventions
- Providing a useful icebreaker on the topic of stress.

TOP TIPS FOR SUCCESS

- Commitment, and a champion, at the top of the organization
- Buy-in to the process at all levels, with active involvement from every level within the organization
- A culture and climate that has a healthy attitude towards stress and the prevention of excessive stress occurring
- Stress measurement is taken seriously: it is not viewed as a paper exercise
- Actions are developed and acted upon as a result of the assessment
- Stress assessment is integrated with associated activities and initiatives such as Investors in People, general health and safety assessments, employee attitude surveys, and annual appraisal/development interviews to pick up individual issues.

The Risk Assessment Process

The purpose of a stress risk assessment is to identify the possibility of employees developing stress-related illness because of the work they are employed to do. Unlike a general risk assessment, a stress risk assessment is more difficult: it requires people to gauge the likely impact on a person's mental well-being. It does, however, follow the same process as a physical risk assessment.

The Management of Health & Safety at Work Regulations 1999 requires that suitable and sufficient stress risk assessments are undertaken.

The process follows the principles laid out in the HSE's publication (2001) that identifies five steps to risk assessment and was reinforced in the *Management Standards for Tackling Work-related Stress* launched in November 2004 (HSE Management Standards www.hse.gov.uk/stress/standards). These identify six key risk factors – aspects of work – which, if not properly managed, can lead to work-related stress. Each standard contains simple statements about good management practice in each of the six areas. Following the risk assessment process helps organizations to identify causes of stress and possible solutions. The HSE does not expect organizations to meet all the standards at the start of the process: they are designed to be goals that organizations seek to achieve through continuous improvement and regular reassessment. The HSE emphasizes the benefits of an approach designed to prevent stress from occurring in the first place.

The five steps in the risk assessment process are:

1. Look for the hazards (risk factors 1–6)

2. Decide who might be harmed and how
3. Evaluate the risk by:
   - identifying what action you are already taking
   - deciding whether it is enough
   - if it is not, deciding what more you need to do
4. Record the significant findings of the assessment
5. Monitor and review

Step 1: Look for the hazards (risk factors)

Factor 1 *Demands:* for example workloads, work patterns and the physical environment

Factor 2 *Control:* how much say the person has in the way he or she does the work

Factor 3 *Support:* includes encouragement, sponsorship, and resources provided by the organization, line management, and colleagues

Factor 4 *Relationships:* includes promoting positive working to avoid conflict and dealing with unacceptable behavior

Factor 5 *Role:* understanding role and avoiding conflicting roles

Factor 6 *Change:* the way organizational change, whether large or small, is managed and communicated in the organization.

Step 2: Decide who might be harmed and how

Anyone can be affected by work-related stress although some may be better able to cope than others, as explained in Chapter 3. Jobs vary in terms of the potential pressure that jobholders are likely to experience (the most stressful jobs are discussed in Chapter 7). Strategies for conducting risk assessments, therefore, need to take account of two elements:

1. The job itself and the potential pressure experienced by the jobholder.
2. The jobholder and the extent to which they personally perceive the job as stressful.

Some organizations initially assess each different job and then assess the individual during a one-to-one appraisal or personal development interview. Others focus on the individual, particularly those who appear to be experiencing high stress levels. A climate of openness, honesty, and trust is essential if organizations are to be effective in identifying individuals who are at risk before the situation becomes too serious. The culture and climate needed to build a resilient workforce will be discussed in Chapter 13.

Step 3: Evaluate the risk and take action

In this step data must be collected to assess the level of risk within the six categories of the HSE Management Standards. In the early stages of stress risk assessment, organizations may need to develop a specific questionnaire to assess the risks. However, once data has been collected, this will set the baseline and monitoring and review can occur by incorporating certain questions into an existing employee attitude survey. For those conducting a stress risk assessment for the first time, the HSE Stress Indicator Tool could be helpful. This is shown in Appendix 8.1 and can be downloaded from the HSE website (www.hse.gov.uk/stress/standards/pdfs/indicatortool.pdf)

Once the problem areas have been identified, action plans must be drawn up to address the issues. Some of the issues may apply to particular departments, for example those related to workload. Others – such as managing change – may apply more broadly within the organization and may need to be addressed corporately.

Background

The London borough of Havering had conducted a stress audit and, as a result, corporate personnel acting on the recommendations established a stress code of practice. To comply with the HSE requirements, the next stage was to establish a stress risk assessment process.

The pilot

The health and safety department designed a risk assessment questionnaire based on an earlier questionnaire piloted by the HSE. A group of managers helped to pilot it and made recommendations for its improvement. They also became champions for the process. The questionnaire acted as a checklist of best practice and helped managers take appropriate action where necessary.

Implementing the risk assessment process

The health and safety department, together with corporate personnel, firmly believed that line managers should take ownership of the process supported by health and safety in conducting the risk assessments. Many of the departments had received Investors in People recognition and undertook personal development planning interviews annually.

Managers were required to attend a half-day training session to be introduced to the risk assessment process and the stress code of practice. The session also raised awareness of stress and the legal responsibilities of managers, ensuring they were aware of the support services available for those staff experiencing excessive levels of stress.

The managers soon realized that most of the actions suggested in the questionnaire represented good management practice and had been undertaken as part of gaining recognition for Investors in People.

It was recommended that managers assess job families and make the sessions a two-way process, allowing staff ample opportunity to discuss the assessment and potential risks. The managers were also encouraged to risk assess individuals when they had concerns that a particular individual was experiencing high levels of stress.

Several managers requested a second training session to help them identify and manage the stress of others. They also required support from health and safety in the early stages of conducting the risk assessments. In addition, workshops were run for staff to help them recognize and manage their own stress and understand their responsibility for informing their managers if they were experiencing excessive stress.

Figure 8.1 **The London borough of Havering's stress risk assessment process**

The example outlined in Figure 8.1 will help those in organizations needing to set up a risk assessment process. The London borough of Havering conducted risk assessments on the basis of job families, in other words, focusing on the job itself. BT took a different approach, focusing on the individual and then building up trends as groups of people completed the stress risk assessment. BT's approach is shown in Figure 8.2.

Background

The stress assessment process within BT is part of an integrated process designed to manage stress and pressure. As an organization BT has undergone massive change in the last 20 years. Since the late 1980s, it has reduced staff numbers in the UK from 250,000 to 90,000 and now operates in a very competitive business sector.

The stress assessment process

The process works on an individual basis. An employee completes an online questionnaire consisting of 40 questions aimed at identifying the person's level of stress and stressors, based on the HSE guidelines and categories for risk assessment. The responses are fed into a central database and the individual and his or her line manager both receive tailored reports based on red, amber, and green.

Those receiving the higher ratings of red and amber are given advice on how to tackle the main stressors. The report thus gives feedback on the level of stress the person is currently experiencing and the best advice for moving forward.

The manager receives a more detailed report giving data on stress levels and the stressors, together with tools to equip him or her to give advice to the person concerned. BT firmly believes that the manager should take responsibility for dealing with stress within his or her area of responsibility.

Approximately 9500 have completed the assessment on a voluntary basis and, so far, there has been a 15 percent reduction in costs due to stress-related absence.

Critical success factors

- The process has been championed at board level by the chief medical officer who is also head of health and safety.
- Great emphasis is placed on gaining commitment and ownership by line management for managing stress
- The online questionnaire is easily accessible
- Comparisons of the HSE stressors can easily be made for different parts of the business
- The approach targets the individual resulting in a solution that fits the needs of that individual rather than having more general solutions
- Data is retained in an anonymous central database allowing one part of the business to be compared with another, for example different call centers.
- Being able to track cost savings following implementation of the broad stress-management program.

Figure 8.2 **BT's stress assessment and management (STREAM)**

Step 4: Record your findings

This is a critical part of the process. Once an assessment has been conducted, it raises expectations that something will happen. The record needs to form a part of the planning process, highlighting:

- The major concerns arising from the assessment
- What has been agreed so far by way of solutions
- The goals, priorities, and key milestones
- The timescales
- How you are going to communicate the plan
- How you are going to ensure that you have the commitment of all key stakeholders including senior management, employees, and trade unions, if appropriate.

The HSE website has a template for an action plan that may be helpful at this stage (www.hse.gov.uk/stress/standards/downloads.htm).

Step 5: Monitor and review

The action plan should be reviewed and the outcome of the total process evaluated. This step may include:

- Checking that agreed actions have been undertaken
- Following up on whether the actions taken have had the desired effect
- Reviewing with specific groups affected by a certain issue
- Monitoring data for trends such as sickness absence, labor turnover and performance data.

At this step a decision will need to be taken on how to monitor stress in the longer term. It may mean repeating a specific stress assessment survey or including certain questionnaires into a broader survey such as an annual employee attitude survey. Actions such as these help to integrate the stress management process into the organization's total people management strategy, and are favored by those who place a high emphasis on employee well-being and work–life balance.

Summary

The main lessons for HR, health and safety advisers and those required to measure stress at the organizational level are:

- Measuring stress is a difficult issue for several reasons
- Audits and questionnaires provide more extensive data about people and likely causes of stress
- Other measures, such as accident rates, labor turnover, and sickness levels, are helpful for monitoring trends
- Commitment at the top and a champion for measuring stress is important

- A culture and climate that has a healthy attitude towards stress and its prevention is essential
- Stress measurement must be taken seriously and not viewed simply as a paper exercise
- The risk assessment process helps organizations to identify the causes of stress and develop possible solutions to alleviate the causes
- Strategies for conducting risk assessments need to take account of the job itself and the jobholders
- A climate of openness, honesty, and trust is essential if organizations are effectively to identify individuals who are at risk before the situation becomes too serious
- Action must be taken following stress measurement, as expectations will be raised that steps will be taken to address issues identified.

APPENDIX 8.1

HSE INDICATOR TOOL FOR WORK-RELATED STRESS

		Never	Seldom	Sometimes	Often	Always
1	I am clear what is expected of me at work	1	2	3	4	5
2	I can decide when to take a break	1	2	3	4	5
3	Different groups at work demand things from me that are hard to combine	5	4	3	2	1
4	I know how to go about getting my job done	1	2	3	4	5
5	I am subject to personal harassment in the form of unkind words or behaviour	5	4	3	2	1
6	I have unachievable deadlines	5	4	3	2	1
7	If work gets difficult, my colleagues will help me	1	2	3	4	5
8	I am given supportive feedback on the work I do	1	2	3	4	5
9	I have to work very intensively	5	4	3	2	1
10	I have a say in my own work speed	1	2	3	4	5
11	I am clear what my duties and responsibilities are	1	2	3	4	5
12	I have to neglect some tasks because I have too much to do	5	4	3	2	1
13	I am clear about the goals and objectives for my department	1	2	3	4	5
14	There is friction or anger between colleagues	5	4	3	2	1
15	I have a choice in deciding how I do my work	1	2	3	4	5
16	I am unable to take sufficient breaks	5	4	3	2	1
17	I understand how my work fits into the overall aim of the organisation	1	2	3	4	5
18	I am pressured to work long hours	5	4	3	2	1
19	I have a choice in deciding what I do at work	1	2	3	4	5
20	I have to work very fast	5	4	3	2	1

(cont'd)

		Never	Seldom	Sometimes	Often	Always
21	I am subject to bullying at work	☐5	☐4	☐3	☐2	☐1
22	I have unrealistic time pressures	☐5	☐4	☐3	☐2	☐1
23	I can rely on my line manager to help me out with a work problem	☐1	☐2	☐3	☐4	☐5

		Strongly disagree	Disagree	Neutral	Agree	Strongly agree
24	I get help and support I need from colleagues	☐1	☐2	☐3	☐4	☐5
25	I have some say over the way I work	☐1	☐2	☐3	☐4	☐5
26	I have sufficient opportunities to question managers about change at work	☐1	☐2	☐3	☐4	☐5
27	I receive the respect at work I deserve from my colleagues	☐1	☐2	☐3	☐4	☐5
28	Staff are always consulted about change at work	☐1	☐2	☐3	☐4	☐5
29	I can talk to my line manager about something that has upset or annoyed me about work	☐1	☐2	☐3	☐4	☐5
30	My working time can be flexible	☐1	☐2	☐3	☐4	☐5
31	My colleagues are willing to listen to my work-related problems	☐1	☐2	☐3	☐4	☐5
32	When changes are made at work, I am clear how they will work out in practice	☐1	☐2	☐3	☐4	☐5
33	I am supported through emotionally demanding work	☐1	☐2	☐3	☐4	☐5
34	Relationships at work are strained	☐5	☐4	☐3	☐2	☐1
35	My line manager encourages me at work	☐1	☐2	☐3	☐4	☐5

Thank you for completing the questionnaire.

This can be downloaded from the HSE website:
www.hse.gov.uk/stress/standards/pdfs/indicatortool.pdf

9 Managing Stress within the Workplace

Introduction

The myriad recent legislation relating to stress within the workplace and the responsibility of employers to assess and manage the risk of stress for their employees has resulted in confusion and concern for many organizations. Cary Cooper suggests that employers are worried because they think all the employee has to do is mention the word "stress" and they are going to be in trouble.

Employers who are willing to take time to consider what is really needed, rather than hastily introducing a suite of policies and procedures in the hope of avoiding litigation, are likely to benefit. Spending time identifying potential causes of stress and developing robust and consistent processes for dealing with issues when they arise should ensure that legal requirements are satisfied. This approach should also ensure that employees will be educated in their role of managing stress within the workplace and can work hand in hand with their employers to make the workplace a safer and healthier environment.

In addition to the considerable amount of legislation in place, there is also significant advice, help, and support available from the Health and Safety Executive (HSE), government bodies, and private companies on how to manage stress within the workplace, with solutions available for all budgets and resources.

This chapter gives an overview of the approaches organizations can employ to manage stress. A range of interventions are outlined to help HR specialists and health and safety experts, as well as consultants, take appropriate steps to manage stress. Several of the steps are covered in greater detail in Part V. Managers may like to skim this chapter to become aware of the interventions and be more proactive in managing stress within their area of responsibility.

Overview of Interventions

- Stress measurement – see Chapter 8
- Developing a stress policy – see Chapter 11
- Dealing with the root causes
- Training interventions
  - stress awareness

    - prevention and coping with stress
    - identifying and managing stress of others
    - building resilience
- Job matching
- Job redesign
- Counselling
- Absence management
- Building a culture and climate for a resilient workforce – see Chapter 13.

Dealing with the Root Causes

University College London (UCL) has produced a set of guidelines, *Managing Stress at Work* (www.ucl.ac.uk/hr/docs/stress.php), which suggest that, in managing stress effectively within the workplace, both managers and staff need to be aware of the potential causes of stress as well as the effects. UCL proposes that the causes of stress can broadly be divided into three main categories:

1. *Personal*
    - Ill health
    - Relationship problems
    - Financial difficulties
    - Family worries
2. *Organizational*
    - Overwork
    - Feeling of being undervalued
    - Poor communications
    - Job ambiguity
    - Conflict with colleagues
3. *Environmental*
    - Poor physical working conditions or job design
    - Heat
    - Noise.

In addition to these causes, there may be common causes of stress faced by the organization as a whole, such as change imposed following a merger or other external pressures. The model of potential causes presented in Chapter 6 could be helpful to managers particularly when trying to identify problems at the team and individual level.

The challenge, therefore, is for managers to identify and respond to potential situations or issues that may come from the employees themselves or the workplace. Managers must work with individuals to encourage them to identify and help them to manage potential stress factors within their own departments or areas of responsibility. In this way, a joint approach to managing stress within the workplace is formed, allowing individuals to understand their own role and accountability relating to workplace stress and, at the same time, enabling them to approach their managers to discuss issues that are causing them stress.

Organizations should be in a position to carry out audits and risk assessments and monitor data and trends that highlight potential problems within the key areas identified (for example absenteeism). It is not possible to provide an exhaustive list of each potential cause and effect, but issues are put forward to illustrate the approach employers can take to ensure that risks are assessed, made aware to employees, and acted upon to prevent recurring problems.

PERSONAL

It is entirely the individual's choice to raise issues with their manager (or with others at work) that might be affecting them personally. However, an organization can ensure its workforce knows that they are able to raise matters confidentially with their line managers or colleagues and, if the company has sufficient resources, they may be able to offer outsourced support, such as external employee assistance programs which offer counselling and guidance. Managers have the responsibility to take note of behavioral changes and discuss these in an appropriate and sensitive way with the individuals concerned. Many managers will require support themselves in dealing with such issues, and expertise from HR and occupational health departments should be available to those who require it. Opportunities for managers to gain development and experience in this area should also be provided.

Publicizing policies and procedures, communicating them effectively across the workforce, and ensuring that staff who raise issues can do so without fear of retribution or embarrassment are important for encouraging staff to confide in managers when they fear stress from personal factors may be affecting their work. Research carried out by the Great Place to Work Institute (2004a) highlighted how important trust in managers was amongst the employees they surveyed:

- The door to management is always open; they listen.
- Management truly encourages and expects individuals to care for themselves before work. They understand personal lives are more important than jobs.
- The company takes care of the people first and the people, in turn, take care of the profits.

The leadership style, integrity, and behaviors of managers at all levels within an organization are critical to the success of establishing high levels of trust. If a company policy states it cares about the welfare of its employees, its leaders and managers need to demonstrate that they mean what they say.

ORGANIZATIONAL

Whilst personal issues might be more difficult to identify initially, it is usually easier to deal with a situation that is confined to an individual. With stress that arises from organizational issues, it may, on the one hand, involve less tangible or immediately apparent behaviors, because the behaviors may be spread across departments and take time to become evident or may only begin to be identified from trends or statistics. On the other hand, it may be easier to anticipate stress caused by organizational issues, for example if major change is planned within the workplace – mergers, redundancies and so on. An example of one organization's approach is given in Figure 9.1.

Although not all companies can afford such an approach, the methodology is one that can be adopted regardless of resources. Most importantly, the learning from the process can be applied within organizations of all sizes: it is critical to establish the correct root cause and provide appropriate, deliverable solutions by dealing with the cause and effect at the same time.

When recruiting within any company, it is important to be realistic and understand exactly what and who you are looking for. If "best fit" can be achieved at this stage, then at least the foundations for moving forward have been established.

Direct Line identified a problem with staff turnover and absenteeism at its call center: "We knew we had employee turnover and absenteeism issues, but weren't able to accurately diagnose why." (Jeff Morris, head of regional resources). The company employed an external consultancy to carry out a stress audit to establish the root causes of the problem and develop an effective strategy to address the problem. Diagnosis included a confidential assessment of the sources and effects of pressure covering 600 employees. It was introduced as a pressure management program and was voluntary. However, the program was openly publicized via a communications campaign that included posters, emails and team briefs. Direct Line also ensured that employees choosing to participate were allowed time away from phones and desks to complete the questionnaire. The main causes of organizational stress were found to be:

- **Lack of recognition – after intensive initial training, employees felt there was little or no opportunity for career progression.**
- **Recruitment – recruiters were found to be raising expectations beyond those the job could deliver and recruiting people looking for stopgap work rather than careers.**
- **Absenteeism – most absenteeism was not health-related. It occurred mostly amongst the youngest group of workers who were often taking full-time employment for the first time and just learning how to create a work–life balance.**

The findings from this program enabled Direct Line to design tailored and appropriate processes that fitted the particular sections of their workforce, rather than a blanket approach across the whole company. Sickness absence management, for example, would not have worked as a method for resolving the absenteeism problem of the call center.

Figure 9.1 **Direct Line's approach to managing organizational stress**

Source: Businesshealth (2002)

ENVIRONMENTAL

Work environments that are obviously noisy, chaotic, or potentially dangerous can easily be identified as a potential cause of stress. However, regular and unabated exposure to more mundane poor working conditions can also result in stress. For example, badly designed workstations present physical stresses to users who sit in front of computers for hours at a time. Guidelines provided by the HSE give employers information on how to carry out workstation assessments and educate employees on how they should be sitting and working.

Taking responsibility for environmental issues and letting employees know what to do should they experience problems from their physical environment and then taking action minimizes the risk of employees experiencing this kind of stress.

Some organizations may be large enough to fund health checks and provide cash towards eye tests; smaller companies can simply educate and eliminate risk to keep problems to a minimum.

Risk assessments should be carried out, as well as assessments of competence in specific areas (for example driving) where individuals can be at risk. Clear record keeping and lines of responsibility are critical to maintaining an efficient process.

Until the more high-profile cases of psychological stress came to the fore, employers focused most attention on being "compliant" with environmental legislation in terms of health and safety. The message now is that they have to achieve a balance with both the physical and psychological welfare of their employees.

The Occupational Safety and Health Service (2003), in Wellington, New Zealand, carried out a comprehensive research program entitled *Healthy Work: Managing Stress in the Workplace*, which looked at managing stress and fatigue in the workplace. A key message that came out of its research was that the management of stress can be built into standard health and safety management systems and should involve employees. It states that to prevent and manage workplace stress, employers and employees must be able to be distinguish between:

- Reasonable and unreasonable demands in the workplace
- Stressors that are unavoidable or outside the employer's control and those that are avoidable within the workplace
- The features and relations between healthy and unhealthy work.

In order to be successful in keeping the workplace healthy at all levels, it is the employers that should take the initiative – but is a shared responsibility to maintain a healthy workplace.

Training Interventions

Appropriate training interventions need to be carefully identified to ensure that specific needs are tackled. Any intervention also needs to be evaluated to be clear that it is making a difference. There are a number of different types of intervention, some of which may be focused on leadership development and management style, that may also have an impact on stress management, and good management practice is good stress management.

STRESS AWARENESS

Organizations can help people to prevent stress levels from becoming excessive, hyper-stress and distress, as well as experience more eu-stress (see Chapter 12 for further information). Typical content of a stress awareness programme would include:

- What is stress? This helps to demystify the concept and gives people a greater degree of control.
- Understanding the physiology of stress helps people to comprehend the link between stress, pressure, and performance and the way they can affect the stress reaction by reducing caffeine, being careful with their diet, and having more exercise and relaxation.
- Recognizing the signs of stress helps people to manage themselves better, be more aware of the level of stress they are experiencing and take action sooner before stress levels become unacceptable.
- Gaining control to keep stress at acceptable levels helps people to understand the extent to which stress is self-generated and the link between thought processes and the stress they experience.
- Strategies for managing stress help people to take steps to prevent or cope with stress. There is a range of strategies available dealing with the emotional, mental, and physical aspects of stress and these approaches are discussed fully in Part V.

This type of intervention may be as short as a half-day workshop, but programs of at least one day in length are recommended to help people to develop action plans for implementation at work and make plans for lifestyle changes.

PREVENTION AND COPING WITH STRESS

Some organizations run longer training interventions and go into greater depth on the changes needed to make a difference. These interventions may be linked to preliminary assessment to pinpoint issues that need to be addressed. Those organizations taking a broader "well-being" approach help people to develop healthy lifestyles. Whilst there is some criticism of stress management development interventions, the authors firmly believe that, with appropriate assessment of the problem areas and the right guidance, people are able to make lifestyle changes that can help them to deal more effectively with stress.

IDENTIFYING AND MANAGING STRESS OF OTHERS

Whilst more organizations emphasize the importance of individuals taking responsibility for their own stress management, they would agree that managers must also be proactive in dealing with the stress of others effectively. This means raising managers' skill sets and awareness.

The biggest challenge, identified in Chapter 8, is assessing the level of stress in another person. Whilst managers can be helped to recognize some of the warning signs and non-verbal cues, people experiencing excessive stress often hide it well. This is a serious situation, as the damage to an individual can be considerably greater when he or she contains the stress within. For this reason, managers are helped to engage in conversations with their staff and adopt the right attitude to stress to bring the problems out into the open. This is discussed more fully in Chapters 18 and 19.

BUILDING RESILIENCE

This type of intervention can both help people to cope with stress and also prevent stress from becoming excessive in the first place. By building resilience, people are able to perform more consistently under excessive pressure and are less vulnerable to suffer from hyper-stress or distress.

This type of intervention is likely to be linked with personal assessment in the areas of:

- Diet
- Exercise
- Rest and relaxation
- Physical, mental and emotional energy
- Diary management – work–life balance.

Chapter 25 discusses the importance of resilience and vitality management in greater detail and gives practical advice on how to raise people's resilience.

Other training interventions closely related to stress management are time management and assertiveness. People often experience excessive stress through a lack of organization and self-management. Paying attention to self-organization can increase the felt level of control and at the same time reduce levels of stress. Helping people become more assertive and increasing their capability to say "no" can also reduce time pressures and overload. Assertiveness training can also help to address other known sources of stress, including relationships with others, ability to deal with conflict, and being the victim of harassment and bullying.

Job Matching

Chapter 7 discussed the level of pressure associated with certain jobs and the authors advised careful selection of people for those jobs. Individuals vary in their comfort zones associated with different levels of pressure: some thrive on the epinephrine (adrenalin) rush, whilst others feel far happier with lower levels of pressure. Care must be taken in the matching of people to jobs to ensure individuals are not placed in situations that fail to maximize their performance. Some of the factors that need to be taken into account include:

- *Skill set* – does the person have the right skills and capabilities for the job?
- *Disposition* – does the person possess any characteristics that will make them more vulnerable, such as anxiety, perfectionism, and overconscientiousness?
- *Experience* – has the person had previous experience and evidence that they have held similar jobs?

During downsizing or reorganization, after a merger or other major change, organizations sometimes redeploy people without giving sufficient thought to the suitability of the person for the given job. Others have redeployed people after a period of sickness absence to a job that the individual will find less stressful with very positive outcomes.

Job Redesign

This can be a useful intervention following a risk assessment. It can address some of the hot spots such as work overload, low control, and role ambiguity. This can be a proactive way of dealing with stress when possible problems are identified. An example is shown in Figure 9.2.

One local authority was aware that operational departments were having difficulty delivering a service and dealing with customer problems that were time-consuming, created overload for the staff, and resulted in high levels of stress in dealing with customer complaints. The authority tackled the problem by setting up a separate, dedicated, customer service department covering all departments in the authority.

The staff were either recruited from internal applicants or from outside. They were selected for their interpersonal skills and capability to handle difficult situations. They achieved job satisfaction by helping the customers to solve their problems. Those new to the authority were given extensive familiarization training to help them handle situations with confidence.

Meanwhile, staff in the operational departments were left free to run their departments without taking up valuable time problem solving. This is an excellent example of a solution developed to achieve an identified outcome of satisfied customers, and at the same time reduced staff stress levels.

Figure 9.2 **Example of job redesign in a local authority**

Counseling and Employee Assistance Programs

This intervention is used when people are experiencing excessive stress. Sometimes organizations have their own in-house counselors, but in recent years organizations have tended to outsource this activity by way of employee assistance programs. The outsourcing option makes this service more confidential, although there may be a reporting back process to the employer. Some organizations allow their employees to self-refer to an occupational health specialist or to HR; others require the referral to be handled by the line manager.

Most organizations agree that line managers do not usually have the skills to deal with a member of their team who is experiencing excessive stress. Sometimes this stress may be the result of a personal problem and the person concerned is likely to feel more comfortable discussing the issue with someone outside the organization. The problem may require legal or financial advice – again, making an external counselor more appropriate.

Absence Management

Absence management is an integral part of managing stress within the organization and has great potential for financial savings. Helping people return to work more quickly will help financially, although any form of absence management will have costs associated with it, Paton (2004), reporting on the annual research conducted by the CBI and AXA, noted that sickness absence is now costing the UK more than £11 billion a year. The findings reported that steps are being taken to manage sickness absence proactively; the evidence found that:

- Early intervention and rehabilitation have been shown to work.
- Involving occupational health in the process of managing absence is critical.
- Absence levels fall when senior managers become involved and absence is monitored.
- 85 percent of employers are now taking action to reduce absence, with return-to-work interviews having the greatest impact on absence levels.
- More than three-quarters of organizations now have arrangements for helping people suffering from stress.

Figure 9.3 provides a good example of an organization developing an integrated approach to managing stress in the workplace.

In 2000 Xerox UK, like many organizations, was faced with massive business challenges and stiff competition in its business sector. A downsizing exercise was undertaken together with a restructure. For the remaining staff, workloads were demanding and many experienced longer working hours.

Xerox UK conducts an employee engagement survey every 18 months and the last survey showed positive results, especially in relation to pay and

(cont'd)

benefits. However, when HR analysed its own department's results, it realized they were unhappy with their long working hours and work–life balance was an issue for them.

HR staff started to share personal ideas on how to manage their time better. They found this approach was helpful and followed it up with a two-day session using the six sigma approach. They brainstormed the key issues and developed ideas for action. The outcome of this session was the development of a workbook: *The Manager's Guide to Managing Workload*. This was a short booklet full of practical tips, which was also put on the company intranet. Briefing sessions were held for line managers.

Having developed the workload booklet, they turned their attention to stress. Conscious that staff were experiencing greater pressure, they were faced with people suffering from excessive stress resulting in sickness absence. This put extra strain on colleagues having to take on additional work. HR staff were aware that by the time they became involved with individuals, they were suffering from high stress levels that made managing it more difficult. They were also aware of the complexity of the stress issue, recognizing that stress affects people in many different ways and that people's ability to cope varies from situation to situation. They also noted that often the source of stress related to factors outside work, but was exacerbated when people were also experiencing problems at the office.

HR staff decided that the first step in tackling the stress issue was to increase their own expertise and ability to deal with the situation. However, from the outset they were convinced of the importance of equipping line managers to deal more effectively with the stress of their staff, realizing that catching problems in the early stages made them much easier to manage. Up until now, HR took responsibility for dealing with staff suffering from excessive stress, but often felt they did not have the skills and knowledge to deal with it.

A briefing session was run for HR and they enlisted the help of occupational health and their legal department. A project team then developed a booklet *Line Manager Guide to Stress Prevention and Management*, which included the following topics:

— Definition of stress
— Sources of stress
— Xerox policy – roles and responsibilities
— Signs and symptoms of stress
— Handling stress
— Looking after yourself
— Absence and rehabilitation.

Knowledge briefings, lasting approximately two hours, were held with line managers: these were interactive sessions and included role-plays. The information was put online and, to raise the awareness of stress, all employees received a short pamphlet (circulated with their pay slips) on stress and how to deal with it. The briefings and information pamphlets have received an excellent response. One-to-one sessions were also conducted with managers on request.

(cont'd)

The HR team have also been working on sickness absence and getting people back into the workplace. This has included:

— Contact with people off sick
— Return to work plans
— Redeployment if necessary
— Follow-ups

Line managers are required to work in consultation with HR and occupational health to ensure that the process is well managed. In addition HR are supported by occupational health and have a BUPA stress line.

Having put all these processes in place, the HR team are now working on refining the stress policy and deciding how best to manage the risk assessment process. Their approach has a number of critical success factors:

— It is a practical approach
— Line managers have been given the tools to take responsibility for managing stress
— It is a time-effective approach: the briefing sessions took two hours
— HR used the expertise of occupational health and the company legal department
— Additional support for managers was also available
— Clear steps were drawn up for managing sickness absence, including the management of staff when they had returned to work
— The policy was refined and put in place once the stress awareness phase had been conducted.

Figure 9.3 **An integrated approach to managing stress in the workplace at Xerox UK**

Summary

HR specialists, health and safety, and occupational health advisers and consultants wishing to develop interventions for managing stress need to remember the following:

- Employers and employees need to work hand in hand to make the workplace a healthier and safer environment
- Significant help, advice, and support is available in the UK from the HSE, government bodies, and private companies on how to manage stress in the workplace
- Organizations of all sizes must establish the correct root cause and provide appropriate, deliverable solutions by dealing with the cause and effect at the same time
- The management of stress can be built into standard health and safety management systems and should involve employees
- Employers should take the initiative, but it is a shared responsibility with employees and managers to maintain a healthy workplace

- Appropriate training interventions need to be identified carefully to ensure that specific needs are tackled
- With appropriate assessment of the problem areas and the right guidance, people are able to make lifestyle changes that can help them to deal more effectively with stress
- Care must be taken in matching people to jobs to ensure that individuals are not placed in situations that fail to maximize their performance
- Job redesign can be a proactive way of dealing with stress, addressing some of the hot spots such as work overload, low control, and role ambiguity.

Managers seeking to be proactive in the management of stress need to remember:

- To identify and respond to situations or issues that may be raised by employees themselves or be evident in the workplace
- They have the responsibility to take note of behavioral changes and discuss these in an appropriate and sensitive way with the individual concerned
- They must be proactive in managing the stress of others. This may mean raising their skill set and awareness of stress to deal effectively with the stress of others
- They must be aware of those occasions when an expert counselor is needed to deal with the stress of a team member.

10 The Legal Perspective: Stress and the Law

Introduction

In the past 15 years, since stress has become an issue that is recognized and openly discussed, awareness has grown of the importance of relevant legislation and the need for employers to act responsibly and take care of the mental, as well as the physical, well-being of their employees. Case law is building gradually, but has not removed all ambiguity. This chapter is particularly important at a time when the number of tribunals for stress is increasing.

The USA experienced litigation first, with the operation of the Workers' Compensation Scheme: a no-fault insurance scheme that compensates for work-related accidents and injuries. It quickly received numerous claims for mental rather than physical injury and, during the 1980s, claims quadrupled as a result of long periods of stress at work and subsequent ill health.

Despite repeated warnings by insurers and research workers, employers were caught off guard when the first UK claims were awarded in the early 1990s. At this stage the Management of Health and Safety at Work Regulations came into force, which explicitly state that employers have a duty of care to protect the psychological health of their employees. Case law since that time, and recent guidance from the Court of Appeal, have influenced the approach that employers need to adopt to meet their legal responsibilities.

This chapter will help both employers and employees to understand their legal obligations. It will:

- ▶ Describe existing legislation that has a bearing on workplace stress and allows employees to seek compensation via employment tribunals or the courts. Failure to comply with this legislation can also result in fines or prosecutions.
- ▶ Discuss notable personal injury actions and court rulings based on common law.
- ▶ Outline Health and Safety Executive (HSE) guidelines.

Key Legislation

The Health and Safety at Work Act 1974 established a "duty of care" towards employees. Employers have a general duty to ensure, so far as is reasonably practicable, the health, safety and welfare of their employees at work. This includes taking steps to make sure they do not suffer stress-related illness as a result of their work. All employees have a responsibility for the health, safety, and welfare of themselves and others while at work.

The HSE (1995), who police the Act through its inspectorate, states:

> *Employers have a legal duty to take reasonable care to ensure that health is not placed at risk through excessive and sustained levels of stress arising from the way work is organized, the way people deal with each other at their work or from the day-to-day demands placed on their workplace.*
>
> *...stress should be treated like any other hazard.*

These are the obligations that arise out of the Health and Safety at Work Act:

- To provide and maintain a safe plant and systems of work: this requires focusing attention on the way work is organized, the content of the job and the worker–machine fit, or worker–job fit
- To provide and maintain a safe working environment
- To have a written policy for health and safety at work
- To consult employees in the identification of hazards and the effectiveness of the remedial measures implemented
- Employees must take reasonable care for the health and safety of themselves and of other persons who may be affected by their acts or omissions at work
- To set up a health and safety committee if required to do so by TUC safety representatives.

The Management of Health and Safety at Work Regulations 1992 and 1999 established a requirement for employers to make a suitable and sufficient assessment of the risks to the health and safety of employees to which they are exposed while at work.

Employers are advised that these risk assessments should be undertaken regularly and particularly reviewed during times of significant change. Those employers with more than five employees must have a written health and safety policy that should include a stress and bullying and harassment statement.

This set of regulations also made clear that employers have a duty of care to psychological as well as physical health.

The Employment Rights Act 1996 protects employees from unfair dismissal and limits the number of potential fair reasons for dismissal. One reason relates to the capability or qualifications of the person for performing the work he or she is employed to do. Capability is assessed with reference to health or any other physical or mental quality. Therefore it is fair to dismiss people who cannot achieve the required performance targets, but also those whose health stops them from doing their job.

It is obviously important that the employer follows a fair procedure for dismissal:

- *Persistent absence*: the following steps will be helpful:
  - Monitor absence
  - Investigate reasons for absence
  - Check that there is no underlying cause in the working environment
  - Discuss the absence levels with employees and, if necessary, warn them that levels are unacceptable
- *Long-term ill-health:* the following steps will be helpful:
  - Investigate the medical condition using medically qualified people
  - Consult with the employee, particularly when it is stress-related and brought about by factors at work
  - Discuss alternatives to dismissal, for example additional support or transfer to another job.
- *Pension provision:* certain occupations, including the emergency services, provide for an enhancement to pensions if staff are injured whilst carrying out their jobs. This includes stress-related illness. There is not a requirement to prove foreseeability and, as such, may be more straightforward than personal injury claims. When ill health pensions are sought, it is usual to have to prove permanent incapacity.

CONSTRUCTIVE DISMISSAL

Under the Employment Rights Act 1996, employees are able to bring a case of unfair dismissal if they resign in response to an action by the employer that entitles them to terminate the contract. Where there has been a breach of the implied term of trust and confidence, stress can be the result, sometimes leading to stress-related illness.

Constructive dismissal cases may be as a result of one incident; but, when the staff member suffers from stress, it is more usual that the situation has been building up over time and the incident cited is the final straw.

In the case of *Leech* v. *CRS*, cited by Earnshaw and Cooper (2001), Leech was a checkout operator who was reluctant to take on the role of cash office supervisor to sort out a problem of cash shortages. She was given insufficient support and training to carry out her additional duties and when there were cash shortages, the police were not called. A new computer system was installed that proved to be totally unsuitable, but Leech's line manager failed to respond to requests for assistance and left her to call in extra help to sort out the problem.

Leech went on sick leave and filed a grievance, but no action was taken. On her return to work the police were called on another matter raised by Leech. Police interviewed her and suspicion was directed at her. She was suspended pending further investigation and resigned at this stage. Suffering a depressive illness, she was unable to work for nine months. She took her case to a tribunal and was awarded compensation that included loss of earnings for constructive dismissal.

The lessons from this case are:

- Employers should avoid forcing employees to take on extra responsibilities

- Employers should provide adequate support and training for new roles
- Employers should avoid making unilateral changes to contracts of employment.

PRE-DISMISSAL ISSUES

According to Seward and Faby (2003), there has been an increase in the number of claims arising from the way in which employers handle pre-dismissal issues. Employees have been claiming:

- The way the employer has conducted the investigation, disciplinary procedure or suspension was a breach of the contractual term of mutual trust and confidence
- It caused unacceptable levels of stress
- The stress resulted in a stress-related psychiatric injury.

There is a distinction between suspension and dismissal. Claims for breach of the implied term of mutual trust and confidence do not apply where the employer is in the process of dismissal. In the case of *Johnson* v. *Unisys* (2001), the House of Lords took the view that as there was a statutory scheme for unfair dismissal, it was not necessary for the courts to develop a common law remedy in negligence or breach of contract. Trust and confidence was concerned with the preservation of the relationship and, therefore, the term had no place in dismissal.

However, if a dismissal does not take place, then the term "mutual trust and confidence' does apply. In the case of *Gogay* v. *Hertfordshire County Council* (2000), the applicant (a residential care worker) was suspended pending an investigation into allegations of child abuse made by a child in her care. The suspension lasted some time, but Gogay was eventually cleared of the charges. She sought damages for clinical depression caused by her suspension and the employer's failure to investigate the circumstances properly. The court found in Gogay's favor as her case related to suspension not dismissal.

The latest House of Lords decision on trust and confidence says that the distinction between dismissal and non-dismissal cases is not always clear-cut. *McCabe* v. *Cornwall County Council* (2004) examines whether the events leading up to the dismissal are sufficiently distinct to circumvent the rules in Johnson. McCabe was suspended following complaints by a number of schoolgirls of inappropriate sexual behavior by him. He was not made aware of the allegations until four months later whilst still suspended. He suffered a psychiatric illness and over the next three years there were three disciplinary hearings. He was finally dismissed although his conduct was relatively trivial. His claim for compensation for psychiatric injury was dismissed by the High Court, but the House of Lords ruled that dismissal is not an automatic bar to a common law claim for breach of contract prior to dismissal.

The lessons learnt from these cases are:

- Procrastination and indecisive management in dealing with grievance,

disciplinary procedures, or dismissal are more likely to give rise to stress and psychological injury claims
- Situations must be thoroughly investigated early on
- Keep the employee involved and handle the situation sensitively.

The Sex Discrimination Act (1995) and the **Race Relations Act (1976)** give people the right of access to employment tribunals. In a statutory discrimination claim there is no need to prove foreseeability. Victims can claim injury to feelings and compensation for any personal injury, and aggravated damages.

Earnshaw and Cooper (2001) reported that discrimination can result in substantial claims. For example, in *Yeboah* v. *Crofton and London Borough of Hackney*, an award was made against a director of housing, Crofton, who had a fixed mental impression that Africans had a propensity to commit fraud. This caused Yeboah great distress, serious public humiliation, and damage to his reputation. The local authority had to pay £380,000 and the discriminator, Crofton, £45,000.

The Disability Discrimination Act 1995 (DDA) states that discrimination occurs when a disabled person is treated less favorably on grounds related to their disability. However, employers may justify less favorable treatment. For example, it could be defensible not to appoint a person who has suffered stress-related illnesses to a job that has the potential to be stressful. Discrimination may also occur when an employer, or someone acting on their behalf, makes "arrangements," or there are any physical features of the premises, that place the disabled person at a substantial disadvantage in comparison with a person who is not disabled. Here, the employer has a legal duty to make "reasonable adjustments." This may require, for example, a phased return to work, extra support, or transferring the employee to another job.

The current Act defines a disability as:

> *A physical or mental impairment which has a substantial and long-term adverse effect on his or her ability to carry out normal day-to-day activities.*

Currently, a mental impairment must be one that is clinically well recognized, and has required psychiatric treatment. However, from October 2005, stress claims will be easier to pursue under the DDA. The UK government has accepted a recommendation that people claiming to have a mental impairment will not have to show they are suffering from a clinically well-recognized illness. It should be noted that the law is now working in favor of disabled people and is very powerful for those with mental illness, such as depression. The authors strongly recommend engaging the services of a specialist employment lawyer when dealing with potential disability discrimination cases.

The DDA could well prove an easier route for pursuing stress claims than the primary legal route. The primary legal route requires a claim for breach of duty of care in common law and, for a liability to exist, the damage must have been reasonably foreseeable and the injury must have been caused by work.

Under the DDA such a strict test is not required: it currently covers all clinically recognized mental health problems and the impairment does not necessarily have to be caused at work. For example, a person suffering a bereavement or break-up of a relationship might be entitled to protection on the grounds that stress is having a substantial long-term adverse effect on the person's ability to carry out a normal job. Compensation is unlimited in DDA cases.

The lessons for employers are:

- Ensure stress risk assessments have been carried out for those people experiencing high levels of stress
- Offer counseling if necessary
- Ensure that people are given an appropriate level of support
- Offer training on stress awareness and strategies for dealing with stress.

WORKING TIME REGULATIONS AND THE WORKING TIME DIRECTIVE (1998)

These Regulations gave rise to wholly new rights and obligations relating to work and rest. Principally, the Regulations cover the following areas pertaining to employee's working time:

- A limit on the average working week to 48 hours
- Entitlement of employees to paid holidays
- Entitlement of employees to minimum daily rest periods
- Entitlement of employees to minimum weekly rest periods
- A limit on average nightly working time, and obligatory health assessments for night workers.

An opt-out provision was made allowing staff to work longer than the 48-hour week. According to *Personnel Today* (2003), two-thirds of employers in the UK ask their workers to opt out of the Working Time Directive, allowing them to work more than 48 hours a week. This is partly to deal with seasonal fluctuations and skills shortages.

Personnel Today (2003) reported that French workers were rejecting the country's 35-hour week and were demanding the freedom to work longer hours. Over a third of French workers wanted a return to the 39-hour working week and this is currently being considered by the French government.

Since 1 August 2004 the Working Time Directive has applied to junior doctors in training, introducing a maximum working week of 58 hours, falling to 48 hours in 2009, with minimum rest periods. Hospitals that breach the Directive will face fines of up to £5000 by the HSE; junior doctors could also take them to an employment tribunal. Hospitals have had to make drastic changes to provide cover at night. The British Medical Association has said it will support overworked junior doctors who decide to take legal action.

At the time of writing the European Commission is reviewing the UK's opt-out from the Working Time Directive. Employers feel that removing the opt-out clause would adversely affect competitiveness and increase staffing costs, as they would be forced to use agency staff. UK attempts to block the changes will be supported by Poland, Malta, and Cyprus.

The HSE sees working longer hours and overdemanding workloads as major stressors. Care must be taken to monitor the hours worked by staff to ensure health does not suffer. There is a growing recognition that working long hours does not equate with productivity.

STRESS AND CRIMINAL LAW

Goldman and Lewis (2003) reported on the move by the HSE in August 2003 to issue an improvement notice under the Health and Safety at Work Act 1974 to West Dorset General Hospital NHS Trust for failing to assess the risk of stress to its staff. This was the first time the HSE had issued such an order against an organization for stress and it arose as a result of a complaint by a former member of staff.

The underlying threat was that if an assessment was not carried out and improvements were not made, prosecution would follow. The maximum penalty for breach of the legislation in a magistrate's court is £20,000 and up to six months' imprisonment. If the case is heard in a crown court, the fine is unlimited and up to two years' imprisonment.

The hospital had an outstanding success rate within the NHS, having earned a three-star rating. However, in reaching these high standards of excellence for treating patients, the penalty appeared to be unacceptably high levels of stress within the workforce. The Trust was given four months to assess the risk of stress and improve it.

Refreshingly, the Trust saw the situation as an opportunity rather than a threat or punishment. Robert Pascall, the Trust's HR director (who had been in post for three weeks at this stage), worked in partnership with the HSE to take the following actions:

- Conduct a stress audit with the University of Exeter, the results of which were fed directly back to staff
- Adopt a new stress policy
- Train executive staff in stress recognition and management
- Introduce bullying and harassment advisors trained by the Andrea Adams Trust, as well as to bring in Royal College of Nursing staff to advise in this area
- Introduce a new appraisal process.

After being given an extension to the improvement notice in order to put these measures in place, the notice was lifted in March 2004. Since then, the stress management program has become a wider initiative called "Shaping the Future", which allows the various directorates of the Trust to take steps to improve employee health and well-being. The Trust has been exceptionally creative and innovative about this and the following measures are all in progress:

- Tai chi classes
- Indian head massages

- Enhanced occupational health (OH) provision
- Self-referral for physiotherapy (the Trust has shown a cost/benefit for this)
- 70 line managers trained in conducting return-to-work interviews.

In an interview for this book, Robert Pascall said that he felt extremely satisfied with the current program, and is pleased to have had an opportunity to make such an impact on the health of the Trust's employees.

The lessons from this case are:

- It has put stress firmly on the business agenda. Organizations who are in pursuit of excellence cannot afford to overlook the pressure that staff can experience in meeting the high standards expected
- It again reinforces the need to be aware of the levels of stress staff are experiencing and to have a process of stress risk assessment.

Notable Personal Injury Actions Based on Common Law

To illustrate the way in which the law is currently being interpreted in the UK, the next section covers:

1. Common law liability
2. Occupational stress and compensation – two landmark cases
3. A landmark guidance from Court of Appeal regarding forseeability.

COMMON LAW LIABILITY

To succeed in a claim for failure to provide a safe system of work, the employee would need to:

1. Show that the employer was, or should have been, aware of the risk (if the employee is of normal health and undertaking a normal workload, there is no apparent risk, and no duty to take preventive steps). For an employee to succeed in a negligence case against an employer, it must be shown that the damage suffered by an employee was foreseeable and foreseeability must be established in each case. It must be shown that the employer could foresee a stress-based illness.

2. Show that the employer has failed to take steps a reasonable employer would normally take to protect them.

3. Show that ill health was caused by the employer's breach of its duty to amend or improve the working conditions. Can it be shown that there is a link between the employer's alleged failures and the behavioral change or illness that is manifest? For example, a heart attack could be related to smoking, diet, or hereditary factors. In the Walker case (see below) the court ruled the nervous breakdown was due solely to work pressures.

4. Establish that he or she has suffered a recognized stress-induced illness, such as a nervous breakdown or eating disorder. In personal injury claims, stress is not viewed as an illness, but it is accepted that it is a cause of psychiatric illnesses.

OCCUPATIONAL STRESS AND COMPENSATION

Walker *v.* Northumberland County Council (1995)

In 1995 John Walker was the first to sue successfully for a stress-related psychiatric illness caused by normal work. He was a senior social worker and area manager, with responsibility for four teams of field social service workers. Over the years his caseload had grown, especially the number of child abuse cases, and no additional staff were provided. Walker repeatedly complained to his superiors of the need to alleviate some of the work pressures his teams were experiencing. He asked for the work to be reorganized, but his request was refused. Walker had a nervous breakdown. Before he returned to work, it was agreed that he would have an assistant and have weekly supervision meetings with his manager. In reality this did not happen. There was a backlog of paperwork from his absence and the workload increased. Walker again went off sick and had a second nervous breakdown; he was forced to retire on grounds of ill health.

Walker successfully sued Northumberland CC for negligence and breach of statutory duty under the Health and Safety at Work Act. This requires employers to provide the employee with a safe working environment and applies to all aspects of work and to all kinds of foreseeable injury, including stress-related clinical conditions. Walker was awarded compensation of £175,000.

The lessons from this case are:

- Northumberland CC should have foreseen the possibility of a second nervous breakdown. It was not liable for the first breakdown because Walker had not indicated to his employers that he was personally having difficulty coping.
- It failed to give adequate support on his return to work.
- After the first nervous breakdown, Walker kept his employers adequately informed and kept notes on the situation.

Lancaster *v.* Birmingham City Council (1999)

Beverley Lancaster started work for Birmingham city council as a clerk in 1971. By 1978 she had progressed to the role of senior draughtsman in the architects' department and supervised ten members of staff. Following the birth of her child she changed to part-time working and a job-share arrangement. After a restructuring and job changes, Lancaster was moved to the housing department where she had to handle rude and demanding tenants. She experienced panic attacks, anxiety, and depression and received medical help. She took early retirement and claimed that her health had suffered due to the council's negligence, that is, Birmingham CC had failed to:

- Assess her ability to do the job
- Provide the necessary training
- Assess the situation – she was experiencing work overload and felt unable to meet the demands put upon her.

Birmingham CC admitted liability; the first time this had happened in a case of stress-related illness. She was awarded £67,000.

GUIDANCE FROM THE COURT OF APPEAL REGARDING FORSEEABILITY

In February 2002 a Court of Appeal ruling set out guidelines for applying the law surrounding stress at work. Four appeals, from different county courts, were all heard together. The Supreme Court of Judicature Court of Appeal 2002 reported that: "In each case a circuit judge had awarded damages for negligence against the claimants' employers after the claimant had had to stop working for them owing to stress-induced psychiatric illness... The Court of Appeal allowed the employers' appeals in three of these cases (Hatton, Barber and Bishop). In the fourth (Jones) it dismissed the employers' appeal not without some hesitation."

In each of the cases, the critical factors were:

- Was this employee's illness reasonably foreseeable?
- Was it reasonable for the employer to do something about it?

One of the appeals upheld was a language teacher, Penelope Hatton, who took early retirement due to depression and debility. The judges ruled that because she never complained to anyone of her workload, which was no greater than other teachers, her absences from school were attributed to other things, such as sinusitis, and she never informed the school of her depression or seeing a stress counselor, her illness was not reasonably foreseeable. The ruling states "This is a classic case where no-one can be blamed for the sad events which brought Mrs Hatton's teaching career to an end."

The second was Barber, a teacher in a comprehensive school with reduced resources and an upcoming OFSTED inspection. He developed depressive illness, and was off work for three weeks. On his return he did tell the school that he was finding it difficult to cope and that the work was affecting his health, but he did not alert the school to his severe symptoms. After a summer holiday period, he did not tell the school that his ill health was continuing, but had a breakdown in November, losing control in the classroom. He took early retirement aged 52. The judges said "it is difficult indeed to identify a point at which the school had a duty to take the positive steps identified by the judge" because they did not have enough information from Mr. Barber. His appeal to the House of Lords was successful (see section below on House of Lords ruling April 2004).

The third appeal upheld was that of Bishop, the factory worker. In this case, the company was taken over and reorganized, and his job no longer existed. He requested to go back to his old work, but was told there was nothing the company could do to bring back his previous role. He was reassured that he was doing a good job in his new role. His GP advised him to change his job but he did not inform his employers of this; he subsequently had a nervous breakdown. The judges ruled that "there was nothing unusual, excessive or unreasonable about the demands" on Mr. Bishop, and "there was nothing the employer could reasonably be expected to do" to rearrange the company to suit one person. It was simply a sad case of someone who could not cope with a change of job.

In the fourth case where the appeal was not upheld, Mrs Jones was employed as an administrative assistant at a local authority training center. She was working excessive hours, trying to do the job of two or three people, as acknowledged by the personnel officer. She complained to her manager, who threatened her with non-renewal of her temporary post if she persisted in her complaints of overwork. She complained to head office and her personnel officer about this. Extra help was arranged twice, but was never actually provided. Eventually, she went off sick with anxiety and depression and never returned to that job. The judges ruled that it was reasonably foreseeable that the unreasonable demands on Mrs. Jones would harm her health, and that there was a breach of duty of care because they did not do anything about it.

This Court of Appeal ruling did, in effect, swing the pendulum in favor of employers, and put more onus on the employee to report any difficulties in coping. A psychological injury is less likely to be "reasonably foreseeable" unless the employer has been informed of the employee's state of mind, or has knowledge of previous psychological illness. But this does not in any way dilute the advice given to managers in Chapter 16 to remain vigilant, ask employees for feedback, never to say there is no resource to help, and never to make promises that cannot be kept.

Mordue (2002) summed up the factors relevant to forseeability:

- Whether the employee is under unreasonable, excessive or unusual pressure
- Signs that others doing the same work are under harmful levels of stress, for example abnormal sickness or absence levels, or a high turnover of staff
- Signs from the employees themselves. These may include specific complaints of stress with clear indications that health is suffering
- Whether the employer has taken reasonable steps to prevent the risk to health, for example time off, transfer of work, redistribution of work, additional help or counseling and mentoring
- Causation is a key step in establishing liability – can the person prove that their stress is caused by the failure of their employer to satisfy its duty of care.

Even when a psychiatric injury is reasonably foreseeable, it is not always the case that an employer will reasonably be expected to act to prevent that injury occurring. The court's view is that an employer is not obligated to dismiss or demote an otherwise willing employee in order to remove him or her from the stressful situation.

Gibb (2002) quoted a spokesperson from Unison, Britain's biggest union which has taken on several groundbreaking cases, who said:

> *Our experience of dealing with stress cases is that they are extremely difficult to prove – most of the cases that go to court are extreme. These sort of cases are very rare and the burden of proof has always been high.*

For instance, the Walker case was successful because he was vociferous throughout and had kept carefully documented notes.

One final very important point to make about the 2002 Court of Appeal ruling is that Lady Justice Hale made the statement: "An employer who offers a confidential advice service, with referral to appropriate counselling or treatment services, is unlikely to be found in breach of duty." This has been cited in more recent cases as guidance, but has also been challenged by judges (see section below on Court of Appeal ruling November 2004).

PRACTICAL LEGAL GUIDANCE

The 2002 ruling by the Court of Appeal does not give the employer license to sit back and ignore the issue of workplace stress. Further advice for employers to stay within the law includes:

- The employer should carry out regular risk assessments for stress, particularly in pressurized environments. Gibb (2002) also reported Tudor Owen, TUC senior health and safety officer, as saying:

  > *Unions will certainly make sure that employers know they must assess the risks of stressful occupations. We will make sure all of our members know that the Court of Appeal has urged them not to suffer in silence but get their complaints about bullying, overwork, inadequate training and unrealistic deadlines on record.*

- The employer should consider carefully the circumstances of his individual employees – particularly those with heavy workloads – and determine whether any of them has a particular vulnerability.
- Be sure to have written foundations for legal protection, including contracts of employment that clearly state sick pay entitlements.
- Have clear policies and procedures that cover stress, bullying and harassment, and whistle blowing.
- Always document situations in writing.
- Keep updated on all legislation and call in legal help early. Geoffrey Bignell of Just Employment Solicitors advises that HR departments must keep managers abreast of important developments, and provide them with workable, robust procedures. However, he says: "it is amazing how often procedures are not followed and this is not viewed favourably in tribunals."

If an employee does become ill, managers may suggest referral to occupational health, or an organization may want a medical opinion on fitness for work (see Chapter 17). An important legal requirement that managers must be aware of is that, if an organization asks for medical information from an employee's GP or specialists, or requests a report from doctors or psychologists assessing the employee, then in accordance with the Access to Medical Records Act 1988, he/she must sign a release form allowing this. The employee has the right to see the report before it is sent to anyone else and can at that point refuse to release it.

Appendix 10.1 is an example of such a release form. Appendix 10.2 is an example of an accompanying letter to the employee explaining his/her rights under the Access to Medical Records Act. Appendix 10.3 is a counterpart letter that could be sent to an employee's GP or specialist. Part IV of the Data Protection Act has more information about this, and can be found in full at www.informationcommissioner.gov.uk.

"An employee does have the right to refuse assessment or treatment, but this rarely happens, except occasionally in alcohol or drug abuse cases," says Geoffrey Bignell, "usually, this is because an employee refuses to admit a problem." When this happens, the employer has to reach a decision without medical advice. Every case is different, however, and a complex case needs the expertise of an employment law solicitor.

Legal Guidance from 2004

HOUSE OF LORDS RULING APRIL 2004

In April 2004, the House of Lords ruled in favor of teacher Barber, overturning the Court of Appeal's decision made on his case in the 2002 ruling. The Lords said that the school had been unsympathetic to Barber's illness, and should have not only made enquiries about his depression, but done something about his workload, in the light of his illness.

The lessons from this case are:

- The employer must remember its duty of care and be particularly vigilant and sympathetic when an employee has suffered a stress-related illness. Barber's employers were not
- Employees must inform their employers when they are suffering from excessive stress and keep appropriate records
- Having received medical certificates indicating work-related stress, employers should take the initiative by investigating what can be done to resolve the problem
- Cases such as this could be avoided if employers and their staff adopt the right attitude and approach to the situation.

COURT OF APPEAL RULING NOVEMBER 2004

The Court of Appeal heard six appeals in cases involving claims for damages for psychiatric injury arising out of stress at work in November 2004. In the case of *Best* v. *Staffordshire University*, the judge said:

> *[The judge in the original case] regarded the availability of counselling as irrelevant on the basis that it was not clear that counselling would have helped Mr Best; what was required was more administrative support ... We agree that on the facts of this case the availability of a counselling service was not fatal to Mr Best's case.*

In other words, Best did not lose this appeal just because the university had a counseling service. It was because Best's breakdown had not been reasonably foreseeable, and the judges explain at length how they reached this decision.

The judges' statement above does not fully challenge the 2002 Court of Appeal ruling, but says enough to warn employers that having counseling available may not be enough on its own to absolve them from their responsibilities. In the authors' opinion, a counseling service to pick up the pieces of broken employees does not satisfy a duty of care to protect employee health. This is like saying that a factory would not need finger guards on its machines if it had surgeons standing by to sew fingers back on!

HSE Guidelines

The HSE (2001) published *Tackling Work-related Stress: A Managers' Guide to Improving and Maintaining Employee Health and Well-being*. In the guide, the HSE recommends a five-step approach based around risk assessment. The *Management Standards for Tackling Work-related Stress* launched on 3 November 2004, modified the approach slightly:

1. Identify the hazards
2. Decide who might be harmed and how
3. Evaluate the risk by:
   — Identifying what action you are already taking
   — Deciding whether it is enough
   — If it is not, deciding what more you need to do
4. Record the significant findings of the assessment
5. Review the assessment at appropriate intervals.

This approach has been a requirement by law for more than ten years under the Management of Health and Safety at Work Regulations. It is a criminal offence to fail to carry out a risk assessment (see Chapter 8 for more detail).

Since 2000, the HSE has been actively consulting to produce standards of good management practice based on the risk assessment approach to tackling work-related stress. Its strategy is to work towards prevention of stress in the workplace rather than coping with stress once it has occurred.

Summary of Steps to be Taken by Employers to Comply with the Law

In summary, there are a number of steps that need to be taken by employers to comply with the law and take care of the well-being of their staff. The HSE who police the Health and Safety at Work Act 1974 and the Management of Health and Safety at Work Regulations recommend a proactive and preventive approach to stress management. For organizations to adopt this approach, they need to do the following:

1. Assess the potential hazards.
2. Identify the jobs most at risk and assess what can reasonably be done to minimize any risk.
3. Review the risk assessment regularly, particularly during times of change.
4. Ensure that people receive adequate training to do their jobs, particularly if they are transferred into new and different jobs.
5. Have a stress policy that is fully communicated to staff, and have clear policies and procedures for bullying and harassment and whistle blowing.
6. Keep up to date with the law and ensure managers do the same.
7. Have a confidential employee assistance program that can be accessed by staff who are experiencing excessive stress.
8. When an employer receives a medical certificate indicating a work-related stress illness, it should be proactive in taking steps to address the problem, giving the employee adequate support if they return to work from a period off sick.
9. Ensure that all cases of stress-related illnesses are handled quickly and decisively.
10. Keep in communication with staff whilst they are off sick.
11. Conduct an individual assessment when a member of staff returns to work after a stress-related illness.
12. Take legal advice early if this becomes necessary.

Summary of Steps that can be Taken by Employees

Employees need to work with employers to ensure that issues are identified in the first place and followed up in a satisfactory manner. This would involve:

1. The employee making the employer aware if he/she is suffering from a stress-related illness.
2. If employees feel they are experiencing excessive pressure at work, drawing this to the attention of their managers.
3. If employees feel they are being dealt with unfairly or they are being ignored, documenting any evidence.
4. If suffering from excessive stress, seeking medical help and taking advantage of any employee counseling services provided by the company.
5. Keeping up to date with legislation.

APPENDIX 10.1

Medical Report
Consent Form

To: ....
(insert your doctor's name and practice address)

I hereby give my consent to my employer, ________________, obtaining a medical report from you in relation to my current absence from work.

*I do/do not wish to see the report before it is supplied to my employer.

Signed: ....

Date: ....

** Delete as applicable*

(Reprinted with kind permission of Just Employment Solicitors)

APPENDIX 10.2

Letter to Employee to Accompany Medical Report Consent Form

Private and Confidential

To: [ ] [Date]

Dear [ ]

I would like to approach your doctor for a medical report in relation to the nature of your current illness and when you are likely to be well again. The purpose of the report is to help me to assess if you are likely to return to work soon and, if so, what steps, if any, I may need to take to help you to return to work.

The provision of a report to me by your doctor is subject to your rights under the Access to Medical Records Act 1988 as follows:

1. Your doctor may not supply the report without your express consent.
2. If you wish to see the report before it is sent to me you must let me know now.
3. If you choose to see the report, your doctor will make any amendments, which he/she agrees with you. If your doctor cannot agree to your amendments he/she will attach your statement about the parts with which you disagree. Your doctor will not send me the report unless you consent.
4. You may request a copy of the report that your doctor sends me at any time up do six months after he/she has sent it to me.
5. Your doctor will not give you a copy of any part of his/her report if in his/her opinion it will be likely to cause serious harm to your physical or mental health or others, or would indicate the intentions of the doctor in relation to you, or would reveal information about another person without that person's consent (unless that person is a health professional).

Please note that, if you do not consent, I will still need to make a decision as to your future employment based on existing information.

If you are willing for me to approach your doctor for a medical report, please sign and return the attached consent form in the enclosed envelope.

Yours sincerely,

Enc.

(Reprinted with kind permission of Just Employment Solicitors)

APPENDIX 10.3

Medical Information Release Form

To [Employee's doctor] Date:

Dear Doctor [ ]

Our employee, [ ], who has been absent from work since [ ] 2005, has given his consent for us to approach you for a medical report in relation to his current condition. We attach his written consent and confirm we have informed him of his rights under the Access to Medical Records Act 1988.

Please provide the following information:

1. The nature of the employee's illness;
2. The likely duration of his illness;
3. In your opinion, how long is he likely to remain off work?
4. What is the likelihood of recurrence and will this affect his ability to work in the future?
5. On his return to work, will he be capable of undertaking a full range of [managerial] duties?
6. If not, what duties will he be capable of undertaking?

Please let us know what your fee will be in relation to preparing your report.

Yours sincerely

Enc.

(Reprinted with kind permission of Just Employment Solicitors)

11 Developing a Stress Policy

Introduction

The Health and Safety Executive (HSE) recommends that organizations have a stress policy as part of their approach to stress management. Many organizations go beyond a separate stress policy and include stress as part of a broader policy related to employee well-being, ensuring that it becomes integrated with policies and procedures for managing people. Having a stress policy forms a key part of the defense in legal cases of stress. Apart from the legal requirement, it should be viewed as having an important role in the stress management process and should not be seen as a paper exercise. For these reasons, it is clear that top management commitment to managing stress is essential. In turn, all employees need to be proactive in helping to prevent stress from occurring in the first place.

This chapter explores the need for a stress policy, its core objectives, and how a policy might be developed, giving an example of a local authority that opted for a stress policy. A summary of the HSE policy guidelines is also included. The contents of policies are outlined and the need to keep them updated emphasized.

This chapter is important for those needing to develop a policy and is essential reading for HR and occupational health specialists. Managers might find the chapter helpful for understanding their responsibilities in managing the stress of others.

The Objectives of a Stress Management Policy

Organizations may decide a policy is necessary because of the growing concern regarding stress. Increased absentee rates and the numbers of employees on long-term, stress-related sickness absence may also prompt organizations to develop a policy.

Sutherland and Cooper (2000) identified three objectives:

1. To prevent stress by identifying causes of workplace stress and eliminating (or minimizing) them, thus dealing with the source of stress.
2. To control stress by ensuring that the stress response does not cause negative impact on the individual, dealing with the response to stress.

3. To rehabilitate employees who are suffering from exposure to stress by the provision of a confidential counseling service. This will deal with the symptoms of stress.

A study by Income Data Services (2002) identified different drivers for developing a stress policy. The Highways Agency introduced its policy after identifying problems caused by a series of organizational upheavals. AstraZeneca noticed an increased number of cases of stress and developed a stress strategy. They recognized the causes – rapid growth and organizational changes, and sheer volume of new work – could put large amounts of pressure on the workforce.

Having a stress policy also makes employees aware that stress is a subject that can be discussed – it is not a taboo subject. Kingston Hospital NHS Trust, urged by the NHS Executive to promote positive mental health at work, introduced a stress policy clearly stating that employees who acknowledged they were suffering from stress would not be disadvantaged. The Royal Sun Alliance's well-being policy aims to create a climate in which stress can be discussed openly.

Some policies also include a section on the nature of stress, recognizing it in self and others, and the causes of stress. They also address strategies – including interventions offered by employers to manage stress. Thus, a policy helps to educate people on how to prevent and deal with stress, particularly when aimed at managers and their staff.

Developing a Stress Policy

The HSE (1997) laid down policy guidelines that provide a good framework for those needing to develop a stress policy. There are five elements of the framework:

1. Effective policies – these set out clear directions for the organization to follow.
2. An effective management structure and arrangements in place for delivering the policy – staff should be involved in the process of policy development. This should be sustained by effective communication and the promotion of competence which allow all employees and their representatives to contribute to the health and safety effort.
3. There should be a planned and systematic approach for implementing the policy – the aim is to minimize risk and a risk assessment should be used to decide on priorities and set objectives for eliminating hazards and reducing risks.
4. Measuring performance – against agreed standards to identify when and where improvement is needed. Active and reactive monitoring should take place to identify both the immediate and underlying causes, and the implications for the health and safety management system. Longer term objectives are also monitored.
5. Auditing and reviewing performance – there should be systematic reviews of performance based on data from monitoring and independent audits.

Performance is assessed by internal reference to key indicators and, externally, by comparing the performance of competitors and best practice generally.

A stress policy should be an integral part of an organization's approach to stress management and, more broadly, should be integrated with other people management policies and procedures – such as performance management, sickness absence, and grievance procedures. It needs to be developed in consultation with others and regularly reviewed and updated. The stress policy can be conceived of as either stand-alone or integrated:

- *Stand-alone policy* – helps to demonstrate that the organization is committed to the management of stress. It is also a good strategy for those taking the first steps in dealing with stress and the well-being of employees.
- *Integrated policy* – introduced by those organizations who want to take a broader view and treat stress as part of tackling employee health and well-being and creating a healthy working environment.

INTRODUCING AND DEVELOPING A STRESS POLICY – TOP TIPS

- In deciding the exact content and the specific measures highlighted in any new stress policy, due attention should be paid to the resources available in the organization to deal with the issue of stress
- Care should be taken when introducing the policy to ensure that management and employee expectations are managed
- How the policy is worded and how it is communicated will inevitably play a part in the development of the "culture" surrounding stress in the organization
- What can be included may well be impacted by the maturity of the organization and the people processes already in place
- While in the early stages of development, a strictly "clean and legal" approach may well be adopted if resources are tight and other people priorities are vying for attention
- In a more established/mature organization, many other people processes and policies will have been established and can be included/integrated into the stress policy
- In these circumstances, it is important that the whole "people offer" is well integrated and coherent, so that approaches to dealing with stress do not appear to be an afterthought.

What to Include in a Stress Policy

The IDS study (2002) noted that the scope and length of policies is extremely variable. The shortest was the Highways Agency document – one large page, whilst the longest was 70 pages. Some organizations back up the policy document with supporting documentation, for example booklets on how to manage stress and sources of help if people experience stress.

The HSE has a model stress policy on its website (www.hse.gov.uk/stress/standards/pdfs/examplepolicy.pdf) which has a number of essential elements:

- Who is covered by the policy
- Definition of stress
- Policy statements, for example the company will identify all workplace stressors and conduct risk assessments to eliminate stress or control the risks from stress. These risk assessments will be regularly reviewed.
- The respective responsibilities of managers, occupational health and safety staff, human resources, and employees
- The function of safety representatives
- The role of the safety committee.

The document should be signed off by the managing director and an employee representative.

Mordue (2002) also considered the following should be included:

- A commitment by the employer to tackle the causes of stress in the workplace proactively and respond with appropriate support and consideration to those suffering from work-related stress.
- A systematic framework for carrying out ongoing risk assessments, to discharge health and safety obligations.
- A framework for the training of managers to identify causes of stress, the signs of stress, and how to deal with individual employees suffering from stress or stress-related ill health.
- Clear guidance to managers on the procedures to be followed if an employee complains of occupational stress or stress-related ill health and how to manage stress-related employee issues such as absenteeism, long-term ill health, and performance issues.
- An explanation of how the policy relates to other policies and procedures, such as grievance procedures, sickness absence review procedures, performance review procedures, alcohol and drug abuse policies, and so on.

AN EXAMPLE

The London Borough of Havering issued a stress code of practice having previously conducted a stress audit. The code of practice is shown in Appendix 11.1 and is an excellent example of what should be included in a code of practice document. In particular, it addresses:

- The aims of the code and the commitment to prevention and control of stress
- The links with other policies
- The educational element, covering the legal requirements and an understanding of the nature of stress

- The risk assessment process
- Ways of preventing and minimizing occupational stress
- Sources of help including strategies for managers and individuals and the internal and external support available for employees.

Three areas could have had greater coverage:

1. The procedure for managers to follow if they are concerned that members of their own teams are suffering from excessive stress.
2. Procedures for managers to follow when people are absent through stress-related illness.
3. Procedures to follow when people return to work after a stress-related illness that should include conducting a risk assessment.

It should be noted that the borough of Havering's code of practice was produced prior to the HSE Management Standards being finalized (HSE, 2004) and, therefore, refers to seven factors, rather than six.

Summary

- It is advisable to have a stress policy from a legal perspective and for managing stress within an organization
- Developing such a policy should not be viewed as a paper exercise; instead it should help everyone within an organization to prevent excessive stress from occurring or to control it, if necessary
- It can help people to discuss stress more openly and take away some of the stigma that can be associated with the condition
- A policy should give clear guidelines of responsibilities and for the procedures to be followed; it can also act as an educational tool
- The stress policy needs to be regularly reviewed and updated.

APPENDIX 11.1

Code of Practice For Managing Occupational Stress

1 Policy Statement

1.1 The Council has an approved strategy with regard to the Management of Occupational Stress. It acknowledges that occupational stress is now recognised as a Major cause of absence from work. It is an issue that the organisation as a whole is committed to addressing with both managers and staff.

1.2 Each service cluster is required to ensure that sound arrangements are in place to prevent and control factors, which contribute to occupational stress. (stress management is not the answer, stress prevention is).

1.3 The Council recognises its responsibilities under the Health & Safety at Work Act 1974 and is committed to ensure that the mental health and well being of London Borough of Havering employees is part of health, safety and welfare management.

1.4 All policies and procedures are aimed at making a positive contribution to the well being of our employees and fulfilling job satisfaction.

2 Introduction

2.1 In 1999 the Council approved a strategy for managing organisational stress. The strategy:

- describes the effects of stress on individuals and the organisation.
- details the key findings of the stress audit undertaken in March 1998.
- details a strategy for the future.

2.2 In 2001 a working group was set up to develop a Code of Practice for managing occupational stress. The group consisted of representatives of the five service clusters, Occupational Health, Corporate Human Resources and Trade Unions.

3 The Aim of the Code of Practice

3.1 The aim of this code of practice is to enable managers and employees to ensure that sound arrangements are in place to prevent and control factors which contribute to occupational stress. In order to do this everybody needs to:

- work together to recognise what occupational stress is
- acknowledge the effect on the individual, the workforce and upon service delivery
- identify and use techniques to minimise the causes of occupational stress
- understand what is required of them to fulfil their responsibilities in managing occupational stress
- undertake a risk assessment to identify occupational stress
- recognise vulnerable people and job roles
- promote a healthy working culture and environment

4 Policies and Procedures Which Support The Prevention and Management of Occupational Stress

4.1 There are a number of polices, procedures and management guidelines available which demonstrate the Council's intention to promote respect at work. Managers should be aware of these policies and procedures as they are models of best practice; these include:

- London Borough of Havering's Core Values
- Health and Safety Policy
- Staff Code of Conduct
- Confidential Reporting
- Employee Assault Policy
- Harassment and Bullying Policy
- Personal Development and Performance Appraisal
- Equal Opportunities and Diversity Policy
- Disciplinary Policy
- Grievance Policy
- Alcohol and Drugs Policy
- Induction and Probation Procedure
- Recruitment and Selection Policy and Procedure
- Managing Absence Policy and Procedure
- Special Leave Management guidelines
- Flexible Working Management guidelines
- Working Time Regulations Management Guidelines

4.2 Where appropriate managers should ensure that they and their employees receive the relevant training.

4.3 School based staff can be employed under different conditions of service which are determined by Central Government and Local Management of Schools, therefore policies and procedures for school based staff may differ from the Corporate policies. In practice, there should be comparable model policies for school-based staff as those listed in 4.1 above, with the implementation of these tailored to meet the needs of the schools.

5 The Law

5.1 Under the Health and Safety at Work etc Act 1974 employers have a general duty to ensure, so far as is reasonably practicable, the health, safety and welfare of their employees at work. This includes taking steps to make sure they do not suffer stress-related illness as a result of their work.

5.2 Similarly all Council employees have a responsibility for the health, safety and welfare of themselves and others while at work.

5.3 Additionally employers must take account of the risk of stress-related ill health when meeting their legal obligations under the Management of Health and Safety at Work Regulations 1999.

5.4 Under Civil Law employers owe a duty of care to their employees, which extends to their mental health.

6 Definition of Stress

6.1 There are several definitions of stress.

6.2 The Health and Safety Executive defines occupational stress as the adverse reaction people have to excessive pressures or other types of demand placed on them.

6.3 This makes an important distinction between the beneficial effects of reasonable pressure and challenge (which can be stimulating, motivating, and can give a "buzz") and occupational stress, which is the natural but distressing reaction to demands or "pressures" that the person perceives they cannot cope with at a given time.

6.4 Stress is not the same as ill-health, but in some cases where pressures are intense and continue for some time, the effects of stress can be more sustained and far more damaging, leading to longer-term psychological problems and physical ill health.

7 Cause of Occupational Stress

7.1 One of the difficulties of dealing with occupational stress is that it is not simple to predict what will cause harmful levels.

7.2 People respond to different types of pressure in different ways and much depends on people's own personalities, experience and motivation and the support available from managers, colleagues, family and friends, and their life outside of work.

7.3 Managers need to be aware of what may make staff more vulnerable to occupational stress, as well as affecting their performance and judgement.

7.4 The factors that may cause occupational stress are detailed in the risk assessment document at appendix A.

7.5 Signs and Symptoms

7.5.1 Occupational stress exists where people perceive they cannot cope with what is being asked of them at work. In principle, everyone can experience occupational stress but the signs and symptoms will vary from one individual to another.

7.5.2 It is important to remember that occupational stress is not an illness, but if it is prolonged or particularly intense, it can lead to increased problems with ill health. For example:

- **physical effects – heart disease, back pain, gastrointestinal disturbances and various minor illnesses**
- **psychological effects – anxiety and depression**

7.5.3 It can also lead to other behaviours that are not helpful to health, such as skipping meals, drinking too much caffeine or alcohol and smoking cigarettes.

7.5.4 Occupational stress can also have consequences for organisations. It may lead to:

- **an increase in sickness absence, which can have a domino effect one person goes off sick which leads to their workload being shared among their colleagues. They in turn may then be unable to cope, which could affect their health, and lead to greater sickness absence.**
- **reduced morale.**
- **reduced performance.**
- **employees seeking alternative employment. Organisations then have the expense of recruiting, inducting, and training new employees.**

8 The Risk Assessment Process

8.1 The Management of Health & Safety at Work Regulations 1999 requires that suitable and sufficient risk assessments are undertaken.

8.2 The process follows the principles laid out in HSE's publication 5 steps to risk assessment. The five steps are:

1 identify the hazards.
2 decide who might be harmed and how.
3 evaluate the risk by:
- **identifying what action you are already taking**
- **deciding whether it is enough**
- **if it is not, deciding what more you need to do**

4 record the significant findings of the assessment
5 review the assessment at appropriate intervals

8.3 The risk assessment is completed on the role not the individual, but not forgetting that ultimately an individual cannot be totally separated from the role.

8.4 The Council's risk assessment document for identifying role stressors can be found at appendix A. The seven risk factors are assessed in this document. Managers who will be required to complete risk assessments should undertake the appropriate training provided.

(i) Identify the hazards
How to find out if there is a problem
There are seven broad categories of risk factors for occupational stress:

Factor 1: **Culture – of the organisation and how it approaches occupational stress**
Factor 2: **Demands – such as workload and exposure to physical hazards**
Factor 3: **Control – how much choice the person has in the way they do their work**
Factor 4: **Relationships – covering issues such as bullying and harassment**
Factor 5: **Change – how organisational change is managed and communicated in the organisation**
Factor 6: **Role – whether the individual understands their role in the organisation and whether the organisation ensures that the person does not have conflicting roles**
Factor 7: **Support – training and factors unique to the individual**
Support – from peers and line management
Training – to ensure an individual is capable of undertaking the core training functions required of the job, to address possible capability issues that could become potential stressors.
Factors unique to the individual – catering for individual differences

(ii) Decide who might be harmed and how
Occupational stress can affect any member of your team. In particular, it might affect those exposed to the seven factors mentioned in Step 1.

At particular times, your employees may be more vulnerable to occupational stress. For example, those returning to work after a stress-related illness, or those who have a domestic crisis, such as a bereavement.

The seven risk factors can affect your employees in different ways. For example, some members of your team may feel anxious about the amount of work they have to do, or the way you will react if they tell you they cannot cope. Finding out how the factors are affecting your team requires a partnership approach, based on openness, honesty, and trust, which explores what the main effects of work are on employees and what areas should be targeted first.

(iii) Evaluate the Risk and Decide if Enough is Being Done

Consider how likely it is that each hazard mentioned in Step 1 could ensure harm in your team. In taking action ask yourself:
– what action is already being taken?
– is it enough?
– if not, what more will you do?

Remember that you should try to eliminate the risks as far as possible. You should try to combat risks at an organisational level at source before considering the training (in terms of pressure management) or counselling needs of the individual employee. You should try to take action that protects everyone, rather than just a few individuals.

(iv) Record Your Findings

Managers must record the main findings of the risk assessment and should share the findings with employees.

You should use this document to monitor progress and help you keep an eye on particular hazards.

(v) Review Your Assessment and Revise Where Necessary

Review your assessment whenever significant changes occur in the organisation, or in the way your team handles its business. Do this in consultation with employees. Consider reviewing the assessment regularly.

9 Preventing Occupational Stress

9.1 There are a number of techniques that will assist in minimising the causes of occupational stress and the management of stress. The two principal ones are to:
- **practice good management skills to create a healthy working environment, and minimise the cause of stress.**
- **use the model of risk assessment to identify the hazards and influencing factors associated with work roles and responsibilities, and the working environment, and to identify whether the mechanisms in place to prevent or reduce stress are adequate.**

9.2 The Council will promote good management practice with the aim of minimising stress in the working environment as follows:-

9.3 Communication
- **ensure there is good communication at all levels in the organisation – bottom up, as well as top down.**
- **work closely with the recognised union representatives to assist in communicating with employees.**
- **develop a communication strategy, which improves internal and external communication.**
- **put a system in place, which ensures line managers hold regular team briefs.**

9.4 Recruitment and Selection
- **enable the appointment of the right person for the job by ensuring the Recruitment and Selection Policy and Procedure is followed.**
- **support new employees to the organisation, through the use of a planned induction programme.**

9.5 Performance Management
- **set clear and realistic objectives throughout all levels within the Council down to each individual team member, ensuring that they are adequately linked.**
- **support all employees participation in the Personal Development Performance Appraisal (PDPA) scheme.**
- **develop action plans to achieve IIP standards.**

9.6 Training and Development

- offer appropriate training and development to employees by identifying competencies required to undertake their role in the organisation.
- establish a management development programme which will be derived from the competency framework for the organisation.
- promote relevant courses such as:
  - stress awareness
  - assertiveness
  - time management
- require managers and employees where appropriate to attend compulsory training such as:
  - PDPA
  - Recruitment and Selection
  - Absence Management
  - Risk assessment

9.7 Policy Development

- encourage all employees to adhere to the principles set out in the Council's Core values.
- ensure that all Policies and Procedures are aimed at making a positive contribution to the well being of employees and the fulfilment of job satisfaction.

10 Sources of Help and Support

10.1 Despite the preventative measures put in place it is recognised that individuals may still experience occupational stress.

10.2 Managers

10.2.1 Managers should develop the skills needed to deal with stressed and distressed members of their team. They should:

- Try not to be panicked by emotion. Acceptance, reassurance and a calm, measured response will be helpful. Ask if there is anyone the person wants to have contacted (if it seems appropriate).
- Ensure that they do not penalize employees for feeling the effects of too much pressure.
- Positively encourage employees to manage their own well-being at work, and provide them with the support they need to do this. Managers need to respond helpfully to employees who are going through stressful times. Simply listening to people can help.
- Ask how they can help rather than just assuming a particular course of action is best. Even in acute distress people can have a clear sense of their own needs.
- At a suitable time, explore whether work is a factor and ensure the employee knows what kind of support the organisation can offer.
- Discuss whether any changes in workload or other adjustments would help. Talk about any resources the organisation has that can help, for example access to counselling, a confidential talk with another employee who is not their supervisor.
- Try to create a culture and structures that enable employees to seek help and manage their own support needs.
- Ensure there are arrangements for employees to have a return-to-work interview after a period of sickness. At that interview, focus on the person rather than on any work problems that arose due to an absence.

- Make sure that people who have been off sick with a stress-related illness feel that they are welcome back.
- If work caused, or was part of the cause, of the ill health leading to absence, address the problems and make alterations where possible.
- Consider referring the employee to Occupational Health.
- Advise the employee of the counselling service.

11 Individuals

11.1 Some of the skills needed for Managers are also appropriate to individuals either when dealing with their own stress or helping work colleagues. Other practical steps individuals can take are:

- Talk to your manager: if they don't know there's a problem, they can't help. If you don't feel able to talk directly to your manager talk to Personnel, ask a trade union or other employee representative to raise the issue on your behalf;
- Support your colleagues if they are experiencing work-related stress. Encourage them to talk to their manager, or an appropriate person.
- See if the Council's counselling service can help;
- Speak to your GP if you are worried about your health;
- Try to channel your energy into solving the problem rather than just worrying about it. Think about what would make you happier at work and discuss this with your employer.

11.2 Internal Support

11.2.1 Occupational Health

If the health of an employee is causing concern, managers should refer the individual to occupational health, via the relevant personnel cluster. Employees can also contact occupational health directly for advice about stress and other work related health problems.

11.2.2 Counselling

The Council has recently increased its counselling service. Individuals can be referred by their line manager or self-refer by contacting the Occupational Health Unit, 12th floor Mercury House. This service is completely confidential.

11.2.3 Trade Unions

Trade Union members can contact their representative or local branch secretary who will arrange for help, advice and information on stress at work.

11.3 External Support

11.4 Listed below are some of the National Support lines that offer confidential help:-

- British Association for Counselling and Psychotherapy – 01788 550899, www.counselling.co.uk
- Relate – 01788 573241
- Samaritans – 0845 790 9090
- MIND – 0345 660163
- NO PANIC Helpline – 01952 590545
- Bullying Helpline: Andrea Adams Trust – 01273 704900
- Alcoholics Anonymous – 0845 7697 555
- Al-Anon – 020 7403 0888
- British Association of Cancer United Patients (BACUP) – 020 7696 9003
- Eating Disorders – 01603 621414

12 The Positive Side of Stress for Organizations

Introduction

Whilst many dispute that stress can be positive, if stress is understood as a reaction to pressure then, at optimum levels of pressure, it can be positive. The authors refer to positive stress as "eu-stress", that is, it can be stimulating and helpful. Excessive negative stress is referred to as "hyper-stress", which is disabling, and after long periods turns to "distress", which can be life threatening. This was discussed in Chapter 3 and will be discussed again in Chapter 18.

This chapter starts by explaining the nature of eu-stress, making reference to the Yerkes-Dodson model and the relationship between pressure stress and performance. Those who are able to experience stress positively will know that it can be described as stimulating and energizing; Csikszentmihalyi describes this feeling as being "in the flow." This is described in greater detail in this chapter, with guidance on how to get into the flow.

Managing talent and the careers of staff are critical issues today. This chapter explains the relationship between careers and eu-stress and discusses ways of ensuring that people are able to continue performing at optimum level at different stages in their careers. It concludes with guidance on strategies that can be used by organizations and managers to help to sustain eu-stress.

This chapter will be of particular benefit to HR specialists with the responsibility for managing talent and performance. Managers will find the chapter helps them to understand the relationship between stress and performance and the motivational aspects of stress. All readers will benefit from understanding how to sustain optimum levels of pressure.

Understanding Eu-stress and Performance

Studies have shown that certain levels of stress enhance performance. In 1956 Selye (MindTools 1, 2004) pointed out that stress does not have to be seen as "bad" – it depends on how it is perceived. He believed that the biochemical effects of stress (described in Chapters 3 and 18) would be experienced irrespective of whether the situations were negative or positive. Thus, the effects of exhilarating, creative work would be beneficial whilst the stress of failure or humiliation would be negative. Selye identified the general adaptation syndrome discussed in Chapter 3. The syndrome operates in response to longer exposure to pressure and has three stages:

1. Alarm phase
2. Resistance phase
3. Exhaustion phase.

Mind Tools 2 (2004) referred to Seyle's research, quoting the example of the reactions of bomber pilots in World War II. After a few missions the pilots settled down, adapted to the pressure and performed well. However, after many missions, the pilots became exhausted and began to show "neurotic manifestations." In the work context, many will relate to being able to perform well for a certain period of time and then exhaustion sets in and performance drops off.

The Yerkes-Dodson Law (Cooper et al., 1988) describes the relationship between pressure and performance and demonstrates that, within limits, performance increases with additional pressure. The original research was conducted on rats and performance was measured at different levels of anxiety. Whilst performance initially increased as anxiety increased, at a certain point performance started to deteriorate. An adaptation of the model is shown in Figure 12.1.

The inverted U curve is a useful way of understanding the relationship between pressure and performance at work. As Figure 12.1 shows, the curve can be split into four levels of stress:

1. *Hypo-stress* – at low levels of pressure, people can become apathetic and bored, with low performance levels. However, although pressure is low, stress levels can be high from the frustration of boredom and lack of challenge.
2. *Eu-stress* – as pressure increases, people start to experience a feeling of being stimulated and challenged and their performance is at its height. At this stage people describe feeling energized and focused: there is enough

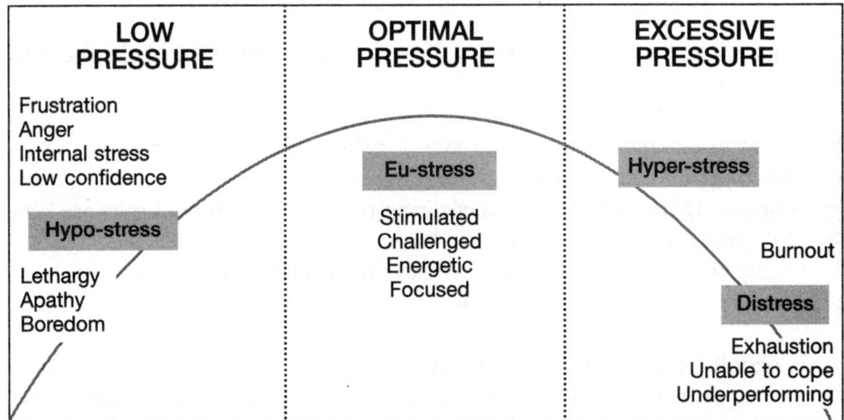

Figure 12.1 **The relationship between pressure, performance and stress**

Source: Adapted from Melhuish (1978)

pressure to perform well, but not too much to feel unable to cope. Some describe the buzz of positive pressure and thrive on the flow of epinephine (adrenalin) when chasing challenging deadlines.

3. *Hyper-stress* – at high levels of pressure, performance suffers and people complain of exhaustion, being out of control, and feeling unable to cope. At this point, people lose their focus and concentration and have to work much harder to achieve the same level of output experienced at optimum pressure. This is particularly noticeable if the work requires people to be creative.
4. *Distress* – if people experience hyper-stress for longer periods, eventually the impact becomes quite serious and the stress has become distress. This can be potentially life threatening; at best, people feel exhausted and unable to perform adequately.

The curve is shown as a smooth curve, but if drawn for an individual it would be different. Further, each individual's curve would have a different shape – some require little pressure to perform at the optimum and could sustain this level of performance for a considerable time; others may have a sharper curve. Tolerance to pressure and stress between individuals was discussed in Chapter 3.

Sustaining Optimum Performance

There are various steps that can be taken to help to optimize performance at different levels of pressure.

If people experience insufficient pressure, managers need to find ways of increasing it by:

- Offering a change of job
- Providing additional responsibility
- Looking for ways of increasing the challenge, perhaps with more stretching targets
- Encouraging people to take more risks.

If people are at optimum levels of pressure, managers can help them to sustain it by:

- Monitoring stress levels and looking for signs of excessive stress
- Ensuring adequate time for rest and relaxation
- Monitoring hours worked and ensuring reasonable working hours are kept
- Holding regular reviews
- Giving recognition and encouragement to sustain performance
- Communicating on a regular basis.

If people have reached excessive levels of pressure, managers need to act fast before distress and exhaustion sets in. Steps must be taken to ensure pressure and, in turn, stress are reduced by:

- Assessing current workload and reallocating work to others if possible

- Ensuring people take a break, if necessary; allowing time off for people to recharge
- Reviewing targets and deadlines and amending them if necessary
- Encouraging people to take steps to increase their resilience
- Discussing the situation, identifying the possible causes of excessive stress and addressing the causes.

Further advice on how to manage stress of others will be covered in Part IV. Particular emphasis is given to best practice models for dealing with stress in Chapter 17, recognizing and assessing stress in others in Chapter 18, and having conversations about stress in Chapter 19. Managers will also find the lessons in Part V will help them give advice to others.

Operating in the Flow

Farmer (1999) made reference to a speech delivered by Mihaly Csikszentmihalyi describing "operating in the flow." When people operate in "areas of best performance," they are able to:

- Be totally focused on the task in hand, with all their energy and abilities channeled on that task
- Be appropriately motivated to avoid distraction
- Be intensely creative and efficient and feel totally satisfied
- Achieve greater inner clarity
- Feel a sense of security – not worry about self-esteem, and experience a feeling of going beyond the boundaries.

The relevance for organizations of people being in the flow is that it is a creative, efficient, and satisfying state of mind. In this state, for example, people are able to make the most creative presentations, develop the best software, and achieve the most impressive performance at work.

Getting into the Flow

One of the frustrations for managers in the 21st century is that they are unable to find quality thinking time. In many organizations it has become an era of intense activity and constantly changing situations, requiring managers to make frequent decisions, often with incomplete information. Managers often complain that they rarely have more than a few minutes of thinking time before they are distracted. Effective managers have developed strategies to be able to get into the flow and sustain optimum performance. These include:

- Taking advantage of flexible working and working from home when possible
- Setting aside part of the day as quiet time
- Delegating major activities to others, thus making themselves more readily available to concentrate on problems as they arise.

Positive Stress and Career Management

The pressure performance curve (see Figure 12.1) can be used as a model for career management. The three zones of pressure identified earlier can be related to different stages in a job:

1. *Newly appointed* – when people are appointed to a new job, they are likely to feel uncertain of what is expected, may not have the skills, are likely to feel out of control, and, in turn, experience high levels of stress. People sometimes describe the experience as "operating on the edge" or "being thrown in at the deep end." In these situations, managers need to provide appropriate levels of support, set realistic targets, and ensure that people receive relevant development to manage the transition effectively. This type of support is less likely at higher levels in the organization, hence the growing need for executive coaching.
2. *Mastery of the job* – after a certain length of time, those able to deal with change, who have a positive outlook and have received the right training to become competent, will be able to operate at optimum performance. At this stage the person is likely to be in control of his or her situation and work takes up much less effort; they can get "in the flow" and achieve exceptional performance. This stage of a person's career must be managed well. Given the flatter organization, managers must ensure that people continue to be stimulated and are, therefore, able to perform at optimum levels. Creative sideways moves must be encouraged whenever possible.
3. *Apathy and boredom* – after a further period of time, the job becomes routine and, without the steps taken above, people can become apathetic, bored or frustrated. This raises stress levels and lowers performance. If a person reaches this stage, urgent steps need to be taken to raise the level of challenge in the job, or it is time for them to move to a new one. This is a good argument for setting targets for job tenure as part of best practice in talent planning.

Positive Stress in Organizations

Positive stress flows from good stress environments, cultivated and sustained by good management practice. Effective managers recognize the need to achieve a certain level of pressure, given the need for a certain level of stress to achieve optimum performance. Goal setting for individuals becomes critically integrated with the vision, strategy, and objectives of the organization, and should be monitored and reviewed, as outlined in Figure 12.2.

As part of managing stress levels effectively, the organization's vision must be identified and clearly articulated to everyone in the organization. The strategy flows from the vision, followed by objective setting and planning – objectives for each part of the organization are set and these are then trans-

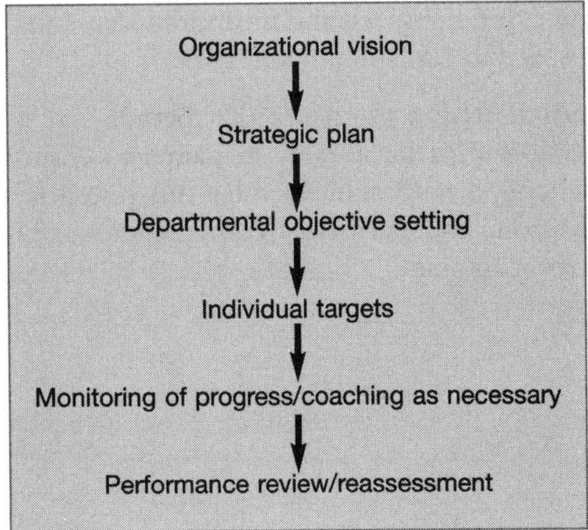

Figure 12.2 **Goal setting for individuals**

lated into individual targets. Great care must be taken to ensure these targets are stretching, achievable, and clearly stated and specific.

Following this stage, managers must ensure their people have the right skills and abilities to achieve their goals, arranging appropriate development, including coaching, if necessary.

Managing performance is a further ingredient in creating a positive stress environment. It requires managers to review progress regularly, reward good performance, and take appropriate action when people fail to achieve targets.

The 21st century has brought with it unprecedented levels of change: change gives rise to ambiguity and uncertainty and, in turn, increases stress levels. Managers must ensure that they communicate well with staff and give them adequate support to help to keep stress at optimum levels.

Summary

- Stress can be positive and help people to achieve exceptional performance, provided it is appropriately managed. This means regular monitoring of stress levels to check that people have not reached exhaustion level (hyper-stress).
- Lessons from the Yerkes-Dodson Law demonstrate that too little pressure can be as bad for performance as too much pressure. Without the flow of epinephrine (adrenalin), people can become apathetic, bored or frustrated and, therefore, stressed. People do, however, vary in the amount of pressure they need to achieve optimum performance: some preferring high levels of pressure to work at their best, whilst others would be overwhelmed by the same level of pressure.
- Strategies can be adopted to keep pressure at the optimum level and encourage positive stress. In this zone people become energized, focused, and creative: this is described by Csikszentmihalyi as being in the flow.

Managers who want to experience this energized and motivated state must allow themselves the time and space to feel suitably relaxed.

- Organizations can adopt various strategies to ensure that people stay at optimum levels. Career progression must be suitably managed to ensure people remain motivated, challenged, and achieve their full potential. Goal setting, open communication, and performance management all help to create a positive stress environment.

13 Creating a Culture and Climate to Build a Resilient Workforce

Introduction

It was noted earlier in this book that the most successful approach for stress management is to adopt a more holistic approach by focusing on the overall well-being of staff. Enlightened companies recognize the importance of a healthy and satisfied workforce as a means of attracting and retaining staff, and achieving enhanced performance through enabling them to withstand the pressures associated with modern life.

This chapter outlines the factors needed within a culture and climate for staff to thrive. This is supplemented by drawing on the criteria used to select the best companies to work for and a major study, *The Whitehall II Study* (CCSU/Cabinet Office, 2004) conducted within the civil service. The example of Microsoft is used to illustrate the approaches and strategies it uses to achieve a resilient workforce. This chapter will be particularly helpful for HR, occupational health specialists, and line managers who want to put the right building blocks in place. It will also help a wider audience to choose an employer that is likely to take care of its workforce.

Understanding Culture

There are numerous definitions of organizational culture: the purpose of discussing culture here is not to define what organizational culture is, but to understand how it sets the context within which individuals work and the requirements needed to build a resilient workforce. In general terms, a set of often unspoken expectations, norms of behavior, and standards of performance reflect a culture. However, no set of rules and no procedure manual can cover every eventuality: it is the culture that fills in the gaps. How well an individual's own values fit with those of the organization is usually an indication of the level of employee satisfaction. The risk of an individual becoming unhappy in their work is greater when the gap is greater.

The HSE has identified six categories of "undesirable work characteristics" or potential "risk factors" that can arise within the workplace:

1. *Demands* – Do you have too much/too little work to do? Do you work too many hours? Are you able to vary your working day?
2. *Control* – Are you involved in deciding what work you do, and when and how you do it?
3. *Support* – Do you get continuous proactive support, for example with new work or everyday issues? What about reactive support, for example if you experience personal problems?
4. *Relationships* – How are relationships conducted at work? Are there problems with bullying/harassment?
5. *Roles* – Are you clear about what is expected of you? Do you have too many and/or conflicting roles/responsibilities?
6. *Change* – Do management communicate and consult adequately about organizational change? Do you feel comfortable with new technologies?

All the characteristics, either singly or collectively, can form the culture of the workplace. For example, is the culture one of long hours, where "harder not smarter" is what counts? Are people perceived as "weak" when they confess to being stressed by whatever problems they encounter? Do the senior people within the organization truly live the values they subscribe to or simply pay them lip service?

Organizational culture is often mentioned in the same breath as organizational change. For employees, a changing culture means they have to be ready to adjust to change and, as it becomes more rapid, the strain on people to adapt to more change more quickly becomes greater. Thus, the risk of stress for employees increases, depending on how open, supportive, and effective the process of change has been.

Sunday Times Survey

The *Sunday Times* (2004) survey, *100 Best Companies to Work For,* compared the performance of these 100 companies with those listed on the FTSE All-Share Index. Five-year compound returns to 31 January 2004 showed a 5.7% negative return for the FTSE All-Share Index companies against a 13.6% gain for the Best Companies. Over three years the returns moved to –11.3% and 6.7% respectively, while in the last year the Best Companies have shown a 44% return compared with 23.1%.

The companies were rated on views of employees on eight workplace factors:

1. *Leadership* – including whether leaders listened more than they talked and responded to the judgments passed on to them by their staff
2. *My manager* – the day-to-day local management
3. *Personal growth* – opportunities to learn, grow, and be challenged
4. *Well-being* – balancing work–life issues, ensuring a good balance between work and home
5. *My team* – immediate colleagues
6. *Giving something back* – to the local community and society

7. *My company* – the way it treats its staff
8. *Fair deal* – pay and benefits.

These elements contributed 80 percent of the final company rankings. The company itself completed a 172-question survey, covering data on policies (for example pay and benefits), processes (for example recruitment and communication), and services and facilities (for example sports and training). Company materials including videos, newsletters, and training materials, supported the submissions.

Using Microsoft, the number one company in 2003 and number 13 in 2004, Figure 13.1 gives an example of some of the ingredients that make it a great company to work for.

What are the people challenges of the business?
Microsoft has to deliver great business results in a tough economic climate and a declining PC market. In particular it has to sustain customer satisfaction in a supply chain where there is little direct contact with the customer. Being an employer of choice is critical for the success of the business, if Microsoft is to attract and retain the best staff.

How is Microsoft viewed as an employer?
There is plenty of evidence to show that Microsoft is getting things right. It was awarded number one in the *Sunday Times 100 Best Companies to Work For* in 2003 in the UK, number 13 in 2004, and was the number one IT company in 2002. It won the work/life balance special award in 2002 and the Giving Back Award in 2003.

What is the people vision for Microsoft?
"Create an environment where great people can do their best work and be on a path to realize their full potential." Three areas are important to realize the vision:

1. *Physical environment* – staff are given the latest technology, including smart phones, enabling them to integrate their work and personal lives, and state-of-the-art, open-plan office space. Other examples include day nurseries, broadband access at home for all employees and their families, and free fruit and drinks available to promote good health.
2. *Emotional environment* – Microsoft is a challenging place to work. In turn, it offers staff the resources to: "proactively manage your health and wellbeing, giving you the knowledge and confidence to lead a healthy and balanced lifestyle." It has a well-being center, an employee assistance program, external mentors for the top five percent of staff, and there is opportunity for flexible working.
3. *Intellectual environment* – Microsoft has to create a favorable environment, offering intellectual stimulation to retain its staff. It provides staff with the latest technology, including laptops and software that has been designed to maximize productivity. The software and processes are kept simple by the three minute/three clicks principle: internal processes or memos should not

take longer than three minutes to complete and processes on the computer (including the website) should be completed within three clicks. Other examples include: stimulating roles and opportunities for career advancement, 70 percent of all development by on-the-job learning, supported by mentoring, coaching, and counseling services for all employees.

How is Microsoft approaching the well-being of its staff?

The philosophy of Microsoft is that staff should be proactive and take responsibility for managing their own well-being. To this end Microsoft seeks to provide active support and shared responsibility to help its staff achieve a healthy lifestyle and way of working. The well-being center and its facilities form an important part of the support Microsoft can offer its staff. The doctor's clinics provide information and advice and work in close liaison with the patient's own GP when necessary. The main center, based at the offices in Reading, supports staff in a range of ways.

Releasing the pressure

Microsoft helps its staff to ensure the work/home ratio is right for everyone. It helps staff through education and support to keep the potential effects of stress and related issues to a minimum. The well-being center offers stress/pressure assessments to increase staff awareness of the issues. Training resources run courses that support the work of the well-being center. The courses help to ensure staff are "fit for life", help them to set life goals and develop personal action plans to achieve their goals.

Regular health checks

The center offers free health checks on an annual basis to help staff to learn more about general health and well-being. Comprehensive procedures incorporate the latest technology, giving accurate results that can provide follow-up health plans and advice. It runs follow-up sessions to monitor blood pressure, cholesterol levels, and weight management. In addition, it offers well man and well woman clinics, pregnancy advice, smoking cessation, and eyesight tests. The center can also provide ongoing medical assistance for staff with medical conditions, for example those with epilepsy and diabetes.

Proactive management of long-term sickness

Staff faced with illness are provided with professional support and advice by the center. The center ensures that staff on sick leave remain connected with their colleagues and the business, and specialist advice helps their recovery and return to work.

Guidance

The center can provide practical help and information on virtually any illness and offers a 24-hour life management and personal support service – the confidential employee assistance program.

Protection against disease

The center is able to provide vaccinations for foreign business travel. It advises on the inoculations needed and, for a fee, gives inoculations for personal travel.

Alternative therapies
The center enables staff to take advantage of a range of alternative therapies specifically designed to address workplace issues, including acupuncture – ideal to promote a sense of well-being and beneficial for a range of conditions from back pain to migraine and fatigue. Other therapies include reflexology and massage (the center also has a massage chair available as a free facility at any time during working hours; it helps to revitalize and/or relax people). A charge is made for the rest of the therapies.

What are the secrets of Microsoft's success?

Microsoft is passionate about bringing its culture to life. The Microsoft HR team are advocates of the Gallup survey approach. This ensures that Microsoft keeps in touch with the views of its staff and drives business change. The company makes extensive use of the StrengthsFinder, developed by Marcus Buckingham, which ensures that people play to their strengths and Microsoft gets the best from its staff. The company recruits talented staff but is aware that to retain this talent, people must be given challenging jobs to do and be looked after well.

Microsoft is investigating innovative ways of developing family-friendly policies and practices and doing real, concrete things to help people achieve a balanced lifestyle. It actively encourages flexible and home working, with priority given to achievement of results rather than time spent at the desk. In implementing this approach, the organization demonstrates a high level of trust.

Microsoft recognizes the importance of communication and works to foster an open, communicative climate, hence the open-plan offices. In addition, communication is streamed on email, TV and complemented by a weekly newsletter, a hard copy magazine and use of the intranet that, again, works on the three clicks principle.

In summary, the approach of the well-being center is to take a proactive approach in encouraging people to become healthy and stay well.

Figure 13.1 **The Microsoft example of creating a great place to work**

Great Place to Work Institute, US, Europe, and UK

The Great Place to Work Institute (2004b), based on numerous independent studies in the US and the UK, believes that:

- A combination of practices is more effective than one single practice at improving bottom line results. These results are greater after three years, indicating that they need to be integrated into the work environment to be beneficial.
- As companies become great, the division between management and other staff fades and the workplace becomes a community.

- Employees are then able to take a pride and pleasure in their work, team and company and want to stay with the company.

The Institute's model (2004c) for a great place to work is based on five dimensions:

1. *Credibility:*
   — Communications are open and accessible
   — Competence in coordinating human and material resources
   — Integrity in carrying out vision with consistency
2. *Respect:*
   — Supporting professional development and showing appreciation
   — Collaboration with employees on relevant decisions
   — Caring for employees as individuals with personal lives
3. *Fairness:*
   — Equity – balanced treatment for all in terms of rewards
   — Impartiality – absence of favoritism in hiring and promotions
   — Justice – lack of discrimination and a process for appeals
4. *Pride:*
   — In one's personal job and individual contributions
   — In work produced by one's team or work group
   — In the organization's products and standing in the community
5. *Camaraderie:*
   — Ability to be oneself
   — Socially friendly and welcoming atmosphere
   — Sense of "family" and "team"

The top 10 companies rated in the *100 Best Companies to Work for in America 2004* (2004d), based on the above criteria, were:

1.	J.M. Smucker Company	6.	Adobe
2.	Alston and Bird	7.	TD Industries
3.	Container Store	8.	SAS Institute
4.	Edward Jones	9.	Wegmans
5.	Republic Bancorp	10.	Xilinx

In the *100 Best Companies to Work for in Europe 2004* (2004d), five organizations were given special awards in five categories:

- *Credibility award winner:* Timpsons – the UK retailer – was given the award for management communication practices, competence and integrity. The company sends out two weekly newsletters, much of which are written by the employees themselves using a simple notepad system. The CEO and president visit the whole of the UK between them for the annual national roadshow meeting with employees, to update them on company news and initiatives.

- *Respect award winner:* Microsoft (Austria, Belgium, Denmark, Finland, France, Germany, Ireland, Italy, Netherlands, Portugal, Sweden, UK) – was recognized for its training practices, flexible working, and reward systems. In France the company spends an average of 6.5 percent of salary per employee per year on training. The company enables many people to work from home: in the Netherlands all employees receive a laptop/tablet PC and a broadband connection for their homes, and the company pays the bills for connection and user costs.
- *Fairness award winner:* American Express (UK and Italy) – received especially high scores for the variety of its efforts to develop a diverse workforce. It has a number of internal employee networks.
- *Pride award winner:* Hexal (Germany) – received its award for its focus on employees with its guideline "Hexal – these are all of us." Employees speak proudly of the on-site gym, kindergarten, and free shuttle service to and from the nearest station.
- *Camaraderie award winner:* Kanal 5 (Sweden) – the Swedish television channel has created a workplace that has a high sense of camaraderie amongst its employees, with numerous parties and social events. To encourage fitness, the station also offers generous payments for employees who exercise; for those who want to relax there is a meditation room.

In a recent survey conducted by the Great Place to Work Institute Europe (2004e) based in Copenhagen, it noted that the number of flexible hours worked had greatly improved on the previous year – the first year the survey had been conducted across 14 European countries. Employees felt more able to take time off work when it was necessary. However, the European countries were seven percentage points behind companies in the US in a survey conducted by the sister company.

WORK, STRESS, AND HEALTH: *THE WHITEHALL II STUDY*

The first of the Whitehall studies began in 1967 with a study of 18,000 men in the civil service. In 1985 a second study commenced, which included 10,308 civil servants across 20 departments in central London: two-thirds were men and one-third women. The *Whitehall II Study* (CCSU/Cabinet Office, 2004) has had seven phases of data collection, the latest phase running from 2002 to 2004. Both Whitehall studies are long-term studies examining the influences on health of circumstances at work, home, and in the wider community.

The participants received medical screening, including blood pressure, cholesterol levels, weight, ECG, walking and lung function, diet, screening for diabetes, and some mental function tests. They also completed a questionnaire covering a wide range of topics. As some people are now moving out of employment, there are additional questions about retirement and activities outside work. The findings of the Whitehall studies are used to influence policy discussions within the government. They are also relevant to organizations in both the public and private sectors and will help employees shape their health, well-being, and quality of lives.

Key findings of the studies are outlined below:

1. **The social gradient** – the studies dispelled two myths. The first is that people in high-status jobs have higher risks of heart disease. The second is that the gradient of health in industrialized societies is simply a matter of poor health for the disadvantaged and good health for everyone else. The *Whitehall I Study* showed that the more senior people were (in employment), the longer they might expect to live; similar findings have been found in the US, Australia, and mainland Europe. The *Whitehall II Study* showed evidence that the way work is organized, the work climate, social influences outside work, and influences from early life – in addition to smoking, lack of physical activity, and obesity – all play a part in the social gradient of health.
2. **Demands and control at work** – the *Whitehall II Study* found that high demands associated with low control at work contributed to stress and ill health at work. Higher up the hierarchy demands increase, while the lower down the hierarchy you go, the lower the control – as measured by degree of authority over decision making and use of skills and opportunity to develop skills. People in jobs characterized by low control had higher rates of sickness absence, mental illness, heart disease, and lower back pain. The incidence of ill health related to the job characteristics and not to the personal characteristics of the jobholders.
3. **Social support at work** – working with supportive colleagues and managers improves health and reduces sickness absence. The study found that good levels of support had a protective effect on mental health and reduced the spells of sickness absence. Lack of support from managers and colleagues is associated with stress at work and, coupled with unclear or inconsistent information, there is a twofold increase in the risk of poor general mental health. Similar studies have also found a correlation between support and ill health, for example research in Sweden showed poor support was related to an increased risk of mortality from cardiovascular disease.
4. **Effort–reward balance at work** – reciprocity is essential to all social relationships. In Germany it has been proposed that a combination of high effort without appropriate reward is stressful and increases the rate of illness. High effort by itself is not stressful: the Whitehall study showed that an imbalance between effort and reward increased the risk of heart attacks. The way work is organized and the climate of feedback in the workplace all potentially affect three crucial aspects of reward: self-esteem, status, and income.
5. **Job insecurity** – secure jobs increase health, well-being, and job satisfaction. When the *Whitehall II Study* was set up, the civil service was still seen as a "job for life." The privatization of the Property Services Agency (PSA) in 1992 suggested the importance of investigating the effects of job inse-

curity on health. Research showed that PSA civil servants suffered more physical ill health than their colleagues in other parts of the civil service in the run-up to PSA privatization. They also suffered adverse changes to risk factors associated with heart disease such as blood pressure. Other research in the UK, and worldwide, confirms that job insecurity increases ill health (particularly mental illness) and use of health services.

6. **Organizational change** – poorly managed change harms health. Whilst widespread compulsory redundancy has been rare in the civil service, there has been a high level of organizational change. Apart from job insecurity already discussed, change also has more widespread effects – including changes to the nature and conditions of work, changes in management style, and, occasionally, changes of employer. Economic recession and deregulation of the labor market during the 1990s resulted in major downsizing of the workforce. Studies in the US, Scandinavia, and Europe showed that major downsizing is associated with an increase in ill health among the survivors, which is reflected in an increase in medically certified sickness, absence, and premature death from heart disease.
7. **A healthy diet, exercise, and quitting smoking all reduce the risk of heart disease and promote well-being** – since the *Whitehall I Study* there has been a decline in smoking. Alcohol consumption varies in terms of drinking patterns and quantity consumed. Lower grades are more likely to consume large amounts in a single session, while higher grades drink more regularly, but smaller amounts that have been shown to be beneficial. Senior women drink more alcohol than those in junior grades. The second study found a wide variation in eating patterns and it was clear from the study that good food habits are a key positive influence on health: a link was found between stress and obesity. Exercise was found to be beneficial in many respects, including reduced body weight and increased cardiovascular fitness including lower heart rate. However, moderately intense activity may be less effective than more vigorous exercise as far as the heart is concerned.
8. **An active social life outside work can have health benefits** – two types of social activity were identified: informal contact with family and friends, and more formal involvement in organized groups and associations. Three dimensions of informal support were found to be important:

   a. Confiding/emotional support – people share interests, boost esteem, and can be relied on
   b. Practical support – helping with problems
   c. Negative aspects of social relationships – family and friends can be a source of worry and the help they can give may be inadequate.

The research showed that having a large circle of friends and seeing them regularly was good for overall health. Relationships offering confiding and emotional support had a larger effect on mental and overall health than practical support. Those experiencing negative aspects of social relationships in close relationships had an increased risk of ill health, functioned less well physically, and were more likely to be absent.

9. **The work–home interface** – stresses from conflicting work and family demands result in poor health. The study investigated how factors associated with home and family life and the interaction between home and work factors affect health. Having control over one's life appeared to be important for health. Having financial problems, and caring for dependant children and elderly relatives predicted low control at home. Work demands may interfere with being a spouse/partner, parent or carer; conversely, family demands may impact on achieving work demands and responsibilities. The Whitehall research found both these conflicts affect mental and physical health of men and women. The negative effects of both types of conflict have been found in diverse countries such as Finland and Japan – despite the different social expectations of the roles of men and women in these cultures.

Building Blocks for Managers to Create a Culture and Climate to Build a Resilient Workforce

The Whitehall study and the criteria used to rate organizations as "great places to work" have important implications for organizations seeking to create the right culture and climate in order to build and sustain a healthy and resilient workforce. The criteria are summarized in Figure 13.2.

Feature	Whitehall study	Great Place to Work, UK	Great Company UK	HSE potential risk factors
Demands and control	√			√
Social support at work	√	√	√	√
Effort – reward	√	√	√	
Job security	√			
Organizational change	√			√
Healthy diet/exercise	√			
Social support outside work	√			
Work–life balance	√			
Credibility		√		
Respect		√		
Pride		√		
Leadership			√	
Line manager			√	
Personal growth			√	
Giving something back			√	
Organization culture			√	

Figure 13.2 **Comparison of the criteria used in the four models**

Summary

The steps that can be taken to help build an appropriate culture and climate are summarized below in three categories – those for action by human resources, managers, and occupational health.

HR needs to focus on the following areas:

1. *Culture and climate* – HR need to engage with the senior management of the organization to ensure that the culture and climate supports resilience within the workforce. An appropriate management style at the top that creates a climate of openness is critical, with senior managers listening to staff and adopting a supportive style
2. *Change management* – most organizations today face constant change. HR need to ensure that this is managed appropriately, with effective communication throughout any change program, in order to keep insecurity to a minimum
3. *Pay and benefits* – these need to reward effort and be seen as fair
4. *Flexible work arrangements* – this could include flexible work patterns, working from home, unpaid leave, and sabbaticals
5. *Training and development* – part of leadership development should address resilience and self-awareness. Staff should be encouraged to play to their strengths, and development should cover stress management at all levels within the organization
6. *Long-term sickness* – proactively manage this in collaboration with occupational health; maintain contact with those off sick and actively support those returning to work from long-term absence.

Managers need to focus on the following areas:

1. *Team climate* – create a climate that stimulates the team and provides mutual support for team members
2. *Resources* – ensure that staff have adequate resources to help support a more flexible lifestyle when this is appropriate, including laptops and mobile phones
3. *Relationships with the team* – listen to the team and provide adequate support when this is necessary. Be aware of staff who are under excessive pressure and ensure they have adequate breaks and time for relaxation. Also be aware of relationships between team members and take any necessary action
4. *Communication* – ensure the team are kept fully informed at all times, particularly during times of change
5. *Respect for the team* – adopt a style that is collaborative, encourages development, and shows a caring approach
6. *Play to strengths* – ensure that all team members are able to contribute in ways that use their strengths
7. *Review the workload of each team member regularly* and assess the degree of the control they have over their work. The review is particularly important for anyone appearing to be experiencing excessive levels of stress.

Occupational health needs to focus on the following areas:

1. *Job design* – provide appropriate advice and support in conducting risk and stress risk assessments
2. *Health education* – provide appropriate advice on healthy lifestyles and managing the work–life balance
3. *Long-term sickness* – work proactively with HR to ensure those off sick are helped to return to work
4. *Employee assistance programs* – ensure that all staff are made aware of any external support services and that any referrals are treated as strictly confidential.

14 Lessons Learnt

This chapter provides those responsible for managing stress in organizations with a checklist of the key points to remember.

Why Do People Experience Excessive Stress?

- Identifying the causes of stress is the appropriate starting point, as any intervention will be getting to the root of the problem rather than treating the symptoms of stress.
- Excessive stress can occur because of a range of factors related to the work, other people, and the person themselves; thus, stress is very person-specific.
- Stress may occur because of one specific situation. More often it is the accumulation of several things happening at once at work and home.
- By being aware of the causes of stress, steps can be taken to minimize the impact.

Which are the Most Stressful Jobs?

- Whilst stress is self-generated, certain jobs expose people to higher levels of pressure.
- Jobs that are consistently rated as highly stressful include the police, doctors, teachers, nurses, and social workers.
- The amount of change experienced by particular occupational groups makes them more vulnerable.
- Working in jobs that have a high level of contact with the public rank more highly.
- Extra vigilance is needed for people in pressurized jobs and staff should be carefully selected on the basis of temperament and resilience.
- Appropriate training and adequate support helps to keep stress at acceptable levels.

How Do We Know Whether There is a Problem Associated with Stress?

- Direct measures include risk assessments and stress audits; monitoring sickness absence related to stress also helps to identify hot spots.
- Indirect measures such as accident rates, labor turnover figures, the cost of

litigation, and the number of people requesting counseling help to build up the picture for an organization.

- Stress risk assessment provides a positive way forward for managing stress within an organization. Once the risks have been identified, action plans can be drawn up to address the problems.
- Stress risk assessment is best tackled as part of an integrated approach to people management, including general risk assessments, annual appraisal, and employee attitude surveys.
- A climate of openness, honesty, and trust is essential if organizations are to be able to identify individuals at risk before it is too late.

What Do We Do About It?

- Organizations need to adopt a systematic approach building on the data gained from the risk assessment and drawing on the extensive help available from the Health and Safety Executive.
- Interventions are most successful if they are based on a thorough identification of the root cause of the problem.
- Managers must be encouraged to take responsibility for managing the stress of their teams by early intervention when a problem arises. Appropriate training for managers is essential to support them in carrying out this role.
- Managers need to recognize the situations when professional help is warranted, before situations become too serious and individuals start to suffer.

What Do We Legally Have To Do About It?

- Keep up to date and within the law and ensure managers do the same. If situations do occur, accurate documentation should be kept and legal advice sought early on.
- Risk assessments should be conducted regularly, especially during times of change.
- A stress policy helps to ensure everyone is aware of their individual responsibilities and the importance of good stress management.
- All cases of stress-related illnesses should be handled quickly and decisively. Contact should be maintained with individuals and there should be a clear strategy for managing the return process.

Does a Stress Policy Help?

- Developing a stress policy is an important part of stress management. The organization may either have a stand-alone policy or develop a policy that addresses general well-being at work.

- It helps people to discuss stress more openly, taking away some of the stigma that can be associated with it.
- The stress policy is a valuable communication tool, making clear the roles and responsibilities of specific groups of people.
- It can be a useful way of educating people to spot the signs of stress and know how to get advice and support if necessary.
- The stress policy needs to be reviewed and updated regularly.

What is the Upside of Stress?

- Positive stress is referred to as eu-stress and helps the individual to achieve exceptional performance.
- Too little pressure can be as bad for performance as too much pressure. The level of pressure to achieve optimum performance varies from person to person: some work at their best at fairly high levels of pressure whilst others have a much lower tolerance.
- Maintaining pressure at the right level to achieve positive stress requires careful monitoring, ensuring adequate time for rest and relaxation and avoiding working excessively long hours.

How Can We Be Proactive?

- The culture and climate must encourage and support a resilient workforce, which includes a management style that promotes openness and supportiveness.
- Change should be appropriately managed and communicated to keep insecurity to a minimum.
- Flexible working arrangements should be supported, together with a fair remuneration package and appropriate training and development to increase resilience and help people play to their strengths.
- Long-term sickness should be appropriately managed and return to work arrangements sensitively handled.
- Managers should be encouraged to develop a supportive and open culture within their teams and ensure that workloads are not excessive.

PART IV

Managing the Stress of Others

15 Introduction

Part IV looks at stress from a manager's perspective. Line managers have a legal responsibility and a moral obligation to try to spot signs that stress may be affecting any team member's health. They have a vested interest in looking for signs that stress may be affecting performance. As Chapter 16 discusses, the law does not expect managers to be mind readers, but to spot signs of stress that any reasonable person would. Part IV begins with the legal responsibilities of managers because it is often the first topic on the agenda when stress and stress management interventions are discussed within organizations.

Beyond what is explicitly required by the law, there are a number of best practice models that managers should use, which should be adopted by every organization. Chapter 17 discusses four elements of best practice for managers to reduce team stress:

1. Policy and procedure, including:
   - stress management, mental health, or well-being policy
   - procedure for managing stress-related illness
   - procedure for stress-related absence
   - individual risk assessment
   - critical incident management procedure
2. Involvement of occupational health (OH) where appropriate
3. Information and support from HR, OH and senior management
4. Training.

Chapter 17 also contains some useful appendices, with templates for stress-related illness and absence procedures, individual risk assessment, critical incident management procedure, and one-day workshop for managers.

Chapter 18 then discusses the typical signs and symptoms of stress that managers may see in their teams, and also the sorts of organizational signs that stress levels are going up overall. If they take the time to listen and be aware of their team's stress levels, most managers will see signs of stress. However, approaching a stressed employee to talk about performance or health can be nerve-racking and most managers welcome help in this area. Chapter 19 covers in depth the issue of having conversations with employees about their stress levels. The tips, ideas, and skills discussed should ease manager's nervousness; they also have application in general management.

Finally, Chapter 20 summarizes the key themes about how managers can grasp the nettle of team stress levels, rather than letting fear, ignorance, or lack of procedure exacerbate pressure and ill health.

16 Legal Responsibilities of Managers in Plain English

Introduction

This chapter will help managers (and those who advise them) to think in terms of their legal responsibilities when dealing with employee stress issues. It sets out how the "duty of care" and the UK Health and Safety Executive (HSE) *Management Standards for Tackling Work-Related Stress* (see Chapter 10) apply to them, and what specific actions they should be taking. All managers should try to safeguard the health of their teams from the effects of stress, regardless of whether the organization has stress policies or procedures. An important point for managers to remember is this: it does not matter if managers are under pressure themselves, if they believe a team member ought to be able to withstand a certain pressure, or even whether they believe stress exists or not. The law may determine that they have acted inadequately, or negligently, in a case of stress-related illness. So it is important that they ensure they take a number of steps on a regular basis and avoid a number of pitfalls.

Managerial Duty of Care

As Chapter 10 discussed, organizations have a duty of care to employees to protect their physical and psychological health. Managers play an important role in this, because they have the day-to-day responsibility for team members' welfare. Whereas the directors of an organization must ensure that policies, procedures, working practices, regulations, and equipment will not harm employee health, a line manager must ensure that all of the above are being used or carried out properly. Geoffrey Bignell, of Just Employment Solicitors, says that managers: "should learn enough about employment law to avoid elephant traps," and if they are lucky enough, their HR departments will keep them abreast of important developments, and provide them with workable, robust procedures. However, he says: "It is amazing how often procedures are not followed, and this is not viewed favourably in tribunals."

The Management Standards (HSE, 2004) set out organizational responsibilities for systems and procedures, many of which will be designed and set in motion by HR or senior management. However, it will largely fall to line managers to carry them out.

The following from the Management Standards are typical examples of this:

- Employees' concerns about their work environment are addressed
- Employees are encouraged to use their skills and initiative to do their work
- Employees receive regular and constructive feedback
- Systems are in place to enable employees to raise concerns about any uncertainties or conflicts they have in their role and responsibilities
- Employees are aware of the probable impact of any changes to their jobs.

These are just 5 of the 31 "states to be achieved" that the standards set out. Managers need to understand all of them, and to be directly involved in nearly all of them. They are simple to understand, and are about good management practice as stress prevention, rather than cure. (The full set of Management Standards can be viewed at: http://www.hse.gov.uk/stress/standards/ index.htm.)

Although these standards are not law, a court of law or employment tribunal would look at whether organizations are upholding them.

Managerial Awareness

Line managers do not have a responsibility in law for every team member's happiness, but they have a vested interest in keeping employee health and morale at optimum levels. Therefore, they need to develop an awareness of and be vigilant about how team members are feeling and behaving. Usually, people begin to feel uncomfortable, out of balance, or out of control before their performance or health suffers obviously. Their behavior may only be slightly out of character when they are in hyper-stress. So managers must know their teams well (nothing new here) and be sensitive to any tensions or early signs of stress (see Chapter 18).

Having said this, managers are not expected to be mind readers or psychotherapists. The law says that they should notice signs and symptoms of stress that any "reasonable" person would notice. A British High Court ruling in February 2002 stated that:

> *Unless he knows of some particular problem or vulnerability, an employer is usually entitled to assume that his employee is up to the normal pressures of the job. and: Generally he is entitled to take what he is told by or on behalf of the employee at face value. If he is concerned he may suggest that the employee consults his own doctor or an occupational health service.*

The trouble is that some managers are aware that their employees are showing signs of stress, but feel powerless to change anything, so they simply do not address it at all. Many are good at pretending that stress does not exist, at least, not in their departments. One senior manager of a large computer firm was discussing with the authors why he had not taken any initiatives to reduce stress in his team, and said: "Not that we are shirking our duty, but today we don't have to." In some ways he is right. There are relatively few successful cases against employers for causing stress-related illness, considering the number of employees who believe themselves to be "stressed." However, it is a shame that this particular manager (and plenty of others) cannot see the benefits of having a healthier, happier team. Furthermore, the number of tribunals for stress-related illness is increasing, and this means increased risk for organizations.

Tony Urwin, BUPA Wellness psychological services director says that:

> *there is a lot of fear from managers about uncovering stress. But it is not rocket science to deal with stress. It is about good, basic management practices. The most stress-free teams have managers who communicate well and give clear messages about roles and objectives. But they also give their teams some freedom – and plenty of appreciation and recognition.*

CULTURE AND ATMOSPHERE

To have the best chance of noticing signs of stress, managers should create a culture of openness where it is OK to speak one's mind. People get a feeling in organizations about whether it will be detrimental to admit to stress, or whether they can say "no" to a project and still have promotion potential. It can be difficult for managers to know whether someone is shirking or truly under so much pressure that they need a reduction in workload; some organizations are introducing systems to try and tackle this issue. Figure 16.1 outlines an example of one such system.

A large London-based consultancy firm has introduced a "traffic light" system to try to take the pressure off its young consultants. Consultancy work is challenging and exciting, but can mean long hours and juggling a number of projects, demanding clients, and deadlines.

The traffic light system provides associates with a better visibility of the expected workload for the next two weeks, in particluar which days are likely to require some late work. This allows associates to bring their social activities into better alignment with the required workload. It also provides managers with a greater visibility of when their team members are expected to work late on other case commitments. This allows managers to identify potential resource issues earlier in the week.

The traffic light is shown in a spreadsheet that is completed by each case team leader no later than Monday morning. Members of the case team complete a similar spreadsheet by the end of each week to monitor the accuracy of the workload prediction.

Figure 16.1 **Good practice in managing employee demands**

Managers themselves still have the greatest power and responsibility to be approachable and create the kind of team culture that will reduce stress. Aspects of this culture are:

- It is OK to ask for help
- The team support each other
- It is OK to say "I am not coping"
- My manager is approachable and I am not afraid of him/her
- It is OK to take reasonable risks and I am not terrified of making a mistake
- It is possible to say no, through discussion and negotiation.

Tony Urwin says that his goal in the industry is:

> *to reduce the stigma of stress, and to see a change whereby employees can tell their managers they are stressed, not just confide in partner or friends. I want managers to understand what stress is – that it is not a weakness, or a personality defect.*

"REASONABLE FORESEEABILITY"

The very word "reasonable" creates a gray area of the law surrounding stress, but it is worth noting that even judges recognize that stress is a legal minefield and have called on the UK government to review it (see Appendix 16.1 for supporting references).

Despite the ambiguity of the words, a large number of tribunals and court cases have hinged on whether an employee's stress-related illness was "reasonably foreseeable." This means: should an organization have known that a particular employee was likely to suffer illness as a result of stress? This might be because of a personal susceptibility, previous stress-related illness, a work system that caused undue pressure, or inadequate training. Two successful cases of this sort are:

1. *Lancaster* v. *Birmingham City Council:* Beverley Lancaster was inadequately trained for her frontline duties and was awarded £67,000 against Birmingham City Council (see Appendix 16.1 or Chapter 10 for more detail).
2. *State of New South Wales* v. *Seedsman:* The judge found that the New South Wales Police Service should have foreseen that Beth Seedsman was likely to suffer psychiatric illness as a result of the exposure to crimes committed against children. She was a young, inexperienced officer who had had very little training. Award: A$125,000 (see Appendix 16.1 for more detail).

However, other cases of stressed employees suing employers fail, because it can be difficult to prove that an organization should have foreseen an illness.

Summing up in the case of *Petch* v. *Commissioners of Customs and Excise*, (1993) the judge said:

> *unless senior management in the defendant's department were aware or ought to have been aware that the plaintiff was showing signs of impending breakdown, or*

were aware or ought to have been aware that his workload carried a real risk that he would have a breakdown, then the defendant was not negligent in failing to avert the breakdown.

In *Pratley* v. *Surrey County Council*, Maureen Pratley, a care manager, sued Surrey County Council for injury due to ill health (depressive illness) caused by negligence. The judge ruled that it was not reasonable to expect her manager, Mrs Elrick, to know that Miss Pratley's health was in immediate danger (fuller details in Appendix 16.1).

Whether successful or not, these cases bring home the point that managers must listen and respond when employees say they are not coping, and then ensure they fulfil their promises. Managers often hold the key to ensuring that employees get the training they need, and that work is organized and allocated to minimize the risk of stress.

NOTE KEEPING, CONSENT TO MEDICAL TREATMENT, AND REFUSAL OF MEDICAL TREATMENT

Examining how a tribunal or court of law views cases of stress-related illness raises another point: if a manager has any fears for employee health, any conversations about work pressures or stress should be put in writing. In *Pratley* v. *Surrey County Council*, there was an issue of only brief and shorthand notes being taken by Mrs Elrick during a crucial meeting where a new system of work was promised. Even though it seems formal, and a manager does not want to damage rapport when having these potentially sensitive conversations, managers should write "minutes" of any meetings and ask the employee to confirm that the minutes contain a correct version of what was discussed and agreed. This can be done sensitively, emphasizing concern for employee welfare.

If an employee does become ill, managers may suggest referral to OH. Alternatively, an organization may want a medical opinion on fitness for work (see Chapter 17). An important legal requirement managers must be aware of is that, if an organization asks for medical information from an employee's GP or specialists, or requests a report from doctors or psychologists assessing the employee, then in accordance with the Access to Medical Records Act 1988, the employee must sign a release form allowing this. The employee has the right to see the report before it is sent to anyone else, and can at that point refuse to release it. (See Appendices 10.1–10.3 for examples of relevant documents.) The Data Protection Act has more information about this and can be found in full at www.informationcommissioner.gov.uk.

"An employee does have the right to refuse assessment or treatment, but this rarely happens, except occasionally in alcohol or drug abuse cases," says Geoffrey Bignell of Just Employment Solicitors. "Usually, this is because an employee refuses to admit a problem." When this happens, the employer has the right to reach a decision without medical advice. Every case is different; however, and any complex case needs the expertise of an employment law specialist.

WAS A MANAGER OR EMPLOYER NEGLIGENT?

The question of what employers, and managers, should practically be expected to do to help stressed employees is another big legal question that was tackled in the UK's High Court ruling of February 2002. Paragraph 33 of that ruling states:

> *Many steps might be suggested [to prevent harm from stress]: giving the employee a sabbatical; transferring him to other work; redistributing the work; giving him some extra help for a while; arranging treatment or counselling; providing buddying or mentoring schemes to encourage confidence; and much more. But in all of these suggestions it will be necessary to consider how reasonable it is to expect the employer to do this, either in general or in particular.*

For legal reasons, the wording in that paragraph is "the employer" rather than "the line manager;" yet the line manager is normally the one with responsibility for implementing or initiating any of those courses of action. Courts scrutinize the actions of managers in stress cases and it is often their individual action, or inaction, that determines whether the employer overall failed in its duty of care.

SEEKING LEGAL ADVICE

The most important piece of advice this chapter could give is to urge managers to seek help not only from HR but from an employment law specialist if there is any doubt as to what steps to take with a stressed employee. Geoffrey Bignell says that although managers should have some knowledge of employment law, "it is not fair to expect the average manager to cope with the legal minefield." Every day spent in tribunal costs roughly £5000, and can cost much more. There is no doubt that getting advice early is cost-effective.

Summary

Managers are in the front line of ensuring that the HSE management guidelines are upheld. They should not pass that responsibility to HR or OH, although they should involve these professionals in all cases where there is any doubt about employee health or fitness for work. They need to create an atmosphere in which employees feel comfortable enough to admit that they are not coping or that their performance is suffering. The earlier managers are aware that there is a problem, the more likely it is that employees can stay in work, properly supported and monitored. A head-in-the-sand approach will nearly always mean damaged employees and organizational cost.

Managers should:

- ▶ Always listen to and act on comments about excessive pressure, not coping, feeling out of control, or similar

- Find an appropriate time to have a more in-depth discussion about these issues (see Chapter 19)
- Focus on how he or she can support the employee in work
- Get help from HR/OH (see Chapter 17) and employment law specialists
- Agree a plan, put it in writing, and ask the employee to confirm agreement
- Make it a part of the regular appraisal system to ask how employees are feeling
- Attempt to implement the HSE Management Standards.

Managers should not:

- Claim there is no resource to help an individual (see Chapter 19 for a list of "things not to say")
- Tackle the issues without HR, OH, or legal advice, if there is any risk of stress-related illness
- Delay contacting employees absent due to stress or psychological illness. They should do this themselves, rather than pass the responsibility to HR, unless there is a good reason for doing so
- Make promises they cannot keep.

APPENDIX 16.1 Summary of Legal Cases Cited in Chapter 16

Lancaster v. *Birmingham City Council*

Beverley Lancaster started work for Birmingham City Council as a clerk in 1971. By 1978 she had progressed to the role of senior draughtsman in the architects' department and supervised ten members of staff. Following the birth of her child she changed to part-time working and a job-share arrangement. After a restructuring and job changes, Lancaster was moved to the housing department where she had to handle rude and demanding tenants. She experienced panic attacks, anxiety, and depression and received medical help. She took early retirement and claimed that her health had suffered due to the council's negligence, that is, Birmingham CC had failed to:

- Assess her ability to do the job
- Provide the necessary training
- Assess the situation – she was experiencing work overload and felt unable to meet the demands put upon her.

Birmingham CC admitted liability to the illness that led to Beverly retiring early on ill health grounds and she was awarded £67,000.

State of New South Wales v. *Seedsman* (2000)

Beth Louise Seedsman was a young, inexperienced police officer who was given little training before being required to work on her own investigating the most unspeakable crimes against children. The judge agreed that Miss Seedsman suffered from post-traumatic stress disorder (PTSD) and that the New South Wales Police Service failed to provide a safe system of work to protect her from such mental injuries. He found that the police service should have foreseen that Miss Seedsman was likely to suffer psychiatric illness as a result of the exposure to crimes committed against children. She was awarded A$125,000.

Pratley v. *Surrey County Council* (2003)

Maureen Pratley, employed as a care manager, sued Surrey County Council for injury due to ill health (depressive illness) caused by negligence. Miss Pratley had complained of stress due to overwork and warned her manager, Mrs Elrick, of injury to health if nothing was done to lighten her workload. Mrs Elrick promised to introduce a new work flow system called "stacking," whereby new cases would not be allocated to case managers unless and until their existing workload had space. This promise was made just before Miss Pratley took a three-week holiday. When she returned, she found that no steps had been taken to put the system in place. Two days later, Miss Pratley went off sick from work with depressive illness. Interestingly, the court ruled in favor of the employer. This was primarily for two reasons. First, Miss Pratley withheld information about the pressure she was under, the extent of her overtime, and previous ill health which her doctor believed to be caused by stress. Secondly, the judge ruled that it was not reasonable to expect Mrs Elrick to know that Miss Pratley's health was in immediate danger. He said:

> *Miss Pratley had not seen fit at that time to go to her own GP, the Occupational Health [OH] Department or the counselling services available. That evidences her own view of her health at the time and is some evidence of the impression she would have given to Mrs Elrick. Her work was not suffering. To find that Mrs Elrick should, in those circumstances, have realized that action had to be taken by the day Miss Pratley returned to work after a three week holiday, would be unreal.*

In contrast, the judge said that it was reasonable for Miss Pratley to expect the "stacking" system to be implemented before her return from holiday, even though this had not been specifically promised. Although the ruling was in favor of the employer, the case brings home the point that managers must listen and respond when employees say they are not coping, and then ensure that they fulfil their promises.

Petch v. *Commissioners of Customs and Excise* (1993)

Mr Petch had two mental breakdowns, being transferred to a different post after the first one. Petch failed in his action for two reasons: he apparently showed no obvious outward signs of stress (although he had manic depression) so the first breakdown could not be reasonably foreseeable. The judge ruled that the second post was not an inherently stressful position, so there was no need to take any steps against a second breakdown and hence no breach of duty of care.

Discussion papers and legal cases calling for UK law surrounding stress to be reviewed:

- Scottish Law Commission, Discussion Paper No 120, *Damages for Psychiatric Injury*, August 2002
- Scottish Law Commission, Paper No 196, *Report on Damages for Psychiatric Injury*, 1 August 2004
- *Marie Flora McDonald* or *Cross and Another* v. *Highlands and Islands Enterprise and Another* – ScotCS 307, 5 December 2000, pp. 52–60.

17 Best Practice Models for Managing Stress in Teams and Individuals

Introduction

Increasingly, organizations are looking for proactive and consistent ways to deal with stress-related illness and absence, and to give managers the skills and knowledge to do this. However, the wheels in many organizations turn slowly and implementing policies and procedures can take months or even years. If organizations would make this a higher priority and speed up the process, there are a great number of employees with stress-induced depression, anxiety, panic disorders, or other illnesses who would benefit greatly from their cases being managed in a structured way. Human resources (HR) and occupational health (OH) have important roles to play, but as mentioned in the previous chapter, the line manager is in the best position to help prevent and initiate support for stressed employees. Unfortunately, in the vast majority of organizations that the authors have worked with, there is no defined procedure for managers to follow if:

- ▶ they suspect a team member is stressed (in hyper-stress or distress)
- ▶ a member of their team is absent due to stress.

The result is decreased employee welfare and performance, increased sickness

Four elements of best practice for managers to reduce team stress:

1. **Policy and procedure, including:**
   - — **stress management, mental health, or well-being policy**
   - — **procedure for managing stress-related illness**
   - — **procedure for stress-related absence**
   - — **individual risk assessment**
   - — **critical incident management procedure**
2. **Involvement of OH where appropriate**
3. **Information and support from HR, OH, and senior management**
4. **Training**

Figure 17.1 **Key stress management best practice elements for managers**

absence, and increased risk of litigation. This chapter will set out four key elements of best practice for managers dealing with stress within their teams (see Figure 17.1), discuss each one in turn and clarify the roles of manager, OH, and HR.

Policy and Procedure

Having a stress policy (see Chapter 11) and procedures for dealing with stress-related illness are critical for helping genuinely stressed employees to get better and be productive employees. It will also manage those are not genuinely stressed, but might be trying to get some extra time off, or who simply do not want to face something or someone in the organization. It is a common occurrence that employees are signed off work for stress when they face a disciplinary hearing. One example of the non-management of stress cases is outlined in Figure 17.2.

A study by the Department for Work and Pensions entitled *Job Retention and Rehabilitation Pilot: Employers' Management of Long-term Sickness Absence* (2004), revealed:

> *There was rather little evidence of active management of sickness absence in the first two to three weeks following self-certificated absence, although some large organizations asked employees about whom they had concerns to see the occupational health service for help … Referral to occupational health typically depended on managers understanding conditions.*

Concerning long-term sickness absence, the report goes on to say:

> *Managers tended to be less certain than Human Resources staff about when activities related to long-term absent employees should begin. Monitoring systems were not always robust, and it was possible for long-term absent employees to be forgotten.*

The full report can be viewed at: http://www.dwp.gov.uk/asd/asd5/summ2003-2004/227summ.pdf.

A large call center near Birmingham, could not understand why so many employees were absent due to stress. It had in place many organizational stress reducers such as flexitime, a crèche, an excellent staff canteen and rest areas, a bright and cheerful atmosphere, and creative financial incentives. One thing it did not do was proactively manage cases of stress-related illness. Employees did not usually get a phone call from their team leader or occupational health until they had been off work for six weeks, and were never assessed by occupational health if they had been signed off by their GPs. It appeared that some employees were jumping onto this bandwagon.

When an occupational health physician (OHP) assessment was put in place for every case of stress-related illness, the incidence fell by nearly half.

Figure 17.2 **Addressing absence in a call center**

As Part III explained, organizations should create a business strategy that seeks to limit stressful working practices and culture as much as possible, and have a policy that clearly states the responsibilities of management and employees regarding stress in the workplace (see Chapter 11). In addition, managers should have a set of guidelines to enable them to uphold these responsibilities. The guidelines could be part of a stress management policy, part of a sickness absence policy, or possibly stand alone.

Organizations should prepare and ensure that all managers are aware of the following:

1. Guidelines for supporting individuals whom managers suspect are stressed, or those who are experiencing stress, but wish to remain at work
2. A procedure for creating structured treatment and return to work (RTW) plans for those absent due to stress
3. Individual risk assessment forms for those considered to be at risk of stress-related illness
4. Individual risk assessment forms for those returning after stress-related illness
5. Contact details of OH, HR, any employee assistance program, welfare officers, mediation services, mentoring schemes, listening ear schemes, helpful websites and telephone numbers of other useful organizations, such as Relate and CancerBACUP
6. A critical incident management procedure.

Template versions of these key documents can be found in Appendices 17.1–17.6. Having these guidelines ensures that all staff are treated equally and fairly. Every case of stress-related illness is different, but treating cases in an ad hoc way is not advisable, both for the sake of employee welfare and legal protection.

The documents in Appendices 17.1–17.6 are for the most part self-explanatory, but it would be useful to discuss individual risk assessment in further detail, since managers often ask: "Am I responsible for carrying out risk assessments on my team, and if so, how do I do it?"

A 2003 report for the Health and Safety Executive by Thomson et al., *Best Practice in Rehabilitating Employees Following Absence Due to Work-related Stress*, provides a detailed and comprehensive report on rehabilitation to work.

WHY HAVE AN INDIVIDUAL RISK ASSESSMENT PROCESS?

Assessing the risk of stress to every individual in an organization is not a requirement under either British law, or HSE Management Standards. It is a requirement for organizations to assess the risk to psychological health of each of the roles within the organization, and any other factors that may cause employees stress, as discussed in Chapter 6. Assessing risk to individuals is carried out differently, because it takes account of factors unique to an individual that the organization would not have to consider in a more general risk assessment. These might be:

- Medical conditions (for example epilepsy) or other considerations under the Disability Discrimination Act (DDA) – such as a history of depression
- The individual's skill level and training needs
- If the individual has significant responsibilities outside work such as caring for children or elderly relatives.

There are typically five reasons why managers or organizations may wish to carry out a more in-depth individual stress risk assessment process on one or more employees:

1. When an organization carries out a risk assessment that is either measuring employee attitudes or objective measures such as absenteeism and turnover, it may identify areas of the business that appear to have higher stress levels, and then decide to seek further information there.
2. There may be good cause, even without having completed an organizational risk assessment, to investigate the levels or sources of stress within an area of the business, for instance during a turbulent period of change, or after the death of a colleague.
3. An employee may show signs of stress that warrant a specific assessment of how he/she could be helped and supported.
4. If an employee has a disability (remember, depression is classified as a disability under the DDA) that might be exacerbated by excessive pressure, an assessment and action plan may help to stem prolonged absences.
5. When an employee returns to work after suffering from a stress-related illness, there needs to be an assessment of that person's needs, and an agreement by all stakeholders about the gradual process of returning to full responsibilities.

TYPES OF INDIVIDUAL RISK ASSESSMENT

There may be any number of ways to carry out an individual risk assessment for stress, but two are discussed here that cover the five situations above. Both are simple and easily carried out by a manager, OH or HR professional.

Information-gathering risk assessment

The first type of individual stress risk assessment follows the HSE's Management Standards and asks for feedback from an individual (or a number of team members) and his/her manager, about whether the standards are being met by the manager or organization, and how the individual is feeling about the various aspects of the standards. The individuals or group then discuss how these standards can be best achieved, given existing resource constraints. They agree a plan, a timetable, and a point at which to assess whether the agreed interventions are making a difference. This type of risk assessment can be applied in the following situations:

- A manager worried about the stress levels of a particular employee and wanting to have a more formal, recordable conversation about how he/she could be supported

- A department or area of the business under a specific pressure, with the manager needing more information to decide how best to alleviate stress
- Following findings of a risk assessment, a more in-depth investigation of an area of the business is needed
- As part of annual or biannual appraisal process.

An example of this type of risk assessment can be found in Appendix 17.3. It can be adapted to an organization by adding specific questions such as: "Has the mentoring program been helpful to you?" or "Does the new matrix management system give you sufficient management input?"

Individual risk assessment supporting return to full productivity

The second type of individual stress risk assessment looks at supporting an employee to return to full responsibilities or productivity. It would apply in the following situations:

- An employee returns to work following stress-related illness
- An employee's performance/productivity has been suffering as a result of stress.

An example of this type of risk assessment can be found in Appendix 17.4. It can be adapted to suit the particular risks in an organization, such as assault, critical incidents, or even hypo-stress (insufficient challenge).

Involvement of Occupational Health

It is important that organizations, managers, and individuals understand that rest is not a cure for distress. Rest might be part of the treatment process, but staying at home, often alone and worried about what is happening at work, is not the way to improve depression, anxiety, or any other psychological disorder. In fact, it can make them worse. Tony Urwin, BUPA psychological services director, says that rehabilitation whilst remaining at work is the first choice:

> *Routine is important in recovering from psychological illness. It may not be ideal for an employee to be in the same boiling water as they were prior to the illness, but for them to go to the workplace and do work of some kind can be therapeutic. The psychological barrier of returning to work is much bigger than the physical barrier.*

In the experience of BUPA Wellness, a leading provider of preventive and corporate health services in the UK, when there is proactive management of stress-related illness and absence – with management and OH working closely together – there can be big cost savings. Dr Jenny Leeser, BUPA Wellness' clinical director occupational health, says that the three biggest problems she encounters in this area are:

Rolls-Royce implemented a company-wide absence management procedure, including action planning for any employee absent for more than four weeks, utilizing OH earlier, and ensuring that all staff were aware of their responsibilities. Rolls-Royce estimates that it cost the company £207,800 to implement (£8700 in staff time to design it and £200,000 to train managers). Employee absence was reduced by about 15 percent, saving the company £11 million.

Full details of this case study can be viewed at: www.hse.gov.uk/businessbenefits/casestudy/rolls.pdf

Figure 17.3 **Reducing absence at Rolls-Royce**

- Organizations tend to avoid stress issues
- Managers are too busy to contact employees absent due to psychological illness
- Managers do not refer to OH soon enough.

She adds: "I think that managers see these issues as too difficult to deal with, and this often leads to resentment on the part of the employee, who feels isolated and uncared for if managers fail to make contact."

Figure 17.3 illustrates how positive OH intervention and management can be have a beneficial effect on the bottom line.

ROLE OF THE GP

The role of a GP is to look after patient health and welfare, and when he/she sees someone in distress, the likely decision is to sign the person off work. Unfortunately, in the UK, GPs often do not have further resources to help stressed patients and referral to a psychologist or counselor can take quite a long time. GPs rarely write to the patient's organization and they can be slow in responding to requests for information. They are not to blame for this state of affairs – they simply do not have the time or resources (although increasingly, GP surgeries have counseling services within them). The result for organizations is that they often stay in the dark about the prognosis. A further issue in dealing with GPs is that they often still use the word "stress" on sickness absence notes, even though stress is not an illness (see Chapter 3). This is sometimes because of the stigma about psychological illness that still exists for some people: patients ask them to write "stress" instead of "clinical depression" or "panic disorder." At other times, the symptoms of stress are varied and it may seem appropriate simply to write "stress". A 1998 Department of Social Security report for the medical policy group stated:

> *The guidance to certifying practitioners, and related educational material for all doctors, should emphasize the need to avoid the vague term 'stress' and to set out the diagnosis as precisely as possible.* **The report can be viewed in full at: http://www.dwp.gov.uk/medical/sreport1.pdf**

ROLE OF THE OCCUPATIONAL HEALTH PHYSICIAN (OHP)

The role of the OHP is somewhat different. OHPs are just as concerned about patient welfare, but because they work within the organization, they focus on getting the person fit for work (best for the individual, best for the organization). Without breaking medical confidentiality, they can be privy to the GP's diagnosis, recommendations, treatment plan, and prognosis, and be able to make recommendations about helpful support, further treatment, and prognosis for return to work. An OH professional is more likely to have success liaising with an employee's GP because he/she can enter into a clinical dialogue and reassure the GP that if an employee comes back to work, he/she will be suitably supported. In reality, what often happens is the OHP can recommend that an individual sees a psychologist and the organization can opt to pay for that outright, or have it paid for by a private medical scheme if the individual sees a psychiatrist first (the usual protocol in the UK). For an organization, a course of psychological treatment or psychotherapy is far less expensive than six months off work.

Information and Support

As mentioned above, information on sources of support needs to be readily available and obvious to managers; otherwise they will not act proactively in stress cases. A high percentage of managers are unsure about how to work with OH to support a stressed employee, or what other resources are available, and tend to turn to HR who they hope will take the whole problem off their hands and sort it out for them.

Organizations should seriously consider the following sources of support if they are not already in place:

1. *Human resources.* If is not viable for the organization to maintain a permanent HR employee, then a remote HR specialist should be used to give advice.
2. *Occupational health.* Again, if an in-house OH nursing adviser or physician is not viable, then it may be affordable to use a remote OH service that can give advice and even manage cases.
3. *Mediation.* This is a service too little used by organizations: it can help to resolve cases of bullying, aggression, and other misunderstandings between employees.
4. *Coaching and mentoring schemes.* These provide a place to turn if managers have a particular challenge supporting a stressed employee. Coaches and mentors will help them to explore a range of solutions.
5. *Listening ear schemes.* Some organizations run their own in-house counseling by training volunteers to act as counselors and to ensure that employees who need help and support are aware what other help is available.
6. *Further sources of support.* Organizations can provide web addresses and telephone numbers of organizations that could help employees in a way that most organizations do not have the resources to do (see Appendix 17.5).

Training

All too often managers will not approach employees who are stressed because they fear meddling in people's private lives, fear the confrontation, or fear opening a can of worms about stress issues that they will find difficult to handle. When employees are absent due to stress, either signed off by their GPs or simply unable to attend work, managers fear harassing employees and making the situation worse, and so, again, often do not make contact with the employee. Also, managers are not usually comfortable phoning someone they think has a psychological illness, because most have had limited experience of it and fear saying the wrong thing.

In order to fulfil their duty of care with the best skill possible, managers need to be trained in how to spot signs of stress (see Chapter 18), depression and anxiety, and to fully understand the procedures outlined in Appendices 17.1–17.3. It is important that enough time is taken so that training can be properly disseminated to them. It will take at least half a day's training for managers to gain an understanding of what stress is (and isn't), how to spot signs and symptoms, and the organizational procedures for managing it. If training is to include coping strategies for stress (both for the manager and his/her team), a full day should be allocated for training. Too often, organizations expect that this training can be done in an hour or two.

There are other useful types of management training that would enable them to protect the psychological health of their teams by developing general awareness of others' thoughts and intentions, and developing communication skills. They include:

1. Basic counseling and coaching skills
2. Relationship building, rapport building, or emotional intelligence
3. Body language.

Figures 17.4 and 17.5 illustrate differing approaches to managing absence, while Appendix 17.7 outlines a one-day stress management workshop covering managerial best practice.

A large London financial company instituted a new sickness absence management program that required employees to be interviewed by their managers for stipulated levels of absence: either three days or more in a 4-week period; three episodes of two or more days in a 12-week period, or any episode of more than 3 weeks. All line managers were trained in the new procedure as well as how to spot signs of stress and how to approach employees about stress-related illness. Ten months on from that training, sickness absence has reduced slightly, but not as much as was hoped. The organization is reviewing the policy because it is thought that the cut-off periods for absence need to be reduced so that management can intervene even sooner. The feedback from the managers has been that it has raised their awareness of stress-related illness and given them an understanding that allows them to speak to employees more effectively about work pressure.

Figure 17.4 **A program for reducing sickness absence**

Occupational health industry development

Some organizations have begun to use an occupational health service specifically for absence management. On the first day of absence, an employee must telephone an OH nursing adviser with the reason for absence. The nurse can then:

- **give medical advice**
- **recommend further assessment by a GP or OHP**
- **recommend counseling**
- **continue to monitor and manage any appropriate cases.**

This should greatly improve the management of stress-related illness cases, as employees will be managed in a structured way sooner.

Figure 17.5 **Developments in the OH industry**

Summary

To sum up, organizations should *proactively* manage stress by:

- Developing a stress (or mental health) policy
- Developing procedures for stress-related illness and absence, including:
  - stress-related illness guidelines
  - stress-related absence
  - individual risk
  - information on sources of support
  - a critical incident management procedure
- Engaging OH and HR support
- Training managers in:
  - how to spot the signs and symptoms of stress
  - organizational policy and procedure regarding stress
  - basic counseling and coaching skills
  - relationship building, rapport building, or emotional intelligence
  - body language.

For further information, a 2003 HSE publication entitled *Best practice in rehabilitating employees following absence due to work-related stress* (Thomson et al., 2003) provides a detailed and comprehensive report on rehabilitation to work.

APPENDIX 17.1 Stress-related Ill health Rehabilitation Procedure

As soon as management suspects that an employee may be ill due to stress, this procedure should begin. It is important not to wait to see if things will get better on their own.

- *Initially, the manager should speak with the employee* to try to assess whether he/she is experiencing difficulties in coping or is experiencing ill health due to pressure at work or at home (although personal details should not be required or encouraged by the manager). If the issue is something that the manager can support alone, this is the preferred course of action.
- *If the individual indicates that he/she is in difficulty or is ill*, the manager should:
  - *Listen and empathize*, but *not* attempt the role of counselor or psychologist
  - *Have a plan in mind*, but first ask the employee what he/she would like in the way of support
  - *Agree a support plan with the employee*
  - *Encourage use of any employee assistance programme (EAP), OH and HR.*
- *If the employee reports illness*, the manager should contact OH for advice, and consider whether the employee should be assessed by an OHP. The OHP would assess the employee's current status and whether support services would be of benefit (for example counseling), recommend appropriate therapies, or referral to a specialist.
- *In helping individuals to remain in work*, support plans can include: reduced number of days, reduced targets, reduced length of day, home/office mix, decreased complexity of work. Goals should be agreed, but it should be recognized that sometimes a plateau is required to consolidate gains.
- *Monitoring and support* include measurable goals such as socializing, hours worked, jobs done at home despite working, life/work decision making, clinical history and demeanor as examined by OHP (if appropriate), measures of performance against plan and liaison with management and HR.
- *Monitoring and support continues* until working normally and (coming) off medication.

The following are important points to remember:

- The employee should be reassured that the organization's aim is to help the individual back to health
- Offering prompt occupational health management avoids development of the belief that the illness and incapacity are permanent
- Every case is different and should be treated as such
- The provision of achievable milestones is the best way to manage the journey and maximize the beneficial outcomes for all concerned.

If an employee is the victim of violence, either from another employee or a member of the public, it is important to enact this procedure, both immediately and later if the employee is displaying any stress symptoms or unusual behavior. See critical incident management (Appendix 17.6) for further guidance.

Adapted from BUPA Wellness procedure

APPENDIX 17.2 Stress-related Absence Rehabilitation Procedure

As soon as management, HR or OH are aware of employee stress-related absence, this procedure should begin. It is important not to wait to see if things will get better by themselves.

- *As soon as* a manager is aware of stress-related absence, he/she should contact HR and OH to seek advice and share information.
- *The employee should be assessed* by an OHP within two weeks to assess his/her current status and whether support services would be of benefit (for example counseling), recommend appropriate therapies, or referral to a specialist.
- At the appropriate time – immediately, or after recovery and further assessment, OH should work with HR and the line manager to *devise a return to work (RTW) plan.*
- Establishing the *RTW scheme may involve further assessment by an OHP or obtaining a report of GP/specialist*, and will be with the agreement of treating doctors, management and the individual (in accordance with the Access to Medical Reports Act – see Chapters 10 and 16).
- *Rehabilitation/RTW* plans need to be considered in context of the DDA but all should be tailored to individual needs and may include: reduced number of days, reduced targets, reduced length of day, home/office mix, decreased complexity of work. Goals will be agreed but it should be recognized that sometimes a plateau is required to consolidate gains.
- *Monitoring and support* includes measurable goals such as socializing, hours worked, jobs done at home despite working, life/work decision making, clinical history and demeanour as examined by OHP (if appropriate), measure of performance against plan and liaison with management and HR.
- *Monitoring and support* continues until working normally and (coming) off medication. If the manager feels that further support is necessary, he/she should contact OH for further advice.

The following are important points to remember:

- The employee should be reassured that the organization's aim is to help the individual back to health and employment, and be made aware of company policy to devise a RTW scheme

- The aim of rehabilitation is to reduce sickness absence by building an individual's confidence during a phased and supported return to work. It is important that the employee is given achievable goals
- Offering prompt occupational health management avoids development of the belief that the illness and incapacity are permanent
- Every case is different and should be treated as such
- The provision of achievable milestones is the best way to manage the journey and maximize the beneficial outcomes for all concerned
- It is critical that the individual is returned to work safely. Cases of severe stress will take considerable time to recover fully. For instance, when an individual has been heavily medicated, he/she may not be able to drive for some time and the DVLA will need to be notified
- Those individuals with a history of self-harm, substance abuse or eating disorders will take longer to recover and in some of these cases, the DVLA would also need to be notified.

Adapted from BUPA Wellness procedure

APPENDIX 17.3 Individual Stress Risk Assessment

This risk assessment should be undertaken jointly between assessor and employee. It will help to detect areas of potential stress that need to be tackled by employee and employer, but does not give an absolute measure of risk. It asks questions about: role, demands, control, support, relationships, and change in accordance with "The Management Standards" contained in the UK HSE's *Management Standards for Tackling Work-related Stress.*

The assessor should complete pale gray boxes, and the employee should complete the dark gray boxes. Both parties should read the completed document, and then jointly write and agree the action plan.

Date:

Assessor details:

Name:

Job Title:

Department:

Employee details:

Name:

Job Title:

Department:

Line Manager:

ROLE

Describe the employee's roles and responsibilities

Are your roles and responsibilities fully understood? **Yes / No**

If not, please elaborate:

Is there any role ambiguity (lack of clarity) or conflicting responsibilities? Yes / No
If yes, please elaborate:

DEMANDS

Have the demands on the employee been assessed as to whether they are achievable within the agreed hours of work? Yes / No

Are the demands achievable within the agreed hours of work? Yes / No

Are the demands challenging enough? Yes / No

Do the employee's skills match the demands?
If not, please elaborate:

Do your skills match the demands of the job?
If not, please elaborate:

CONTROL

Are you consulted about work patterns? Yes / No

Do you have control over pace of work and when breaks are taken? Yes / No

Are you encouraged to use your skills and initiatives? Yes / No

Are you encouraged to develop new skills in order to take on new and challenging work? Yes / No
If no, are you satisfied with your current level of challenge? Yes / No

If any of the above answers are "no", please set out assessor's view and possible solutions:

SUPPORT

What systems are in place to formally support and appraise employees (such as formal appraisals, 360° feedback, employee assistance programs, manager's "surgery" time, mentoring, coaching, team meetings, training needs assessments)?

Do you know what support is available to you, and how to access it? Yes / No

Is there adequate support in place for you in your role:
From managers? Yes / No
From colleagues? Yes / No
If not, what would you propose to improve this?

Do you have adequate resources to do your job? Yes / No

Do you receive adequate feedback and appraisal of performance? Yes / No

RELATIONSHIPS

Are you aware of policies and procedures that help to prevent or resolve unacceptable behaviors in the workplace, and do you know the content? Yes / No

Are you aware of policies and procedures that help to prevent or resolve unacceptable behaviors in the workplace, and do you know the content? Yes / No

What systems are in place that encourage employees to share information?

Are there adequate systems in place that encourage employees to share information? Yes / No

Would you know how to report behavior you considered to be unacceptable? Yes / No

CHANGE

Are you provided with information that enables you to understand the reasons for proposed changes in the organization, and the probable impact on you? Yes / No

Are you consulted about changes and given an opportunity to influence proposals? Yes / No

How would employees be supported or retrained if this were needed as a result of organizational change?

ACTION PLAN

What are the key areas of risk as identified above?

Role:

Demands:

Control:

Support:

Relationships:

Change:

How will they be tackled? Give step-by-step action plan for each risk identified. Information to include:

- ▶ Specific objective in tackling the risk
- ▶ Information to be gathered, if any; completion date
- ▶ Conversations or negotiations decided on, and deadline date
- ▶ Actions to be taken; deadline date
- ▶ Date for review of whether measures are working

APPENDIX 17.4
Individual Return to Work Support Form

This form should be completed jointly by assessor and employee, if possible.

Date:

Assessor details:

Name:

Job Title:

Department:

Employee details:

Name:

Job Title:

Department:

Line Manager:

ROLE

Describe the employee's roles and responsibilities

DEMANDS

What are the sources of pressure in this role?

Have the demands on the employee been assessed as to whether they are achievable within the agreed hours of work? Yes / No

Do the employee's skills match the demands? Yes / No
If not, what are the plans for training?

CONTROL

Does the employee have control over the pace of work and when breaks are taken? Yes / No
If not, how could this be increased?

OTHER RISKS

Is there anything else about the role that could pose a risk to mental health? Yes / No

Does the employee suffer from any condition that could increase the risk of stress-related illness? Yes / No / Unknown

Does the employee suffer from any condition that can be classified as a disability under the Disability Discrimination Act? Yes / No

DESCRIPTION OF THE SITUATION

Describe the situation that led to stress for the employee

Describe the illness, disability or reduced function that led to absence

Give details of the employee's current state of health and any medical recommendations

Give details of any relevant individual circumstances that may affect return to work

RETURN TO WORK PLAN

How will the employee return to work?
How will the employee be welcomed back?
Is there a planned timescale for phased return?
Will the employee have reduced responsibilities? If yes, give details

How will the employee be supported in work?
Mentoring, coaching, training, help from colleagues, shadowing?

How will the employee be supported personally?
EAP, GP, other specialist help?

How and when will the employee be assessed?

OH assessment:

Managerial interview:

Work appraisal:

REVISED SUPPORT PLAN AFTER SUBSEQUENT ASSESSMENT

Date:

How will the employee continue in work?
What new changes will be made?

How will the employee be further supported in work?
Mentoring, coaching, training, help from colleagues, shadowing?

How will the employee be supported personally?
EAP, GP, other specialist help?

How and when will the employee be assessed again?

APPENDIX 17.5 Routes to Help

INTERNAL

- Manager
- Human resources
- Occupational health
- Employee assistance program
- Listening ear scheme
- Intranet

EXTERNAL

- GP
- Counseling – self-refer
- Helplines
- Local support organizations
- Internet

There are many organizations that provide counseling for a wide variety of needs. National numbers are listed, but some have local representation.

Alcoholics Anonymous	www.aa-uk.org.uk	0845 76 97 555
The British Association for Counselling lists all trained and qualified counselors throughout the UK	www.bacp.co.uk	0870 443 5252
The British Association for Behavioural and Cognitive Psychotherapies lists qualified psychotherapists throughout the UK	www.babcp.org.uk	01254 875277
CALM was set up to tackle stress and depression in young men, but anyone can use their confidential counseling helpline between 5pm and 3am	www.thecalmzone.net/Home/index.php	0800 58 58 58
CancerBACUP provides cancer information, practical advice and support for cancer patients, their families and carers	www.cancerbacup.org.uk	0808 800 1234
Cancer Link provides emotional support and information to cancer patients, their families and carers. They produce a range of publications on cancer	www.londonhealth.co.uk/cancerlink.asp	0800 132 905
Cruse Bereavement Care for anyone affected by bereavement	www.crusebereavementcare.org.uk	0870 167 1677
Directgov for practical information on death and bereavement	www.direct.gov.uk/Homepage/fs/en	
MIND mental health charity information line	www.mind.org.uk	0845 766 0163
Narcotics Anonymous	www.ukna.org	020 7730 0009
National Debt Line is a free, confidential telephone helpline for people with debt problems in England, Wales and Scotland	www.nationaldebtline.org.uk	0800 074 6918
Parentline Plus offers support to anyone parenting a child	www.parentlineplus.org.uk	0808 800 2222
Quitline for help with smoking cessation	www.quit.org.uk	0800 002200
Relate relationship counseling, courses and workshops	www.relate.org.uk	0845 130 4016
Saneline offers information and advice on all aspects of mental health for individuals, family or friends	www.sane.org.uk	08457 678000
Samaritans	www.samaritans.org.uk	08457 90 90 90

Adapted from BUPA Wellness

APPENDIX 17.6 Critical Incident Management Procedure

This procedure, or process, has three stages: initial, middle, and final. If a traumatic, distressing or upsetting incident occurs at work, the manager should get involved as quickly as possible to help with the **initial stage**, namely to:

1. Comfort and console distress
2. Provide care for physical needs
3. Offer practical help for next steps
4. Protect from further threat and distress
5. Facilitate reunion with loved ones
6. Ask: Does the employee
   - need time to be alone?
   - have a safe way home?
   - have further safety concerns?
   - have work concerns?
   - have health concerns?

Managers should be formally trained in order to be able to provide the correct level of support at this stage. They should be able to:

1. Educate the employee about the normal responses to trauma
2. Help the employee to understand that his/her reactions are normal
3. Know exactly what support will be available to the employee
4. Explain to the employee that they can get help at any stage (that the refusal of help now does not mean that they will not be eligible later)
5. Understand that at this initial stage, they should not be trying to elicit details of the incident from the employee, or initiate any psychological intervention.

After this initial stage, advice should be sought from OH to facilitate the **middle stage**, which involves:

1. Telling details of the incident to the manager or counselor depending upon the nature of the incident, this may be inappropriate unless handled by a psychologist or trauma counselor)
2. Allowing the victim to vent feelings

3. Ensuring the victim has access to all support available
4. Monitoring employee behavior and performance and help with feeling competent

The **final stage** is about ongoing monitoring and support, to identify whether any further intervention is needed. The manager should remain vigilant to changes in employee behavior or stress/trauma symptoms.

APPENDIX 17.7 Stress Management Workshop for Managers

Introduction
Clarification of delegate objectives and preview of the day

Defining stress
A model that explains the difference between pressure and stress

Stress effects
The physical and behavioral/psychological effects of stress
The science of epinephrine (adrenalin) and its importance in the stress response
Identifying the stressed employee
The signs of excess pressure in an organization

Stress and the law
What is a manager's duty of care regarding stress-related illness?
A best practice model for managing stress
How do the latest guidelines from the HSE affect management practice?

BREAK

The three key determinants of stress: Perception, resilience, and acceptance
How they relate to coping strategies for stress

Coping strategies for stress

- *Personality management* – The type A personality and susceptibility to stress; questionnaire on personality
- *Emotional intelligence* – How are the relationships on your team reducing or increasing stress levels?
- *First principles of peak performance* – Eating, drinking, playing, sleeping, and relaxing. Where does your team get its energy?
- *Managing the workload* – Do your team members ask each other for help? What happens to team dynamics when the pressure is on?
- *Mental gymnastics* – such as challenging flawed thinking, stopping worry, solution-orientation, humor and anger management.

LUNCH

Stress management policy introduction

- Aim and commitment of the policy
- Management of work-related stress
- Responsibilities of managers and employees
- Confidentiality

Approaching the stressed employee

- What to say
- What not to say
- Body language basics
- Counseling skills for managers – role play to illustrate how stressed employees might be approached

BREAK

Mediation for managers

- Facilitative versus directive
- The rules
- Monitoring progress
- Case studies and role play

Dealing with difficult people

- Aggressors, complainers and clams
- Sticking to the aim

Individual action plans

Closing summary and questions

Total time 7:00 hours

Adapted from BUPA Wellness

18 Recognizing and Assessing Stress in Others

Introduction

As Chapter 16 made clear, it is important for managers, in upholding their duty of care, to be able to spot signs and symptoms of stress early, before an employee is in distress. A big challenge for managers is that people are good at hiding signs of stress – from others and themselves. A frequent comment from those people who have had nervous breakdowns or suffered other serious stress-related illness is, "I didn't see it coming." Part of the reason for this is that once people feel stressed, their brains do not work completely logically. They may understand that they feel under pressure, their stomach hurts every afternoon, they are getting frequent headaches, or their home relationships are deteriorating, but they may not equate this to being near "distress." Because they want to be capable and perform well, they often think they just need to work harder in order to regain control! People can be resistant to the idea that they are stressed: on being asked: "How are you?," the stressed person is likely to answer: "Fine." (Chapter 19 will look at how managers can build rapport and get more realistic and honest answers about employee stress levels.) This chapter explores:

- ▶ Individual signs and symptoms of stress that may be detectable in others
- ▶ Organizational symptoms of high stress levels and what managers can do.

Why Managers Should be Vigilant

Nearly every manager will have experience of employees who are unproductive, rude, uncooperative, withdrawn or absent, but how can a manager be sure of the causes of these kinds of behavior? Are they due to stress, or something else? As Stephen Williams and Cary Cooper state in their book *Managing Workplace Stress* (2002), "How can a line manager tell who's about to fall off the edge because of excessive demands or who's frustrated because they are insufficiently challenged?"

In order to manage effectively, managers must seek information and feedback from their teams about stress levels, know their teams well, and *observe them carefully*. Simple observation of body language and behavior may make all the difference in noticing that something is not quite right with an employee, and saving him/her from "falling off the edge."

Signs of Stress in Others

As Chapter 3 explained, there is an important physiological element to stress. When an individual feels under threat, he or she will release stress hormones with resulting physical effects that make up the fight or flight response. This physiological response to threat is covered in detail in Chapters 3 and 22, but as a brief reminder, the main responses are:

- Increased heart rate and blood pressure
- Increased breath rate and shallow breathing
- Muscle tension
- Increase of blood flow and fuel to major muscle groups
- Decrease of blood flow to extremities, brain cortex, other major organs and digestive system
- Senses hyperalert
- Decreased sensitivity to pain.

Even though many of the above responses are invisible, and despite the fact that people are good at hiding stress, there are usually visible effects from stress. Managers (and colleagues) should look out for any of the following:

- Face looking tense, worried, pale
- Strained, higher pitched voice
- Severe fatigue
- Body tension; shoulders high, sitting and/or leaning forward
- "Protective" or closed body language, meaning chest covered or protected, shoulders turned away, little eye contact
- Withdrawal, little verbal communication
- Little contribution to team discussion
- Reduced productivity, creativity
- Increased rate of mistakes, accidents
- Missing deadlines, or renegotiating them at the last minute
- Irritability, aggression or violence
- Belligerence
- Negativity
- Sarcasm
- Weight loss or gain
- Increase in smoking or drinking
- Any change in personality
- Illogical or unreasonable behavior
- Lack of self-care
- Excessive hours
- Recurrent lateness, leaving early
- Extended breaks.

The above list can also be found in Chapter 4, and incorporates Sutherland and Cooper's (2002) summary of behaviors displayed by people who are experiencing excessive stress. It is repeated here because it is such an important reminder for managers who are looking for stress in their teams.

After a period of time being stressed (weeks, months or even years) high levels of stress hormones can cause, or be a factor in, a number of physical and psychological conditions or illnesses. Figure 18.1 describes common stress-related illnesses and behaviors that cause absence or decreased productivity, and explains how they are linked to stress. This does not mean that these conditions and behaviors cannot have other causes. Managers should not jump to conclusions, but be aware of the following links and use the information as part of a wider picture of an individual.

Readers will notice that the right-hand column is interconnected, with some "links" being the same as the conditions themselves. This is because stress is often multisymptomatic and can be the result of a vicious spiral. For instance, someone can become very tired as a result of working long hours and, therefore, be more susceptible to depression. The depression can cause even more fatigue and, perhaps, difficulty in rising in the morning. This means recurrent lateness, with resulting guilt and frustration, and possibly working later to get things done. Thus the spiral goes on and can be difficult to break. A final point about detecting stress in others is that it is a common misconception that stress is the same thing as depression. Stress is not an illness, but can lead to illnesses and undesirable conditions and behaviors.

Illness, condition or behavior	**Link with stress**
Fatigue	Poor quality or broken sleep
Despondency	Possible hypo-stress, underchallenged
Upper limb syndrome/repetitive strain injury	Chronic muscle tension
Headache and migraine	Muscle tension, high blood pressure and restriction of blood flow to brain
Weight loss or gain	Digestive disorders/comfort eating
Shaking or trembling	Muscle tension
Belligerence, aggression, negativity, sarcasm	Severe anxiety or frustration; possible low self-esteem
Withdrawal/little contribution/closed body language	A protective response, and possible signs of depression
Panic attacks	An extreme fight or flight response
Frequent crying	Brain is operating out of its emotional centre, the limbic system; possible sign of burnout or depression
Depression	Mental and physical exhaustion make this more likely
Recurrent lateness, lack of self-care	Fatigue or possible sign of depression
Personality changes/illogical behavior	Brain is operating out of its emotional centre, which causes changes in perception
Missed deadlines	Loss of ability to think logically, concentrate, manage time, delegate or ask for help

Figure 18.1 **Common stress-related conditions and behaviors and their link to stress**

Managerial Awareness and Acceptance of Stress

Managers should understand that stress has wide-ranging, short-term and (some serious) long-term effects, and these effects may be very different from what they themselves experience when they are stressed. There are still some managers (directors and board members) who say that they do not believe stress exists. The authors have heard this in many types of organization from government agencies to investment banks. It may be due to a lack of understanding of what stress is, or a fear that it is too complex to tackle effectively. What they fail to grasp is that if individuals think they are stressed, they are! Stress is about perception and is completely subjective. Often senior managers see stress purely as a cost to the organization and not as an opportunity to be an employer of choice by creating a positive environment. If an individual is only claiming to be stressed in order to avoid work (for whatever reason), then a robust procedure for stress-related absence is an excellent way to reveal this (see Chapter 17). Stress as an organizational issue is not going to go away and the faster some of them learn this, the better. As Steve Sumner from the Employers' Organization for Local Government said in a press release in 2004: "the bottom line is, would you rather have people at home off sick, or do something about it?"

Signs of Stress in an Organization

When stress levels rise overall in an organization, there are also telltale signs. Stress tends to be infectious, since the behavior of one person can put pressure on others. The result can be a sudden change of climate and culture. The catch-22 is that often the cause of stress is a significant restructure or lack of resource that means everyone is so busy, no one has time to remedy the situation. Organizations should look for and monitor where possible the following *organizational stress indicators:*

- Increased sickness absence rate
- Increased turnover rate
- Increased accident rate
- Increased numbers of musculo-skeletal problems including back strain and upper limb syndrome
- Many employees working very long hours
- Increase in blame culture
- Increase in office politics
- Decreased communication and information sharing
- Departments working reactively, not proactively or creatively.

Some of these organizational symptoms are more tangible than others, but the sad truth is that the majority of organizations (even large, blue-chip organizations) are not even monitoring sickness absence rates, or the number of hours employees are working. It is difficult to evaluate whether any interventions to reduce stress are working if there is no relevant data to monitor.

The Manager's Role in Reducing Organizational Stress

If organizations do not monitor sickness absence rates, or any of the things on the list above, managers can (and should) do it for themselves. To manage well, and to manage stress well, they should keep abreast of all those things. A good checklist for managers wanting to assess stress levels of their teams is:

- Monitor all the points on the above organizational stress indicators list
- Use an appropriate range of questions based on the HSE's management guidelines as part of annual/semi-annual appraisal – see Chapters 6, 8, 16, 17 (in particular Appendix 17.3, individual stress risk assessment) and 19
- Frequently ask team members on an informal basis how they are coping, whether their goals/roles are clear, what other support they need, and whether they understand any changes occurring – see Chapter 19
- Get to know team members to increase the ability to spot when behavior is out of character
- Monitor personal stress levels and take corrective action if necessary.

This final point seems obvious, but managers sometimes do not see the effect their own stress is having on their teams. In an interview for this book, a senior consultant in a large London consultancy firm said: "Well, actually, I am quite stressed, but I don't show that to my team." What he obviously does not realize is that he *is* showing it to his team: they will pick up on his body language, voice pitch, and plenty of other clues that will make them aware – even if they do not know the cause. Also, as was mentioned earlier, stress is infectious. Of course, the manager cannot necessarily change the organization, its structure or resources, but he does have control over two things: how he handles stress within himself, and how he manages and leads his team. A well-led and managed team is a less stressed team. The next chapter will address the specific conversations managers should have with team members in order to help prevent and manage stress levels.

Summary

There are a wide range of stress-related illnesses, conditions and behaviors, discussed in detail in Chapters 3 and 22. Many of them are not visibly detectable in another person, but others are, and it is these (listed in this chapter) that managers must be alert to. Managers and organizations should do their best to understand what stress is and is not, and to detect it early before individuals reach distress. Where organizations are not monitoring those things commonly affected by high stress levels (also listed in this chapter), managers can (and should) do it for themselves.

19 Building Rapport and Having Conversations about Stress

Introduction

> *Dealing with people is probably the biggest problem you face … in business.*
> Carnegie (1982, p. xiv)

As discussed in Chapter 17, managers should be open to the idea that stress can have grave negative effects on health and performance, and be willing to discuss it with team members. Otherwise, employees are more likely to hide the fact that they feel out of control or unable to cope. Managers should never think that stress audits, risk assessments, or any stress management interventions are a substitute for direct and meaningful conversations about demands, control, support, relationships, role and change – the six major factors in stress management identified by the Health and Safety Executive (HSE) in its *Management Standards for Tackling Work-related Stress* (2004). This chapter will set out clear guidelines for managers about:

- How to build rapport
- Creating an environment where stress can be discussed openly
- Important factors to consider when having conversations about stress
- Key positive messages to convey (and what not to convey) when discussing stress or stress-related illness (SRI).

Managerial Involvement in the Management of Stress

Throughout the HSE's Management Standards, references are made that indicate the importance of direct managerial involvement to help manage the six factors. For instance, some of the "states to be achieved" that the HSE has set are:

- Systems are in place to enable and encourage managers to support their staff
- Employees receive regular and constructive feedback
- Systems are in place to enable and encourage managers to deal with unacceptable behaviour.

For all six factors, the HSE wants systems to be in place to respond to individual concerns. For most situations, the first port of call for concerns due to stress should be an individual's manager.

Of course, sometimes the concern is the individual's manager. In these cases, the manager's manager may be the first point of communication and, ideally, human resources (HR) or occupational health (OH) would be options, too. Managers, however, should not think that HR and OH are there to have meaningful conversations about stress with their team members for them. One of the most common issues seen by the authors in helping organizations to manage cases of stress-related illness is of managers trying to pass the issue over to either HR or OH to handle independently. From the psychological perspective of the stressed employee, it helps significantly if the manager is directly involved in proactively managing sickness absence due to stress. This is because a big fear for most people returning to work after SRI is that their manager and team members will somehow think less of them, and they may not be accepted back into the team. They also worry how they will cope back at work, and if they have not communicated with their manager for some time, that fear is increased.

Barriers to Effective Communication

There are, however, a number of barriers to managers communicating well with stressed employees. First, managers are often nervous (even terrified) of asking a team member about stress levels or symptoms because they fear opening "a can of worms" to do with work or personal issues. Second, there are rarely written procedures for managers to guide them as to what do in a case of stress-related illness or absence (as discussed in Chapter 17). Third, managers often fear that if they involve themselves, they will be drawn into spending endless amounts of time on the issue, they will have to become psychoanalysts, or be asked provide a solution that they cannot (such as more resources).

This presents a good case for training managers in how to initiate conversations about stress and/or potential illness, what the organization expects of them, and what is clearly not their responsibility. Managers often have little experience of counseling conversations, so they do need guidance. They need to experience some role play in this area, or at the very least, think about how they could approach someone suffering from stress. They need to know what to say and, more importantly, what not to say.

Positive Messages to Stressed Employees

The single most important message that the manager must give the employee from the first conversation about stress onward, is that it is the employee's welfare that is the concern – more important than performance or absence – and that the organization wants the employee to be well. In a large British food distribution company, managers have been known to ask, after a delivery vehicle has been involved in an accident, about damage to the vehicle before asking how the driver is. The managers there are surely not callous, but have not had explained to them the potentially negative effect of this approach on the driver. It is easy to say that they should know this anyway, but some people do not know it.

Another message the employee should understand – although it needs to be handled sensitively, is that the organization wants the employee to come back to work. This sounds simple and obvious, but there are a large number of organizations that are not managing cases of stress-related absence at all, and the unsaid message to the employee might be: "You don't necessarily need to come back." One senior manager in an investment bank confided to the authors that, sometimes, he would rather certain individuals stayed off work, because he felt better off without them and once they were off work for three months or so, it is not paid for from his budget as the long-term health insurer picks up the tab. This attitude is damaging in many ways: foremost because the employee is ill at home, not being treated, and possibly getting worse. Even if that individual is fraudulently claiming to be stressed and ill, he/she is not being challenged, developed, or helped to be a productive member of an organization or society.

Of course, organizations will not want employees to come back to work before they are well enough, but the message should be clear that the organization will proactively manage cases, use OH and other specialists, and formulate a return to work (RTW) plan in line with medical guidance. If the employee has an SRI but has remained in work, the principle holds true for returning the employee to full duties, or full performance. Obviously, this is not the message to emphasize in the first, or first few, conversations with an employee who is ill from stress. Every case of SRI is different, and managers must use their judgment about when to begin to talk about RTW plans. If it is at all unclear as to whether an employee is fit for work, OH professionals should be asked for guidance.

Factors to Consider in Conversations about Stress

When managers initiate conversations about stress, they need to be aware of, and have a plan in mind for, a number of factors, namely:

- The environment
- Their language and tone of voice
  - What to say
  - What not to say
- Their body language
- A possible support plan
- Possible routes to help
- Contact names and numbers
- Preferred outcome of the meeting (that is, agreement reached).

The environment. *Managers should consider:*

- A suitable meeting place which has complete privacy, not necessarily the manager's office. The employee may associate going into the manager's office and the door being closed with being disciplined. They may also worry about what other employees will think. Consider meeting off site
- An environment which is as comfortable and quiet as possible
- Chairs of the same height, with no desk or barrier in between the two parties. Sitting together at a small table is fine
- Placing chairs/knees at slight angles, or if directly facing, not too close together
- Overall, as small a distance apart as seems comfortable to both parties, especially the employee
- Employee should be offered water or other drink, but not alcohol.

Body language, language and tone of voice. *Managers should consider:*

- Be more aware than usual of the feelings they are projecting, since they are likely to be nervous about this conversation
- Make every effort to relax their breathing, shoulders, jaw, and forehead
- Be prepared to listen quietly, nodding or saying uh-huh to encourage employee to speak more
- Use a soft, low tone of voice
- Do *not* cross arms or legs
- Have an "open" posture with chest and shoulders facing the employee
- Use gestures such as hands softly folded (when listening), palms up (when speaking)
- Have direct eye contact to convey paying attention.

What to say – use phrases such as:

- "I am concerned about you"
- "You seem down/sad/angry/harassed/more pressured than usual"
- "I've noticed that ..." (especially useful when employee is denying that anything is wrong)
- "How can I help/support you?"
- "Have you seen your GP? Used the EAP? Seen the OH nurse?"
- "Have you tried ...?"
- "Would you like to talk about it?"
- "If it is a personal matter, you don't have to tell me the detail, but tell me how I can help."
- Be prepared for silences; be patient and wait for the employee to speak. Filling silences can make it more difficult for the employee to say what is for them, distressing or embarrassing.

What not to say – avoid phrases such as:

- "You look really stressed/You are obviously very stressed"
- "I wish I could help you but..."
- "Pull yourself together"
- "What does your GP say? Are you on medication?"
- "I think you should..."

- "Your colleagues are under more pressure", or "Work is piling up"
- "Everyone else is coping"

Possible support plans and routes to help

- Involve HR by informing them that someone is absent due to suspected stress-related illness, check on any required procedures and availability of OH, EAP, mediator (if appropriate), or any other support
- Involve OH to help to manage the case. They may possibly write to GP, do a health assessment or fitness for work assessment, or recommend counseling or another specialist
- Ensure employee has details of any employee assistance programme (EAP) for counseling, if appropriate
- Give employee details of any other helpful numbers or websites (see Appendix 17.5), if appropriate
- Use temporary administrative staff to decrease workload
- Temporarily allow employee to work fewer hours/days
- Call a team meeting to redistribute work
- Meet a specific training need
- Provide a mentor or coach
- Use mediation if the issue is a personality clash or suspected bullying.

Meeting outcomes

The aim of any meeting between manager and stressed employee should be:

- Manager and employee agree a specific support plan as per above

  or
- Manager and employee agree to take no specific action for the time being. This suggestion should come from the employee, not the manager.

In all cases:

- Manager and employee should agree when to reconvene to assess whether the plan is working
- Manager and employee agree when and how the employee will be contacted
- Minutes of the meeting should be prepared, and the employee asked to sign them (see Chapter 16).

Building Rapport

An important point to make about all these suggestions is that conversations about stress and people's feelings and fears are much more than having a strategy for a conversation and a list of things to say. A manager must already have a rapport with his/her team members and have built their trust. This is not something that is built in an instant. It is something that is built through a range of actions and behaviors, many of which are listed in Figure 19.1. This is not meant to be a comprehensive list, but it is a good starting point for any manager.

Getting to know the employee

- Spending time with him/her
- Showing interest in his/her career
- Showing interest in his/her life outside work
- Always seeking to understand his/her motivation

Earning trust in the manager

- Manager being honest with the team
- Manager keeping promises and appointments
- Manager looking out for and protecting team members

Raising the self-esteem of the employee

- Seeking his/her point of view and ideas
- Recognition of his/her contribution
- Regular thanks and appreciation
- Genuine and sincere praise of him/her

Giving constructive feedback to the employee

- Active listening
- Motivating him/her (using information sought above)
- Recognizing his/her individual talents and giving opportunities for them to be used
- Never directly criticizing, but mentoring and developing in a caring way

Language, body language and tone of voice

- Shoulders and body focused on the employee
- Tone of voice friendly and positive
- Use of humor
- Smiling
- No cutting remarks or ambiguity

Figure 19.1 **Building rapport**

> *You can have policies and procedures and any manner of stress management interventions, but without the right management attitudes and behaviours, there will still be the likelihood of stress.* **Learning and development specialist**

Further Guidance

- Procedures are important for ensuring that everyone is treated fairly and equally. However, each case is individual and there needs to be flexibility in the approach. People vary in their ability to recover from illnesses, particularly psychological illnesses.
- Even when employees are not ill, a good manager will be collecting information on a regular basis about how employees are faring in their work. This will come from:
  - — Frequent informal conversations about how they are coping, whether their goals/roles are clear, what other support they need, and whether they understand any changes occurring

— An appraisal system run annually or semi-annually. If an organization does not have an appraisal system, a manager may set up a less formal system of talking about demands, control, support, relationships, role and change (see Appendix 8.1, the HSE Indicator Tool for Work-related Stress).

Summary

Managers must be in the front line for detecting stress in employees, both by observation and regular conversations, formal and informal. They must also be in the front line when it comes to having conversations about stress-related illness, absence, and underperformance. It is critically important for team relationships that managers do this themselves and do not try to pass the responsibility to HR or OH. There is, however, an important role for these professionals to play. HR do need to be informed right away when employees are debilitated in any way due to stress, and they should be a source of information, support, and resources. OH should be utilized – always sooner rather than later:

- To determine the current state of health
- For referral if appropriate to a psychologist, counselor or other professional
- To establish fitness for work
- To help formulate a RTW plan.

In any conversations about stress, the two most important messages for the manager to convey are that employee health is paramount, but the organization wants the employee back at work. When having these conversations, managers should consider:

- The environment
- Their language and tone of voice – conveying care and support, not guilt, retribution or apathy
- Their body language
- Possible support and RTW plans
- Possible routes to help
- Contact names and numbers of any resources such as EAP
- Preferred outcome of the meeting, and ensure that minutes are taken.

Any positive foundations laid in the relationship between manager and employee will be important when it comes to these potentially tricky conversations. Managers who establish and maintain a good rapport with their teams will find it easier to have a more open, relaxed conversation about employee health and ability to cope. Because every case of SRI is different, managers need all the information they can in order to make the right judgments about the best way to give support. There are a wide range of things that managers should do to build rapport, a good summary of which is listed above.

20 Summary of Managing the Stress of Others

Introduction

Part IV looked at stress from a manager's point of view. In the authors' experience, even seasoned managers can have difficulty in recognizing stress and are nervous about talking to employees about it. They fear opening a can of worms that they cannot handle very well. Alternatively, they stay silent because they do not think there is anything they can do about the organizational stress issues. If an employee is absent due to stress, managers often do not make contact because they fear harassing the employee or saying the wrong thing. In the words of Dr. Jenny Leeser, clinical director of occupational health for BUPA Wellness, these situations "can end up in the too-difficult box" for managers.

Part IV covered:

- The legal responsibilities of managers
- Best practice models that should be adopted organization-wide and learned well by managers
- How to spot signs of stress in others
- Building rapport with team members and having conversations about stress.

This chapter summarizes the most important learning points from Part IV.

Legal Responsibilities of Managers

- It is a legal responsibility of managers to recognize symptoms of stress that, according to UK law, "any reasonable person would."
- Many tribunals and court cases have hinged on whether an employee's stress was "reasonably foreseeable." This remains a gray area of the law, so managers should be extra cautious and develop an awareness of any early signs of stress.
- It is advisable for managers to learn enough about this area of law to avoid major pitfalls. This could be done through an organizational training scheme, through updates from HR, or self-study of HR publications.
- The way a manager handles a case of stress-related illness can be scrutinized in a tribunal or court of law.

- The HSE Management Standards (HSE, 2004) set out organizational responsibilities for reducing stress, but most of them need to be carried out by managers, so managers need to read and understand them. They can be viewed at: http://www.hse.gov.uk/stress/standards/index.htm.
- Although the standards are not law, a court of law or employment tribunal would look at whether organizations are upholding them.
- Stress management is about good, basic management practices that enhance employee performance in any case.
- To have the best chance of noticing signs of stress, managers should create a culture of openness where it is OK to talk about stress and ask for help.
- Managers must ensure that employees get the training they need to do a job, and that work is organized and allocated to minimize the risk of stress.
- If a manager has any fears for employee health, then conversations about work pressures or stress should be put in writing.
- In the UK, in accordance with the Access to Medical Records Act 1988, an employee must sign a release form allowing his/her employer to request medical information from a GP or specialists, or a report from doctors or psychologists assessing the employee's health.
- Managers should seek help from HR and an employment law specialist if there is any doubt as to what steps to take with a stressed employee.

Best Practice Models for Managing Stress in Teams and Individuals

Policy and procedure:

- Having a stress policy and procedures for dealing with stress-related illness is critical for helping genuinely stressed employees to get better and be productive employees.
- Organizations should prepare and ensure all managers are aware of the following:
  1. Guidelines for supporting individuals who managers suspect are stressed, or those who are experiencing stress, but wish to remain at work.
  2. A procedure for creating structured treatment and return to work plans for those absent due to stress.
  3. Individual risk assessment forms for those considered to be at risk of stress-related illness.
  4. Individual risk assessment forms for those returning after stress-related illness.
  5. Contact details of occupational health, human resources, any employee assistance program, welfare officers, mediation services, mentoring schemes, listening ear schemes, helpful websites and telephone numbers of other useful organizations, such as Relate and CancerBACUP.
  6. A critical incident management procedure.

Template versions of these key documents can be found in Appendices 17.1–17.6.

Individual risk assessment:

- It is a requirement for organizations to assess the risk to psychological health of each of the roles within the organization and assess any other factors that may cause employees stress.
- When warranted, organizations should assess risk to individuals and take account of factors unique to an individual, such as medical conditions, skill level, or care responsibilities outside work.
- Reasons that an individual risk assessment might be warranted include:
  - High stress levels in a team from organizational risk assessment information or due to a stressful or tragic event
  - Employee showing signs of stress
  - Employee has a disability
  - Return to work following stress-related illness.

Involvement of OH:

- If employees are absent from work, then proactive management of stress-related illness and absence – with management, HR, and OH working closely together – will make all the difference.
- Occupational health advice and intervention should be sought at an early stage if an employee is, or is suspected to be, stressed.
- Rest is not a cure for distress. Isolation and solitude can make some psychological illnesses worse.
- Occupational health physicians (OHPs) focus on getting employees fit for work (best for the individual, best for the organization), whereas GPs focus on saving their patients from distress, so are more likely to sign a person off work.
- OHPs can be privy to GP's diagnosis, recommendations, treatment plan and prognosis, and be able to make recommendations about helpful support, further treatment, and prognosis for return to work.

Training:

- Managers need to be trained in how to spot signs of stress, depression, and anxiety, and fully understand procedures for dealing with stress-related illness.
- Other useful training for managers includes:
  - Basic counseling and coaching skills
  - Relationship building, rapport building, or emotional intelligence
  - Body language.

Recognizing and Assessing Stress in Others

- A big challenge for managers is that people are very good at hiding signs of stress – from others and themselves.
- Managers should understand that stress has wide-ranging, short-term and (some serious) long-term effects, and these effects may be very different from what they themselves experience when they are stressed (see list in Chapter 18).

- In order to manage effectively, managers must seek information and feedback from their teams about stress levels, know their teams well, and observe them carefully.
- There are also telltale signs when overall stress levels rise in an organization, and they are listed in Chapter 18.
- If organizations do not monitor stress levels, managers can (and should) do it for themselves.

Building Rapport and Having Conversations about Stress

- It is critically important for team relationships that managers speak to stressed employees themselves and do not try to pass the responsibility to HR or OH.
- In any conversations about stress, the two most important messages for the manager to convey are:
  - — Employee health is paramount; and
  - — The organization wants the employee back at work.
- In any conversations about stress, managers should consider:
  - — Making the environment conducive to openness
  - — Using language and tone of voice that conveys care and support, not guilt, retribution or apathy
  - — Awareness of body language and that it conveys care and openness
  - — Possible support and return to work plans
  - — Possible routes to help
  - — Contact names and numbers of any resources such as EAP
  - — Preferred outcome of the meeting
  - — Taking minutes of the meeting for legal reasons.
- Managers who establish and maintain a good rapport with their teams will find it easier to have a more open, relaxed conversation about employee health and ability to cope.

PART V

Understanding and Dealing with Stress

An Individual Perspective

21 Introduction

Organizations are made up of individuals, so to manage organizational stress as effectively as possible, each individual needs to learn how best to manage stress. Of course, each employee has a unique personality, outlook, responsibilities, and set of circumstances, so each person's solution to pressure and stress will be quite different. Part V was written largely to speak to the individual reader, but the explanations and suggestions will also help managers and colleagues to understand and help others. Part V also presents a case for giving all employees the benefits of learning about coping strategies for stress through a training program.

Understanding what stress is and the effects it has is an important starting point for anyone in managing stress. Chapter 22 discusses the symptoms of stress that many people feel, but would not necessarily be obvious to the outside world. It explains how those symptoms are linked to the physiology of stress and suggests how individuals could assess stress in themselves.

Chapter 23 tackles the question of whose responsibility it is to manage stress levels and suggests how one can feel more in control. Chapters 24 and Chapter 25 cover a large range of individual coping strategies for stress. Nearly all coping strategies for stress will fall into one of four broad categories:

1. Managing and improving personal perception
2. Managing emotions and increasing emotional energy
3. Building physical and mental resilience
4. Acceptance of circumstances and ability to be peaceful.

Once an individual decides on a set of strategies, those strategies must be put into action, and that is where many people go wrong in managing their own stress levels. They know what it is they should be doing, but they do not do it. Chapter 26 will look at some of the excuses, and real reasons, for failing to look after one's self and manage stress effectively. Part V concludes with a summary using a question and answer format.

22 Recognizing and Assessing Individual Stress Levels

Introduction

This chapter was written with the individual reader in mind, because everyone needs to be able to recognize stress before it results in ill health. However, as the introduction to this section pointed out, it can also help managers and colleagues to understand and help others. Most people are good at hiding the signs and symptoms of stress from others – and themselves. The authors have seen many cases of extremely stressed individuals who were insisting they were absolutely fine. For those people, it is only when they hit rock bottom – "distress" in the form of a nervous breakdown, panic attacks, depression, or some other severe physical or psychological illness – that they realize the pressure they were under was not sustainable. When they recover, they usually say that they have learnt to spot the signs of stress early, and implement coping resources to get back to "eu-stress".

Instead of learning from the experience of stress-related illness, it is much more desirable to learn to see stress in ourselves early, noticing changes in performance and mood before we get ill. Self-awareness is all-important here and, for many people, this means developing a habit of checking in with oneself for feedback on wellness, mood, concentration levels, energy levels, and the level of control that one feels. Chapters 23–25 will cover these areas, and much more on coping resources. This chapter will cover signs and symptoms of stress, some important points about the physiology of stress and ideas about how to measure individual stress levels.

Individual Stress Symptoms

When stress (or perception of a threat) causes the release of stress hormones, the collection of physical reactions known as the "fight or flight response" is inevitable. These symptoms are listed in Chapter 3, but are repeated here because they are the first thing that individuals may notice:

- Tense muscles (for fighting or fleeing)
- Rapid and shallow breathing, or holding breath
- Tightness in the chest

- Pounding heart (to pump more blood to the muscles)
- Sweating
- Dry mouth
- Butterflies, stomach ache, or other digestive problems
- Need to empty bladder or bowels (to be lighter!)
- A panicky feeling.

Other aspects of the initial fight or flight response that individuals may not notice are:

- Increased blood pressure
- All senses hyper-alert (but sometimes tunnel vision)
- Decreased sensitivity to pain
- Pale face
- Pupils dilated
- Blood diverted away from extremities, digestive system and brain cortex (the higher brain responsible for logic, reason, and learning) to the major muscle groups (hands and feet may feel cold)
- Increase in clotting ability of blood (hence the association with heart attacks)
- Decreased concentration and ability to think logically or creatively
- Decreased energy spent on:
  - Cell repair
  - Immune system rejuvenation
  - Fertility and libido (sex drive).

Why Stress Hormones Cause So Many Problems

The body is designed to withstand the fight or flight state for short periods of time only. It is excellent for survival, but physically and mentally tiring. When stress hormone levels have been high for some time, the body literally gets worn down and internal equilibrium and health are neglected for the sake of maintaining the emergency state. There is a wide range of conditions that can result from this lack of physical and mental renewal; individuals may experience:

Physically:

- Poor sleep (nervous system speeds up and makes sleep difficult)
- Chronic muscle tension, typically in neck, back, and shoulders
- Headache and migraine
- Skin conditions such as eczema, psoriasis, and impetigo
- Appetite loss or increase, therefore weight loss or gain
- Increased susceptibility to viruses
- Digestive disorders such as indigestion, ulcers, and irritable bowel syndrome
- Decrease in fertility or libido
- Chronic high blood pressure
- Poor circulation (due to blood being diverted from extremities and retained in major muscle groups)

- Numbness or tingling in extremities or different parts of the body
- Trembling or shaking
- Heart disease (due to arterial damage from high blood pressure)
- Stroke (again, due to arterial damage)
- Cancer (possibly due to reduced immune system response).

Psychologically:

- Severe anxiety
- Severe frustration
- A feeling of dread
- Feeling out of control
- Judgment and memory impairment
- Increased number of mistakes
- Panic attacks (an extreme fight or flight response)
- Frequent crying (brain is operating out of its emotional center, the limbic system – see below)
- Irritability, anger, and aggression (again, the reaction from the limbic system)
- Depression (mental and physical exhaustion makes this more likely).

THE INVOLVEMENT OF THE LIMBIC SYSTEM

As Chapter 3 discussed, any perceived threat causes the amygdala, a part of the brain's limbic system, to become much more active. The limbic system houses the fight or flight response, emotions, and emotional memories. The amygdala becomes the "command and control centre" in an emergency, because it can respond much faster than the neocortex (the logical, reasonable, learning part of the brain). This explains why people do not think reasonably or logically when stressed and why they can become irritable and aggressive (think about road rage, violence in sport) or tearful (think about the end of a day when everything went wrong).

Measuring Individual Stress Levels

As mentioned above, if individuals can become aware of their own stress responses, they are in a position to try to remedy that stress. There are a myriad of stress tests, quizzes, and audits available – both from the internet and in the many popular books on stress, as well as in magazines. The authors' view is that it can be unhelpful to "test" whether an individual is stressed, because it is so difficult to devise a questionnaire that is completely valid for everyone. Everyone's response to stress is different, so questionnaires end up creating false positives (the questionnaire says the individual is stressed when he is not) and false negatives (the questionnaire says the individual is not stressed when she is). It is far better to consider a range of questions such as the following:

- On waking: Do I feel rested? If not, why not?
- Am I looking forward to work most days? Or dreading it?
- Do I understand my aims, purpose, and goals (daily, weekly, and annual)?
- Do I have positive, supportive relationships at work? If not, can they be improved?
- Do I have positive, supportive relationships at home? If not, how can they be improved? These really must be worked on, because it is nearly impossible to sustain a poor home relationship without feeling stressed.
- Am I challenged adequately, and am I developing in my career and in life?
- Do I feel organized?
- Am I able to say no, or do I take on too much?
- Am I being realistic about what I think I can achieve?
- Do I feel in control of my life?
- If there is a particularly stressful situation going on in my life, how am I minimizing its impact on me?
- Am I taking time out for renewal, relaxation, and recreation?
- Am I eating healthily (plenty of fruits and vegetables, wholemeal carbohydrate foods, beans, nuts, seeds)?
- Am I drinking plenty of water?
- Am I keeping fit?
- Am I happy?

Appendix 22.1 is a questionnaire that asks these sorts of questions and, although it is not a definitive barometer of stress for the reasons given above, it can be used to raise awareness of likely responses to stress.

Considering Coping Strategies

It can also be helpful to assess what coping strategies are being used to minimize the impact of pressure, rather than focus too much on the sources of pressure and their impact. There is such a wide range of coping strategies and they can be highly individual. Without wanting to place a limit on the number of methods of reducing stress, the following categories will help the reader to understand the range:

- Health and well-being
- Relaxation
- Recreation and hobbies
- Relationships and emotional support; social life
- Humor and fun
- Self-awareness; knowing one's strengths and weaknesses
- Assertiveness and communication
- Personal organization and time management
- Mind management; attitude and outlook.

Appendix 22.2 is a questionnaire designed by BUPA Wellness, a leading provider of preventive and corporate health services. Entitled Personal Effectiveness Questionnaire, it helps to assess which coping strategies an individual uses effectively and which of them could be utilized more fully.

Another similar questionnaire was developed by MR Dynamics, where the focus is on avoiding and reducing stress. The survey gives a pathway to enable people to choose, compared to others, how they approach the world and what actions they can take in key areas where the mind and the body interact. They are:

- Perceived ability to cope, as an overarching factor
- Physical health
- Creativity
- Efficiency
- Peace of mind
- Relationships with others
- A sense of control and direction.

Feeling in control, with clear sense of purpose and values, can be a massive antidote to potentially stressful situations. The 25-question, online survey can be accessed free of charge at www.mrdynamics.com. The personal survey report generated from completing the survey leads naturally to the development of personal action plans.

A comprehensive list of specific coping strategies can be found in Chapter 25, along with more detail on increasing self-awareness.

Summary

This chapter has looked at individual stress symptoms and their physiological explanations. Even more importantly, it has discussed measuring individual stress levels and explained that developing a broad self-awareness of stress responses and symptoms is the most accurate way to monitor stress. The appendices to this chapter are two questionnaires that help to develop that self-awareness, but do not attempt to say definitively whether someone is stressed or not. This is difficult because individual reactions are different, and most people fluctuate between hypo-stress, eu-stress, and hyper-stress on a monthly, weekly, or even daily basis. It is at the point of distress that people become debilitated for a significant period of time. Then, a diagnosis of some illness or debilitating condition can almost certainly be made.

This chapter also encouraged the focus to be on coping resources, rather than absolute levels of stress. The following three chapters delve into the sorts of coping resources that exist and how to incorporate them for better mental health and peace.

APPENDIX 22.1 Spotting the Warning Signs of Excessive Stress

Read each of the statements listed below. If the statement applies, or has applied to you in the previous twelve months, or at a time when you know you were experiencing intense pressure, then tick the statement. Be as honest as you can when you respond to each statement.

1.	I am easily irritated	
2.	I have difficulty concentrating for any length of time	
3.	I feel tired even when I wake up in the morning	
4.	I seem to have boundless energy	
5.	I cannot take fairly trivial decisions	
6.	The quality of my sleep has deteriorated. I have difficulty getting to sleep and/or I wake during the night and am very restless	
7.	I am achieving far more work than usual	
8.	I am losing my temper very frequently and feel powerful negative emotions	
9.	I feel generally run-down and rather unwell	
10.	I am able to concentrate fully on what I am doing	
11.	Life seems to be quite hopeless. Nothing seems worthwhile and I feel really low	
12.	My eating pattern has altered. I have lost my appetite or I seem to be eating more food to comfort myself	
13.	I have difficulty in absorbing new data	
14.	I suffer from frequent headaches	
15.	I am able to respond quickly to the demands placed upon me	
16.	I have difficulty recalling information when I am required to do so	
17.	I am drinking more alcohol than usual	
18.	I experience dramatic mood swings – sometimes I feel quite elated, at other times I feel really depressed	
19.	I often feel exhilarated about what I am doing	
20.	I have missed, or been late for, one or two important appointments	
21.	I feel wound up and am unable to relax properly	
22.	I am unable to achieve my normal level of creativity	
23.	I suffer from backache regularly	
24.	Ideas seem to flow more easily than usual	
25.	I feel inadequate and unable to cope	
26.	I have taken time off work	
27.	I frequently suffer from indigestion	
28.	I seem to lack the capacity to focus on a particular problem – my mind keeps wandering onto other issues	
29.	The least little thing sends me into panic. I feel as if I am unable to cope anymore	

30.	I have been smoking more cigarettes than usual	
31.	I have frequent need to urinate	
32.	In discussion with other people, I constantly repeat myself	
33.	My driving is rather erratic and my judgment impaired	
34.	I seem to have so many things to worry about	
35.	I am mentally and/or physically very active	

Directions for Scoring

Wherever you put a tick alongside a statement, put "1" in the appropriate space in the table below. Each number corresponds with the numbered statement. When you have done this, enter the totals of each of the columns in the spaces at the bottom of the column.

PROFILE OF WARNING SIGNS

Emotional reactions	**Disruption of thought processes**	**Physical reactions**	**Behavioral reactions**	**Positive reactions**
1 ( )	2 ( )	3 ( )	6 ( )	4 ( )
8 ( )	5 ( )	9 ( )	12 ( )	7 ( )
11 ( )	13 ( )	14 ( )	17 ( )	10 ( )
18 ( )	16 ( )	21 ( )	20 ( )	15 ( )
25 ( )	22 ( )	23 ( )	26 ( )	19 ( )
29 ( )	28 ( )	27 ( )	30 ( )	24 ( )
34 ( )	32 ( )	31 ( )	33 ( )	35 ( )
TOTAL				

WHAT DOES YOUR PROFILE MEAN?

A score of 0–2: If you scored zero in the first four categories, there are a number of interpretations. You may have been dishonest with yourself, or you may be unaware of the signs you are manifesting. Alternatively, you may be managing your stress levels very effectively already. A score of 2 in any of the first four categories shows a tendency to react in a particular way in stressful situations. A score of 0–2 in the final category, Positive reactions, does not necessarily indicate stress, but it may be worth thinking about why this score is not higher.

A score of 3 to 5: If you scored 3 or more in any of the first four categories, it is an indication of stress, but is not untypical. It may mean:

- you react in different ways to different situations
- you may have been suffering from excessive stress for a long time, and it is now manifesting itself in several ways.

A score of three or more in the final category, Positive reactions, shows a very healthy ability to deal with pressure.

A score of 6 to 7: A score of 6 or 7 is common for some people from time to time, so do not add to your stress by worrying. However, scores of this level are not desirable or sustainable over time, so it is advisable to develop a range of coping strategies (see Chapter 25) to reduce stress.

APPENDIX 22.2 Personal Effectiveness Questionnaire

Personal Effectiveness Questionnaire

BUPA Wellness

Score the statements below on the following scale:

Never	*Rarely*	*Sometimes*	*Often*	*Nearly always*
0	*1*	*2*	*3*	*4*

A1	I am able to set my own priorities	0	1	2	3	4
A2	I take exercise regularly	0	1	2	3	4
A3	I have realistic expectations of my abilities	0	1	2	3	4
A4	I am able to say "no" when I want to	0	1	2	3	4
A5	I can talk openly about concerns or problems I may have	0	1	2	3	4
A6	I have interests or hobbies other than work	0	1	2	3	4
A7	I am satisfied with my ability to solve problems	0	1	2	3	4
A8	I enjoy my interests or hobbies outside of work	0	1	2	3	4
B1	I manage my time well	0	1	2	3	4
B2	I get the sleep I need	0	1	2	3	4
B3	I reward my successes	0	1	2	3	4
B4	I avoid words like "should", "ought", "can't", "must"	0	1	2	3	4
B5	I am satisfied with my social life	0	1	2	3	4
B6	I feel committed to my organisation	0	1	2	3	4
B7	I am able to identify which issues are important	0	1	2	3	4
B8	I actively practise some form of relaxation	0	1	2	3	4
C1	I am well organised	0	1	2	3	4
C2	I have a healthy diet	0	1	2	3	4
C3	I consider problems as opportunities	0	1	2	3	4
C4	I state my views clearly when it is necessary	0	1	2	3	4
C5	When I leave work, I look forward to going home	0	1	2	3	4
C6	I am satisfied with how much my boss includes me	0	1	2	3	4
C7	I tackle difficult problems efficiently	0	1	2	3	4
C8	I can relax between leaving work and arriving home	0	1	2	3	4
D1	I plan ahead	0	1	2	3	4

D2	I am satisfied with my drinking and smoking habits	0	1	2	3	4
D3	I know my strengths and what I have to offer	0	1	2	3	4
D4	I value myself	0	1	2	3	4
D5	I have resources and people I turn to for advice	0	1	2	3	4
D6	I am able to make my own decisions at work	0	1	2	3	4
D7	I react objectively in critical situations	0	1	2	3	4
D8	I take time out when I feel too pressured	0	1	2	3	4
E1	I meet or beat my deadlines	0	1	2	3	4
E2	I keep my weight within acceptable norms	0	1	2	3	4
E3	I accept that there are situations I cannot change	0	1	2	3	4
E4	I tell people how I'm feeling	0	1	2	3	4
E5	I ask for help when I want it	0	1	2	3	4
E6	I enjoy the work I do	0	1	2	3	4
E7	I am good at prioritising	0	1	2	3	4
E8	I slow down when I have to	0	1	2	3	4

Totals:
Q1 ___ Q2 ___ Q3 ___ Q4 ___ Q5 ___ Q6 ___ Q7 ___ Q8 ___ Overall ___

Personal Effectiveness Skills

1 Personal organisation
2 Health
3 Self awareness
4 Assertiveness
5 Social life
6 Satisfaction
7 Problem solving
8 Relaxation

Scoring method

A1 + B1 + C1 + D1 + E1 = Total score for skill 1

A2 + B2 + C2 + D2 + E2 = Total score for skill 2 etc.

Scores of 2 or below on any skill and/or 12 and below on any section indicate possible areas for improving personal effectiveness.

23 Taking Responsibility, Developing Control

Introduction

Over years of running workshops and asking delegates: "What is stress?", one of the most common responses is that stress is "being out of control." Nearly everyone can understand that this is a big part of what stress feels like. The catch-22 is that once someone is stressed and feels out of control, the logical, thinking part of the brain (the cortex) is not fully engaged because the emotional part (limbic system) has taken over – as if preparing for an emergency (see Chapters 3 and 22 for fuller discussion). This means that there is little hope of generating a logical, reasonable response to the pressures causing stress and, thereby, regaining a sense of control. The limbic system is also likely to generate feelings that "this is being done to me," as a victim mentality takes hold. Alternatively, it can invoke feelings of simply being inadequate – that everyone else is coping while one's own world is crumbling. This chapter will first discuss taking responsibility for personal health and happiness, and then finding ways to feel in control and capable, and escape a victim mentality.

Whose Responsibility is it?

Many employees have the attitude that it is the organization's responsibility to keep them healthy, and a typical comment the authors hear from employees is that "they" (the management) should do something about the stress everyone is suffering. Under current legislation in the UK and elsewhere, organizations do have a responsibility for ensuring that systems of work are safe. However, they are not responsible for every employee's state of mind and therein lies the difficulty of trying to legislate against organizations causing employees too much stress. How much pressure is too much?

Unless there has been specific negligence such as:

- failing to stop bullying or harassment
- failing to train adequately for the rigors or pressures of the job
- failing to act when stress-related illness was "reasonably foreseeable"
- failure to support traumatized employees
- applying more than "reasonable" psychological pressure to an individual,

then individuals need to assess their own levels of stress and happiness, and decide if a job is right for them. Lady Justice Hale said, in a highly significant High Court ruling in February 2002, that:

> *If there is no alternative solution, it has to be for the employee to decide whether or not to carry on in the same employment and take the risk of a breakdown in his health or whether to leave that employment and look for work elsewhere before he becomes unemployable.*

In other words, if one finds walking into burning buildings stressful, the fire service is probably not a good choice of career. The authors believe that employees have a responsibility to be aware of their own state of mental health and take action early if mental health seems threatened. It cannot be for the employer to read minds and, even though there are barriers such as stigma, or potential loss of promotion or earnings, employees must be honest about whether they are stressed and seek help.

The other side of the argument can be found in Chapter 18: that managers should be vigilant, communicate with team members, and try to help employees who appear to be stressed but have not communicated about it. Managers are responsible for seeing signs of stress that any "reasonable" person would. When people become mentally ill, they do need help and there is no suggestion that when people become acutely distressed, they must sort themselves out or even know what to do to get better. Since no one can know someone's state of mind as well as that individual, it is in every employee's interest to develop an "early-warning radar" for stress. That involves the habits and skills discussed in the rest of this chapter and Part V.

Developing Control

This section will speak of "developing control" or "feeling a sense of control," but the most important thing to learn about control is that there is no real control over anything except one's self. When people "feel" in control they feel better, but there is quite a difference between being in control and being organized or feeling able. There is also a difference between control and influence. This section will look at these differences in turn, as well as learning to "feel" in control when a victim mentality is evolving.

CONTROL VERSUS ORGANIZATION

Quite often the sense of being out of control comes from "too much to do and too little time." Although there is no blame being laid, this is a result of overcommitment, lack of managing expectations, or lack of negotiating workloads and deadlines. There needs to be an acceptance that one human being can only achieve so much. Everyone has to make a choice about what to focus on and what to put in the "not possible" pile, or "I choose not to do this" pile. There is an apt expression: "Every 'yes' is a 'no' to something else."

Once commitments are pared down to a reasonable level, it is much easier to organize those commitments such that things fall into place more often, customers are happy, and levels of work satisfaction are far higher. It can be helpful to ponder what the expression "less is more" means to one's self. When people focus on fewer things – the really important things – there is a much greater sense of achievement and direction. Sometimes, when individuals are in hyper-stress, the result is a determination to work even harder to regain control, when what is more likely needed is rest and regrouping. People who handle stress well have the ability to shelve problems and projects until they have the capacity to deal with them.

Two tricks for learning to focus on the truly important things are:

- Identify daily, weekly, monthly, and annual goals. Write them down and refer to them.
- Throughout the day, check in with the question: "What's the best use of my time right now?" This will help to keep one on track because it is incredibly easy to be sidetracked by a thousand and one tasks that masquerade as important.

CONTROL VERSUS FEELING CAPABLE

Some people's stress is caused by:

- feeling that they are in over their heads
- feeling unskilled in some area
- a general low self-esteem.

The authors have used the term "impostor syndrome" to identify those who worry that, one day, everyone at work will find out that the individual has no idea what he/she is doing. An example of this is given in Figure 23.1.

> **Two British government organizations were being merged; a senior accountant in one of them was dreading the merger and developing signs of stress. His big fear was that his new boss would uncover weaknesses in his performance or skill base. This man had been an accountant for 25 years and had good to excellent work appraisals all along. He admitted that he felt undeserving of those appraisals, and worried if he could live up to them. After stress management coaching, he decided to be (somewhat) honest with his new boss. The phrasing he used in their first meeting was that he was committed to high performance, wanted to stay abreast of relevant legislation, and improve his IT skills. He asked his new boss to "mentor" him in those areas and to focus on his continuing development. In that way he opened up channels of communication for his boss to give him more feedback – something that can become difficult at senior levels. It then allowed him to relax, knowing that through mentoring conversations, he could assess how his performance was perceived.**

Figure 23.1 **A case of "impostor syndrome"**

There can be other reasons for feeling incapable and (once again) it is important to try to identify the reason. It could, for example, be a fear of failure or experience of criticism. Once this has been identified (or guessed by intuition), the use of something called "affirmations" has been shown to be highly successful in reversing a particular mindset. Affirmations are statements that bring mental focus on a particular belief, value, or goal. They take the focus away from negative thought patterns and create a new habit of more positive thought. Psychologists believe that new "neural pathways," or patterns of thought, are created by repeating affirmations. These neural pathways eventually become the "preferred" route instead of the old negative ones. Classic affirmations have the following qualities:

- Present tense ("I am", rather than "I will be")
- Positive ("I am successful", rather than "I am not a failure")
- Personal ("I am a successful salesman who is expert at establishing rapport")
- Playful ("I am a successful salesman who is amazing everyone with my charm and expertise")
- Challenging (I am a successful salesman who is winning £1,000,000 of new business this year).

Some examples of this kind of affirmation are:

I am calm

I am happy

I am capable

I solve problems

I choose my reaction

I find the right people at the right time

I am winning

I feel totally energized

I can re-evaluate

Although these affirmations conform to the "rules" listed above, there is no reason not to break the rules if it generates the desired results. Other types of statements repeated frequently, used as a screen saver, or put up on a refrigerator door can reduce stress and help with a sense of control and direction. Examples are:

You can't please everyone

Things don't have to be perfect

What doesn't kill you makes you stronger

He who angers you conquers you

There is all the time in the world

I am too blessed to be stressed

Courage brings confidence

I don't know the key to success, but the key to failure is trying to please everyone
Obstacles are those frightful things you see when you take your eyes off the goal

Through this sort of "positive brainwashing," people can begin to feel more in control because they are more confident about their capabilities and more accepting of human limitations.

CONTROL VERSUS INFLUENCE

For managing stress, the importance of letting go of trying to control others cannot be emphasized enough. Although there is no real control over other people or events, focusing on influencing people and situations with the right behaviors is usually worth the effort. Chapter 24 discusses the concept of emotional intelligence, which is partly about the ability to manage others' emotions. This skill lends itself to influencing others, but it must be pointed out that this does not mean manipulation. Manipulation is one way to influence, but it does not tend to be lasting because most people are quick to recognize it, which reverses its effect. Influencing with the right motivations (goal achievement, developing others, creating a positive culture/emotional climate) can work like magic and, again, gives a feeling of control and confidence.

Developing the habit of attempting to influence in a smart way rather than a manipulative one (such as invoking sympathy, using others' weaknesses, or being aggressive) is not complicated. It simply requires a realization that this is a more lasting, stress reducing way of moving toward goals, and the use of reminders to view situations in a new way. Two excellent references for exploring this concept further are Dale Carnegie's *How to Win Friends and Influence People* (1982) and Daniel Goleman's *Working With Emotional Intelligence* (1999).

Stephen Covey (1992, p. 122), in his book *Principle-Centered Leadership*, says this about influence:

> *As we focus on doing something positive about the things we can control, we expand our circle of influence. Direct control problems are solved by changing our habits of doing and thinking. Indirect control problems require us to change our methods of influence. For instance, we complain...that "if only the boss could understand my program or my problem ..." But few of us take the time to prepare the kind of presentation that the boss would listen to and respect, in his language, with his problems in mind.*

Summary

This chapter has emphasized the importance of taking personal responsibility for one's mental health and stress level. Since no one can understand someone's state of mind as well as him or herself, it is up to that individual to notice it and try to influence it positively. And it is particularly important to develop an early-warning system for stress, so that measures can be taken, or help sought, before mental or physical illness results.

Developing a feeling of being in control is a particularly important part of stress management, but one must remember that there is no absolute control over other people or events. If this is fully accepted, then the benefits of control over self can be explored. This is discussed as the "self-control" aspect of managing emotions, found in Chapter 24. The control over what one thinks and feels is powerful and can be used to positive effect for reducing stress (and for success and happiness). This can be achieved through recognizing negative thoughts that generate stress (including the desire to control others) and the use of affirmations to change those thoughts to positive ones. Affirmations are positive statements of intentions, beliefs, values, and goals that are repeated in order to shift focus onto desired outcomes. There is a range of examples of affirmations within this chapter.

24 Managing Emotions

Instead of condemning people, let's try to understand them. Let's try to figure out why they do what they do. That's a lot more profitable and intriguing than criticism; and it breeds sympathy, tolerance and kindness. Carnegie (1982, p. 17)

Introduction

Because stress causes people to be more emotional (see Chapter 22), and even lose control of emotions, managing emotions is a key part of managing stress (whether in one's self or others). Suppressing those emotions as a way of controlling them is absolutely not the answer since, ultimately, stress is exacerbated. Neither is letting them all go in an outburst. Often, this doesn't give real relief from stress and it tends to alienate or exhaust others.

This chapter is about managing personal emotions in a sustainable and positive way and about getting the best out of others by managing emotional interactions. This will help to create synergistic, productive (and happy!) relationships. The chapter will discuss three key elements of managing emotions, as well as bringing out the best in people and dealing with difficult people.

Three Key Elements of Emotions Management

Over the past 30 or 40 years, psychologists have been investigating the idea that there are many aspects to intelligence, rather than just one single measure: the IQ. One major work in this area was Harold Gardner's *Frames of Mind: The Theory of Multiple Intelligences*, written in 1983. In the book, he proposes that there is a range of intelligences including linguistic, musical, bodily kinaesthetic, spatial, logical-mathematical, interpersonal, and intrapersonal. Speaking to the American Educational Research Association in 2003, Gardner said that since 1983, he has expanded his theory to include naturalist intelligence and a possible existential intelligence (the intelligence of big questions). Of all these "intelligences," the greatest popular interest has been generated by the inter- and intrapersonal intelligences, more commonly known now as emotional intelligence or EQ.

EQ is the ability to understand and motivate self and others, and create the conditions for others to thrive and work well together (to be a leader). Three key elements of EQ to be discussed in this chapter are:

1. *Self-awareness* – recognizing negative and positive emotions and behaviors

2. *Self-control* – choosing a response instead of simply being reactive; living a chosen path according to personal values
3. *Understanding others' emotions* and helping them to be positive.

SELF-AWARENESS

Chapter 22 discussed self-awareness in terms of checking for signs and symptoms of stress. As part of that process, it is important to add questions about feelings and the reasons why one might be feeling them – particularly negative feelings. Throughout the course of a day, one might feel disheartened, angry, guilty, resentful, pensive, and much more, and stress can intensify those feelings. No matter how people might try to hide them, emotions do leak out and they affect performance and sometimes health.

There is nothing complex about becoming self-aware. It is a habit that can be practiced and developed so that it becomes an automatic part of one's existence. For some people it comes naturally, but others will need consciously to ask themselves questions on a regular basis until it becomes a natural habit to do so. These questions could include:

What am I feeling right now?

What have I been feeling lately?

Why am I feeling this?

How can I improve my mood, or maintain a good mood?

What is going right or wrong in my relationships?

What new action could I take, or what habit could I develop, to feel more positive emotions?

Could I choose to feel something different?

SELF-CONTROL

The final question above is, in some ways, the most important, because it is about the power to choose one's reaction, response, and feelings in any given situation. And that gives people the power to make themselves happy, positive, and solution-oriented, no matter what. Consider what Viktor Frankl, author of *Man's Search for Meaning* (1959) wrote about his experiences in Nazi concentration camps:

> *everything can be taken from a man but one thing: the last of human freedoms – to choose one's attitude in any given set of circumstances.*

Arguably, there couldn't be a worse set of circumstances and the book is an inspiration for those who feel victims of circumstance without a choice about how they feel.

Choosing a positive response when a negative one would be more automatic is an empowering habit, to be practiced alongside self-awareness. The following questions might help:

- Could I "reframe" this issue? Could it be a "challenge" or "opportunity" instead of a "problem" or "disaster"?
- Could I let go of this negative emotion (anger, sadness, resentment, guilt)?
- If not now, could I let go of it in the future? When?
- What would it feel like to let go of the negative emotion?
- What positive emotion could replace it (forgiveness, hope, peace, determination)?
- Then, imagine feeling this new positive emotion until it becomes easier and easier actually to feel it. If this seems impossible, it is probably necessary to go back to the first question.

Self-control involves other skills and habits, too. It is about having integrity, being trustworthy, and truly living one's values. For example, someone might value health, but then fail to look after their health. This indicates that either they value other things more than health, or they lack the self-discipline to live what they value. The implication here is that it is important to be clear about values, personal convictions, and the qualities one wants to embody. This will entail spending time thinking about them and how they will practically be lived. Appendix 26.1 is a worksheet that will help in the thinking process of naming one's values. In the authors' experience, workshop delegates say that spending time on this exercise is one of the best things they ever did for themselves. It pays dividends in the following ways:

- Helps to direct attitude and behavior when feeling negative or lost
- Helps to direct attitude and behavior when dealing with difficult people
- Helps to keep one's overall aim in mind, and assess whether current behavior or situation is leading there
- Helps in difficult decision making
- Increases self-esteem and confidence.

Finally, self-control involves anger management. For some people, emotional outbursts happen quite regularly, whether in the form of tears or shouting. It is exceptionally difficult to stop these outbursts after they begin, because of the physiology of the brain when it is stressed (see Chapter 22). A better way to control these strong expressions of emotions is to examine underlying expectations and ability to accept the world the way it is. Those people who lack acceptance have a greater tendency to cry, scream, or have tantrums when things do not go their way. Practicing acceptance is an important pillar of self-control. Acceptance does not mean never trying to change anything, or accepting unhappiness or injustice unquestioningly. It means letting go of what we cannot change or influence, in order to gain inner peace. Not a bad trade, really.

UNDERSTANDING AND MANAGING OTHERS' EMOTIONS

Handling, guiding, motivating, and leading others (major factors in EQ) are key determinants of whether someone will be stressed, and also whether they will be successful (Goleman, 1999). People have different skill sets for this: some very limited and some, seemingly, with charismatic power. Everyone, though, can improve relationship and communication skills. Again, there is nothing particularly complicated about it. The simple steps are:

1. Notice how others may be perceiving you and seek feedback
2. Decide on the EQ skill to be improved, to achieve the results you want
3. Focus on that skill or habit daily.

A good example of how these steps can work is found in Figure 24.1.

Increasing EQ will help to decrease stress because of the increased ease of communication, less conflict, and more comfortable feelings around people. It

George W. is a middle manager for an IT company in Hampshire. He was having trouble meeting time targets and felt his team was not performing to its full potential. He was becoming increasingly frustrated and stressed trying to motivate them and wondered if they needed more training – or replacing! He could not work out why no one wanted to speak in team meetings, that no one seemed to have any innovative thoughts. Here is how he went through the above steps:

1. **First, he asked himself how he was perceived by his team. Some intuition helps here, and George's first thoughts were that perhaps his manner was off-putting. Perhaps he was too loud, sounded too aggressive or authoritarian, or talked too much. But he felt unsure about what the reason might be, so he sought feedback from a few close colleagues (one was a team member) on how he was perceived by others in the business. The feedback was (from the honest, brave person) that he did talk rather a lot, never really listening to people's answers, and perhaps people gave up trying to be heard.**
2. **George realized that listening was the key skill for him to work on, along with patience that allowed people more time to formulate answers or overcome shyness.**
3. **He began to focus on listening more in every conversation he had and started trying to calculate the percentage of a conversation for which he had been speaking and trying to keep it in proportion to the number of people present. He developed the body language of a good listener: eye contact, head sometimes cocked to one side, nodding, smiling, saying "hmmm," and pausing to encourage more input from others. Above all, he reminded himself daily of what he was learning by listening rather than speaking so much and of what he had to gain from letting his team do the talking. He even put an affirmation by his bathroom mirror that said: "I learn by listening." Fairly quickly, he didn't consciously have to think about it quite so much – it became part of his skill set.**

Figure 24.1 **An example of the benefits of developing relationship skills**

will increase success because it brings out the best in people and motivates them toward desired goals. It may be helpful to the reader to discuss more fully these two points:

- Bringing out the best in people
- Dealing well with difficult people.

Bringing Out the Best in People

Given the right emotional climate, people tend to work to their full potential. This ultimately helps everyone to be less stressed and more successful.

To bring out the best in someone, it is imperative to know something of the person, understand what motivates him, what she is passionate about and what goals he has. Many managers make the mistake of thinking that everyone is motivated the same way they are. Another common managerial failing is treating people like children and not exploring the myriad of things that might get people truly excited about their work. Yes, it takes longer in the short term to find out what makes a person tick and motivate him/her accordingly, than to use a dictatorial style. However, it probably takes less time in the long run and almost certainly produces better, more creative results.

The following list of skills would be useful for anyone trying to create a positive emotional climate in which teams thrive:

- Awareness of how people perceive you and each other
- Listening well
- Awareness of body language
- Regularly seeking feedback
- Having a clearly defined mission that is understood by all
- Having a vision that people identify with
- Having understanding and empathy
- Powerfully motivating one's self and others
- Giving recognition and appreciation
- Ensuring everyone feels a benefit
- Ensuring everyone is developed
- Leading by example
- Creating an environment in which:
  - people trust
  - people can say what they feel
  - it is OK to take risks (depending on the job function)
  - it is OK to ask for help
  - collaboration is encouraged.

It would be helpful to look at the list and think about which of these skills were used in a recent meeting and which could be practiced more. Bear in mind that anyone can use these skills. They do not require the title "manager" or "director."

A final point to make is that some people have a hard time bringing out the best in others because of their own lack of self-esteem. They may have a need to make others look worse in order to look and feel better. It is part of growth and maturity to realize that by helping others to be at their best, one can also shine and get desirable results. Managers would do well to remember what William James (1842–1910), the psychologist and philosopher, said about motivation:

> *The deepest principle in human nature is the craving to be appreciated.*

Dale Carnegie, in his book *How to Win Friends and Influence People* (1982, p. 239) said:

> *Be liberal with your encouragement ... let the other person know that you have faith in his ability to do it, that he has an undeveloped flair for it – and he will practice until the dawn comes in the window in order to excel.*

Dealing with Difficult People

This is a part of life everyone has to face, but most people could improve their ability to deal with those who might potentially drain energy and cause stress. There are a number of classic types of difficult people, bearing in mind that "difficult" is about perception and that people always have a reason for behaving as they do – even if it might be difficult to understand or agree with. Figure 24.2 is a list of types of difficult people that has emerged over the years from workshop delegates.

Aggressors	**Dishonest/false**
Complainers/cynics/negative people	**Awkward/stubborn**
Clams (those who do not give much information about what they think or how they feel)	**Clowns** **Shirkers/lazy** **Attention seekers**
Opinionated	**Drama queens**
Immature	**Poor me/pathetic**
Emotionally barren	**Saboteurs**
Don't seem to care/no passion	**Don't like change**
Insecure	**Perfectionists**

Figure 24.2 **Types of difficult people**

The discussions about how to handle these sorts of people (or people we perceive to be like something on the list above) are always interesting, because in a room full of calm people, the best and most logical methods for dealing with even the worst behaviors emerge easily. And the number one piece of advice for dealing with difficult people is always:

REMAIN CALM

This is because, when one is calm, accessing the clever, creative, reasonable part of the brain (the cortex) is much easier. If the emotional brain (the amyg-

Remain calm, or find a way to take a short break in order to calm down
Adapt behavior
Listen
Seek to understand the person
Find a way in to their way of thinking
Find common ground
Sympathize/empathize
Mirror body language, but not if aggressive
Make the person feel heard and valued
Emphasize positive traits or behaviors – praise something about the person
Stay solution-focused
Summarize and get agreement for future actions and behavior
Keep it specific and in the present – don't dredge up old arguments except to use specific examples
Don't personalize – talk about what you observe of someone's behavior, not what kind of person he/she is
Keep a perspective
Keep a sense of humour

Figure 24.3 **Suggestions for dealing with difficult people**

dala) is controlling things, conversation ends up as a shouting match, a seething trade of insults, or a negative silence.

One of the most important tips above after "remain calm" is "seek to understand the person." Working out why someone is behaving in a certain way is half the battle. For instance, if someone is behaving aggressively, it may be because of a perception of a threat, a need to feel in control, a habitual defensiveness due to past experience, or an accumulation of life stresses. Assessing the cause will allow either reassurance that there is no threat, giving the person a way to feel in control, inviting the person to view the situation on its own merit, or offering help for external stresses. Attempting to understand a difficult person will make him/her feel heard and valued, another fundamental aspect of improving communication. Once someone feels heard and understood, then the next critical steps can be taken, which are:

- Begin to focus on solutions
- Agree on future steps and desired outcome.

A fuller list of suggestions for dealing with difficult people can be found in Figure 24.3.

Summary

Managing emotions is easily the subject of a book on its own, but this chapter has attempted to cover the key points in order to manage stress more effectively. The three important aspects of managing emotions – self-awareness, self-control, and understanding others' emotions – were discussed in turn, and two significant aspects of managing others' emotions were covered: bringing out the best in people; and dealing with difficult people.

Self-awareness involves being aware of one's own emotions and how they are leading to behaviors. Making a habit of asking one's self for emotional feedback on a daily basis will develop self-awareness.

Self-control has a number of aspects, including honesty, integrity, and choosing one's reaction and attitude. It is about living proactively, guided by goals and values. That way, no matter what happens in life, the values and ultimate goals remain. The alternative is a reactive life that has no real fixed principles, where happiness is a result of external circumstance rather than inner peace and sense of direction. The benefits of living one's values are increased self-confidence and self-esteem, help with difficult decision making, and with deciding how to behave and respond in challenging circumstances. Self-control is also about developing an acceptance of the world the way it is, so that anger and disappointment can be handled maturely.

Understanding and managing others' emotions is something that most people develop with age and experience, but also something that can be deliberately learned in order to better manage stress and be more successful. The three simple steps to take in order to improve this aspect of managing emotions are:

1. Notice how others may be perceiving you, and seek feedback
2. Decide how you would like the communication or relationship to improve, and decide what skill could be developed to achieve the results you want
3. Focus on that skill or habit daily.

This is not rocket science, but it takes persistence and focus to make new ways of behaving and thinking become a natural habit.

Utilizing skills to bring out the best in people is also not rocket science, but can always do with practice. Realizing that everyone is motivated differently is the first step. Then getting to know the person and using that information for motivation produces better, more creative results. A list of skills to consider in order to bring out the best in people can be found in this chapter.

Discussions about dealing with difficult people nearly always keep peoples' attention, because it is a part of everyone's life. The crucial points to remember are:

- ▶ Remain calm
- ▶ Seek to understand the reasons for behaviors (ask questions and listen well)
- ▶ Make the person feel heard, and valued
- ▶ Focus on solutions to the current situations
- ▶ Seek agreement on future steps.

A more comprehensive list of tips can be found in this chapter. A final quote to think about, taken from *Working with Emotional Intelligence* (Goleman, 1999), is this:

> *In short, out-of-control emotions can make smart people stupid. As Doug Lennick, an executive vice-president at American Express Financial Advisors, put it to me, "The aptitudes you need to succeed start with intellectual horsepower – but people need emotional competence, too, to get the full potential of their talents.*

25 Building Resilience

Introduction

Developing resilience to pressure is a life skill that everyone needs. Everyone has pressure; pressure that will almost certainly increase greatly from time to time in life. Everyone has frustration, sadness, anger, fear, grief, or pain that needs to be dealt with in order to bounce back to full capacity, energy, and glory. This chapter will define resilience for the purpose of discussion (bearing in mind that it might mean different things to different people), set out some simple steps for building resilience, and suggest a wide range of practical actions that can be used by even the busiest and most pressured individuals.

Steps to Resilience

Resilience is the ability to restore energy and equilibrium after setbacks, disappointments, and pressures. It is absolutely not the ability to bury frustration, hurt or sadness, or to be stoic and impervious to feelings. But neither is it dwelling on negative feelings, thereby creating a self-perpetuating cycle of stress. Resilience is a process that can be practiced and strengthened. It has a series of steps that can become an automatic way of thinking and doing. These steps could be described as follows (to be discussed in turn below):

1. Recognizing a lack of balance (either hypo-stress or hyper-stress)
2. Considering the reasons for this lack of balance
3. Making a conscious decision about how to restore balance and vitality
4. Getting on and doing it
5. Taking that learning process on life's journey for future reference; commonly known as growing wiser.

STEP 1 RECOGNIZING A LACK OF BALANCE

Stress can be viewed as a lack of balance between pressure and coping resources. Sometimes, recognizing it is obvious and easy, for instance after bereavement, redundancy, financial loss, meeting a big deadline, or taking exams.

At other times there can be an almost complete lack of awareness of stress symptoms. This can be because they have built up gradually and the individual has grown accustomed to these symptoms, perceiving them as "normal." Chapter 22 discusses the effects of stress, and also suggests a regular "check-in" process to assess whether one is in "eu-stress" or not. Mentally weighing

Before I had a breakdown, I never used to even consider whether I was OK or not, or how I was coping. "I'm a capable person, and I can handle anything" I guess I was thinking. Now I do a whole range of things to stay in balance: I take time for myself, exercise, and have a quiet time every day. But the most important change I have made is that I don't just assume I am going to cope with all the pressure. I have a dialogue with myself on a regular basis, at least every week, and I'm honest with my answers. I don't want to go back to where I was. Project manager in financial services sector

Figure 25.1 **Example of recognizing a lack of balance**

up life's pressures and personal feelings against current coping resources will bring positive mental and physical health benefits. Even when in eu-stress, this process is helpful, because it identifies what is going right, and these behaviors and patterns can be continued and strengthened. Examples of recognizing a lack of balance, and recognizing when things are right, are given in Figures 25.1 and 25.2.

There is a story about an international rugby team, and a new way of thinking about playing and winning that helped to turn their poor fortunes at the time. When a new coach took over, he noticed that when the team lost, they spent a lot of time going over what had gone wrong, but when they won, they did not spend much time reviewing what they had done right in order to win! They just went straight to the bar to celebrate. So one change this coach made was to bring the team together to analyse their formulas for success. This helped the team to have a more positive focus when playing: to think about doing this which will help us win, rather than think about not doing that, which might lead to a loss.

Stephen Covey, in his bestseller *The 7 Habits of Highly Effective People* reminds readers that "We go toward what we focus on", and clearly the rugby coach understood that. In order to make a behavior change, it is far easier to work toward the desired behavior (articulated and visualized) than to refrain from the unwanted behavior. This method had a significant positive effect on the rugby team's results and is one that can build resilience for everyone. It is effective not only for things like smoking cessation, dieting, and limiting behaviors such as perfectionism or workaholism, but when pressure levels are high, or a setback has been suffered, it will bring focus, energy, and a path back to success and feeling in control.

Figure 25.2 **Example of recognizing when things are right**

STEP 2 CONSIDERING THE REASONS FOR LACK OF BALANCE

As in step 1, the reasons for this may be obvious. It may be a life event, or unfortunate circumstance, in which case one could move straight to step 3. If the reasons are not obvious, or seem obvious but are displaying a pattern, the real source of the stress or imbalance needs examining. The following questions might help in this process:

- Am I taking on too much, trying to "do it all"?
- Am I expecting perfection from myself?
- Am I afraid of failure?
- Am I constantly keeping busy to avoid the really important work?
- Am I blaming others?
- Do I waste energy worrying?
- Do I say to myself, "I must do this or that"?
- Do I rarely ask for help?
- Do I "catastrophize" situations, that is, perceive them as worse than they are?
- Why?

The example in Figure 25.3 outlines the value of going through this self-examination and questioning process.

> Sally was a successful PR manager, but felt under too much pressure and was aggrieved because she felt a lack of support from her manager. This was the supposedly obvious reason for feeling stressed – it was someone else's lack of action and support causing excessive pressure. Going through these questions, Sally answered yes to expecting perfection from herself, fear of failure, but even more importantly for her, to rarely asking for help.
>
> Through the dialogue that ensued, it emerged that Sally had had three unsupportive bosses in a row. This was certainly a pattern and Sally discovered that it was probably more to do with her own lack of assertive communication about what she needed and wanted from her managers, than a fault of theirs. It took some preparation, but Sally was able to begin communicating her needs better. Just being able to say this to her manager made her feel less stressed and she reported that, to a great extent, the communication worked. She felt more supported and learned to ask her own team for more help, too.

Figure 25.3 **How to uncover a lack of balance**

STEP 3 CONSCIOUSLY DECIDING HOW TO RESTORE BALANCE AND VITALITY

This third step is arguably the most important in the process, because it is about building solutions. Figuring out the best route to take to restore balance may be easy and obvious, or might be a trial and error process. Either way, it is about matching up needs with resources or new habits. A key ingredient is that people take personal responsibility for their choices and results, no matter what personal circumstances there may be. It is too easy to say:

- I can't help it: I am a born worrier, short-tempered, perfectionist, and so on
- I would take better care of myself, but I don't have time
- Because of this awful occurrence, I cannot be happy
- It's not my fault. Somebody else should do something.

However, every excuse in the book won't bring happiness or peace. It may be a slow process to restore energy and balance, but getting on the journey is the important part; and every journey begins with the first step. Step 4 outlines a wide range of suggestions that will reduce stress and increase resilience and vitality.

STEP 4 ACTUALLY DOING IT

Step 4 is about actually taking that first step to self-help, and developing rituals and routines that enable and maintain eu-stress. Ideas and suggestions for how to stay in balance are helpful, but there will be no change in balance or vitality levels unless the behaviors are practiced and maintained. The barriers to this are discussed in detail in Chapter 26, because even the best routines and discipline sometimes falter and need bolstering again.

The following are two lists of ideas and health habits for increasing vitality and resilience to pressure. The first list, Instant rebound, is for restoring energy in just a minute or two in those moments of feeling overwhelmed, frazzled, negative, or just flat. The second, Sustained vitality, lists those things that need to be sustained over time to bring energy and well-being.

Instant rebound

- Number one: have a break! But not a Kitkat.
- Take a moment to assess what you most need right now. Do you need a stretch, to move around, fuel, hydration, a mental pause, collaboration, or attitude adjustment? Read on ...
- If you need fuel, eat fruit, nuts, seeds, or a high carbohydrate snack with no refined sugar. Sugar will give a short-term energy high followed by a low.
- Have a stretch. Stretch your arms up, roll your shoulders, stretch your back. Try *Office Yoga* by Darrin Zeer or *Office Yoga: At-your-desk exercises* by Diana Fairechild (see Chapter 29 for further information).
- Take a 60-second walk. Up and down stairs is good. Outside is even better.
- Have a drink of cold water
- Have a herbal tea with lemon or other citrus/tangy fruit, ginger or ginseng.
- *60-second relaxation:*
  — Check posture is upright, shoulders back and down, head in line with spine, feet flat on floor, back supported by the chair, hands ideally in lap

— Close your eyes
— Be aware of your breathing and let your stomach rise and fall with each cycle
— Mentally check for areas of muscular tension
— Imagine letting go of that tension
— Visualize a relaxing scene
— Say a trigger word to yourself on each exhalation, like "calm" or "relax"
— Enjoy this feeling for a whole minute, or more
— Use your trigger word later for further relaxation.

- *60-second supercharge:*
  — Check posture as above
  — Close your eyes
  — Be aware of your breathing, and let your stomach rise and fall with each cycle
  — Visualize an energizing moment in your life (sailing, skiing, winning an award)
  — Rerun the scene, and the feelings associated with it
  — Say a trigger word to yourself on each exhalation that will help you to recall these images and feelings
  — Enjoy this feeling for a whole minute, or more
  — Use your trigger word later for an even faster energy boost.
- *Aromatherapy break*
  — Put 5–8 drops of your chosen essential oil in a container of hot water
  — Enjoy the break and savor the scent. Just don't mistake it for herbal tea.
- Phone a friend. Say it is a two-minute call to get some energy, and to give that person a positive message, too.
- Send a loving text to your partner, child, or a friend.
- Ask for help. Brainstorm who could help you and phone that person right now.
- Call your team together to brainstorm with you. Have a 5–10 minute pow-wow. Openness brings energy.
- Consider: What is the best use of my time right now? Only spend your time on the very best use of it at any time. Don't spend it on what would be a "good" or "OK" use.
- And reconnect to your overall purpose(s). Is what you are doing now getting you there in some way?
- Have a laugh. Try: www.laughlab.co.uk.
- Enjoy five minutes of pleasure reading.
- Slip on some headphones and listen to five minutes of uplifting music.
- Consider what your feelings are right at this moment. Are you sad, angry, resentful, afraid, stressed? If it is a negative emotion, consider letting go

of it, and replacing it with a positive one. Could you be forgiving, grateful, peaceful, sympathetic, brave, passionate, committed?

- Read your affirmations. If you don't have any, write one! See Chapter 23.
- Think about your impact on others right now. How would you like to impact on them? Connection to others brings energy.
- Right now, do you have more optimistic or more pessimistic thoughts in your head? Do you need to change the balance?
- Is the pressure you feel external or internal? Assess your expectations of yourself and ask if you are expecting something superhuman or unachievable.
- Are you distracted by something? Either deal with it right now to get it out of your head, or write it on a list somewhere and mentally put it aside.
- Set a time limit on the task you are working on if it is an unpleasant one. Promise yourself to work on it for x number of minutes, with a reward at the end. No, still not chocolate, but some kind of enjoyable break.

Sustaining vitality

These are some tried and true paths to vitality that are not necessarily instant. They are habits and ways of living life that will help to build and sustain energy. Everyone needs to find and develop individual paths to vitality, balance, and success.

First, the basics: We are all human, and there's no getting around these.

- Do *aerobic* (continuous, rhythmic) *exercise* such as walking, jogging, cycling, or swimming for 30 minutes, three times per week. See recommended reading list for more on exercise.
- Also *develop strength, flexibility, and balance* with activities such as weight training, martial arts, yoga, dancing, or gardening. Consult your physician before beginning any exercise program, particularly if you have not exercised for some time.
- Eat a diet with a high percentage of *complex carbohydrates:* 50–60% of your intake. The rest of your intake should comprise 25–30% fat (predominantly healthy monounsaturates) and 10–20% protein. Eat six to eight times per day, staying within your daily calorie limit. For more on diet and nutrition, see Chapter 29.
- Get good quality *sleep.* This means waking up feeling like you have had enough.
- Find a time to *relax* each day, even if for only 10 minutes.
- Drink two litres of *water* each day.
- *Reduce caffeine* intake to four cups per day, and none after 5 pm.

Don't think of these things as a life sentence. Think of them as nurturing yourself during your one and only life.

Next, a range of habits to consider:

- — *Connect* daily or weekly *to your values* so that you remember what you are doing on this planet. Otherwise, life can be just one big treadmill.
- — Think each day about *proactive activity*. Be clear about your goals, and spend your time moving toward them. Being reactive is not energizing!
- — *Every "yes" is a "no" to something else.* Think about what you are saying "yes" to.
- — *Work no more than 50 hours per week.* After that, your productivity diminishes exponentially. At more than 55 hours per week, your health, your child's development, and your special relationship(s) are all at risk.
- — *Develop your support network.* This means personal and professional support and will include family, friends, colleagues, mentors, coaches, personal trainers, massage therapists, and others. This takes time and energy, yes, but the rewards are great. Make sacred time with your family. Make the effort to connect with your friends regularly. Ask colleagues to collaborate. Ask someone you respect to mentor you. These things boost mental, emotional, and spiritual energy.
- — *Give others praise and recognition.* Just try it and see what happens. If others are not displaying some characteristic that you want to encourage, praise them for it anyway: "Thanks John, it's really helpful when you show …". They'll remember this and do more next time.
- — Consider it a medical prescription to *LAUGH* daily. In all our busyness, we can forget to see the funny side of life and we don't feel we have time to swap jokes or watch a comedy video. But laughing raises seratonin levels (seratonin is a neurotransmitter that stabilizes mood and reduces depression) and strengthens the immune system (really!). It's also contagious, and enhances the productivity of yourself and those around you.
- — *Recreate.* Think of the origin of the word recreation and do some. The world is your oyster.
- — Develop the habit of always arriving *10 minutes early for appointments.* Then use the time in some valuable way – make a phone call, read, review the objectives for the meeting, talk to the receptionist and gather some valuable information, or just relax!
- — Never schedule meetings back to back.
- — Do some regular thinking about where you are blocked, or not progressing as you would like. Then tap into that support network and *get some help to move forward.*
- — *If not now, when?*
- — Develop an awareness of what you are feeling by checking in with your-

self, and asking if any *attitude adjustments* are necessary. Emotions are contagious, positive or negative.

— If a relationship isn't working for you, how could you behave, or what could you say to try to make it better? You have nothing to lose but another drain on your energy.

— *Be aware of people who drain your energy* and try to minimize their impact on you, or give them feedback if you are in a position to do so.

— *Be aware of people who energize you* and spend more time with them!

— Take *one day per month to blitz* the small stuff that is distracting you.

— Improve your *living and working environments* so that you feel good in them.

— *Take a mental break every 60–90 minutes.* This is in line with your natural energy rhythms, and it will increase your productivity and creativity.

The reader might notice that the ideas in these two lists in step 4 are not all to do with physical energy. While physical energy is certainly important in developing resilience, there are other types of energy that need to be renewed daily, too, and they are mental, emotional, and spiritual. It may be helpful to describe and discuss these four energies for a better understanding of how to increase them. Again, these descriptions are meant for clarification and discussion, and are not meant to be absolutely definitive.

Physical energy:
Stamina, strength, flexibility, suppleness and *speed.* It is positively embodied as a relaxed bodily readiness, quickness, lightness, feelings of physical confidence and wellness – of vitality. This is the one we tend to understand the best, but fail to do the things we know would increase it. It is best maintained by uncompromising rituals that practice "the basics" of sustaining vitality listed above.

Mental energy:
Thinking, pondering, learning, alertness, analysis, creativity combined with mental focus and concentration, logical process combined with intuition. It is embodied as a feeling of progress, "flow," challenge, certainty, even "eureka!" It requires the skills of flexible thinking, moving between external and internal focus, between broad and narrow perspective, and a "realistic optimism." Practicing these skills and habits is easier under the following conditions:

1. Clear goals and objectives
2. Discipline over where our time is spent, and the ability to say "no"
3. Regular "time out" to regain perspective and rest the brain.

Emotional energy:
Positive relationships, personal connection, teamwork, partnership, collaboration. It is embodied as fulfilment, satisfaction, happiness, synergy, and also peace, warmth, feeling valued, liked and loved. It is enhanced by:

1. Self-awareness, self-confidence, and self-control
2. Empathy and seeking to understand others
3. Ensuring others feel valued and developed
4. The ability to motivate and influence others
5. Conscientiousness.

Spiritual energy:
Inspiration, aspiration, enthusiasm, future vision and possibility, optimism, hope and joy, meaning to life. It is embodied in many different ways for different people; as a god or higher purpose in the universe, or a higher purpose of a life, or as unswerving principles, truths, or values about how to live one's life. As with emotional energy, it is associated with peace and love. Capturing spiritual energy is also highly individual, but some conduits may be:

1. Considering perspective on life and what gives happiness
2. Understanding today in the context of a wider life and time-line
3. Knowing one's values
4. Relaxation, meditation, prayer, and time out in nature
5. The ability to be playful and laugh.

Energy drainers
One final point to make before moving on to Step 5 is that some common coping strategies which appear to give quick relief, are actually negative and tend to cause a vicious spiral of stress. They include:

- Caffeine
- Alcohol
- Procrastination
- Saying "I'll get back to you"
- Shouting, or using aggression or fear to get things done
- Trying to do everything at warp speed
- Total task-focus without considering the human element.

STEP 5 GROWING WISDOM

The final step in the process of building resilience is learning from experience and becoming wiser. Much of what people call "wisdom" is about:

- Understanding one's own strengths and weaknesses
- Playing to strengths
- Quietly but persistently working on weaknesses
- Seeing the bigger picture of life and working out what is important
- A realization of one's spiritual nature. This does not necessarily mean organized religion, but can be a practice of meditation, seeking peace, spending time in nature, understanding how the world is interconnected, and feeling thankful

- Learning from experience that one can overcome setbacks and cope with tremendous pressures
- Learning to listen: to others and to one's own heart.

Acceptance

Ultimately, life can feel overwhelming, or unfair, even if resilience is high. When faced with situations or people that are not going to change, having acceptance is the ultimate way to have resilience. Acceptance does not mean a completely fatalistic attitude, never trying to work toward something better. It does mean making the best of what one has and being happy anyway, despite the circumstances of life.

Acceptance can be strengthened by learning to recognize negative attitudes and emotions, then consciously letting go of them as often and as quickly as possible. Letting go of anger, fear, resentment, worry, dislike, or hate is a critical aspect of resilience, and will enhance happiness, health, and inner peace.

Summary

Building resilience – the ability to restore energy and equilibrium after setbacks, disappointments, and pressures – is essential for long-term stress reduction. To build resilience:

- Learn to recognize a lack of balance
  To improve this:
  — practice having conversations with one's self about state of emotions, health, and happiness
  — use self-assessment of whether one has an optimum level of stress (see Chapters 3 and 22).
- Consider the reasons for this lack of balance
  To improve this:
  — Be honest about the "real" issues one might have
  — Consider personality traits that may exacerbate stress (see Chapters 3 and 24)
  — Consider personal perception of events and how others might see them.
- Make a conscious decision about how to restore balance and vitality
  To work on this:
  — Write an action plan. There are so many paths to destressing: each person has to find the range of coping strategies that will fit with individual schedules and preferences, and that are sustainable
- Get on and do it
  To work on this:
  — Schedule things in a diary, put reminders up by the desk, refrigerator, bathroom mirror, as a screen saver

- — Persist and recommit every time it is needed. Everyone benefits from this
- — Ensure that all four "energies" are restored every day.

- ▶ Grow personal wisdom
  - — Make a habit of seeing the bigger picture of life and stay focused on what is really important
  - — Learn to accept that some aspects of life are negative and will probably not change.

26 Committing to Action

Introduction

If all the New Year's resolutions and all the promises made for better health habits were kept, the world would be a very healthy, stress-free place. Unfortunately, there is a human tendency to slip into quite unhealthy habits when it comes to exercise, diet (including caffeine, alcohol, and nicotine), sleep, proper relaxation, attitude adjustment, and acceptance (see Chapter 25).

Why develop a lifestyle that will only add to fatigue and stress? It is partly because of the pleasure associated with certain unhealthy habits (the high of caffeine, the buzz of alcohol, the fun to be had when staying up very late), and partly because man is programmed to conserve energy and seek out the tastes of sweet and fat. Once upon a time these things helped man survive. Now, because of their non-stop availability, they can be detrimental to health.

The fight or flight response (see Chapters 3 and 22) also adds to fatigue and stress levels. It is very useful to man when he is in physical danger, just as much now as in the Stone Age. However, in the work environment, the threats are usually non-physical (unless working in professions like the military or police) and the fight or flight response is more detrimental than helpful.

In the authors' experience, committing to taking care of oneself and reducing stress become top priority (at least for a time) when there is a serious and immediate threat to health, for instance a heart attack scare or a nervous breakdown. Without that spur, the commitment will usually come from an understanding of the connection between habits and health and then the willpower to maintain those proactive habits. Sometimes these good intentions are lasting, and sometimes they are not.

This chapter will examine the most common reasons and excuses for not taking action to reduce stress or increase well-being and vitality. It will then use two exercises (examining values and creating a plan) to demonstrate the principal steps in taking action. They can just as easily be applied to projects and goals as to well-being and vitality.

Excuses for not Taking Action

> *Regret for the things we did can be tempered by time; it is regret for the things we did not do that is inconsolable.* Anon

"I don't have time" is the number one, most used excuse heard by the authors in all their years of experience. However, the way people spend their time is their own choice. In truth, people always have time for what is truly important to them. It is illogical to say that family and health are important, when all available time is spent at the office. For some people, it might need considerable rearranging in order to make time for health and relaxation. However, they should not pretend that it is impossible, in order to make themselves feel better about not doing those things.

"I will do it when ..." is a variation on the "I don't have time" excuse. A common example of this is "It's a particularly busy time. I will have more time in a few months (after this project, or whatever) to look after myself." The problem is that things never really slow down. Health, relaxation, happiness, and fun can be delayed endlessly, but the body still keeps score. People need balance all the time – more so when life gets busy.

"I can't change" is the next most-used excuse. People will say they have tried to give up smoking but cannot; tried exercise but did not like it; they just do not like vegetables (except French fries); they cannot sit still; cannot relax; have never slept well; were born with a fiery temper; and so on. However, these excuses all boil down to either "I won't try very hard to change," or "I truly do not believe that I have the power to change."

To aid the change process, it is useful to try and work out the perceived benefits from not changing. For instance, by not dieting, there is no "failure" to lose weight. By continuing to smoke, one can chat with the smokers at breaktimes at work.

Another key to changing is understanding that one does have control over behavior and attitude (see Chapter 25). This can help to assuage the frustration that can come from failure. Focusing on the great benefits can encourage another try.

> *Our biggest fear is not that we are inadequate, but that we are powerful beyond measure.* Williamson (1996)

Another excuse often heard is, "If I live in such a healthy way, I will never have any fun. I don't want a life sentence of healthy but boring." This one probably requires an attitude adjustment about what is boring and what is fun. If going to the pub to socialize with friends is the activity of choice, then working out why that is fun is important. If it is the socializing, then perhaps drinking alcohol the entire time is not so vital – even a hindrance. If feeling part of the group by smoking is what feels "fun," perhaps that could be replaced by pub games or developing a joke-telling ability to be "in." Of course, pub games and jokes will not give the same buzz as nicotine, but they do not cause emphysema either. Laughter, however, does have an immediate mood-lifting ability and other health benefits (see Chapter 25).

Living a low stress, healthy life does not mean no alcohol, no chocolate, no fatty foods, meditating and exercising every day without fail. Except for smoking, enjoying treats and alcohol in moderation is fine – and possibly beneficial. Proactive habits such as exercise and relaxation are valuable when done as little as three times per week.

Grasping at straws, some clients use the following excuse, "Even if I maintain all those healthy habits, I might still die young of some disease, or get hit by a bus tomorrow. Just last week I read about a super-fit guy who died of a heart attack at 42." It is true that no matter how one lives one's life, one might die before the bad habits seriously impact on health. However, if one does live to a ripe old age, would it not be much more fun to be functionally fit, flexible, and pain-free?

Steps to Taking Action

STEP 1 VALUES

No matter how it is diced up, the key to deciding how to live proactively for happiness and health is examining one's values. Values are the things someone would not want to live without. They might be virtues such as honesty and integrity, aspects of personality such as sense of humor and courage, or irreplaceable things like family, partner, health, or inner peace.

Appendix 26.1 is an exercise for examining and articulating one's values. Appendix 26.2 is a list of commonly held values, although it is not intended to be in any way prescriptive. Time spent defining values is not wasted and the authors have heard many comments along the lines of: "It was the best thing I ever did in my life" and "It helped me immeasurably to understand myself." Knowing one's values is the first step in living a proactive life: taking action toward goals and attitudes, rather than simply reacting to the circumstances of life.

STEP 2 ACTION PLAN

The right sort of action plan makes it many times more likely that any action will be taken. Creating a plan takes time, energy, and creativity, and many people prefer just to get on and "do". However, the likelihood is that they will run out of steam and direction after a short time, reverting to old habits and reactivity.

The "right" sort of action plan is not rocket science, however; just a few basic principles are required.

- *Specific, measurable goals.* Most people make the mistake of stating goals like "spend more time relaxing." This idea is fine, but the goal needs to be something like, "spend ten minutes every day meditating, relaxing breathing and muscles."
- *A specific series of actions to arrive at the goal,* to include real dates and times on which the actions will take place. These might be to buy a few relaxation tapes and try them out; explaining the new routine to partner or children; putting your briefcase by the door the night before to allow time for the early morning meditation.
- *Contingency plans for overcoming obstacles.* Build defences for excuses before they have a chance to take hold. This might be to work with a partner, seek instruction, or block out time in the diary.

Appendix 26.3 is a pro forma for creating an action plan. It is meant to be simple, but to challenge the reader to make a commitment. It can be adapted to work or personal goals. Appendix 26.4 is a special action plan worksheet for increasing energy and vitality.

STEP 3 MAINTAINING MOMENTUM

Having achieved a more relaxed feeling, or any other health goal, does not mean that the actions will be maintained. Inventing reminders for maintaining habits, or finding ways to grow and improve with the habits is helpful and sometimes essential. Going back to the example above where the goal was to meditate for ten minutes every day, the following might be considered:

- A screen saver that asks "Have you meditated today?"
- Meditating with your partner so that you encourage each other
- Developing "affirmations" that are a reminder of the benefits of meditation (see Chapter 23).

For some positive habits, "resetting" can be helpful. It is easy to drift into poor nutritional habits, weight gain, negative patterns in relationships or not getting enough sleep. From time to time, reassessing energy and "destressing" needs, and recommitting to action will have huge benefits.

Ultimately, because people are in complete control of how they live their lives, the only things that stop good habits are thoughts and decisions. One can make new decisions at any time, and it is never too late.

Summary

Failure to take care of one's self is quite illogical, but so common and easily done. Despite the facts that people know to be true about how to decrease stress and increase well-being, they continue to use a range of excuses for not taking any action.

This chapter examined the commonest reasons for failing to look after health, namely:

I don't have time.

I will do it when I am less busy.

I can't change.

It's no fun.

I might die tomorrow anyway.

It then looked at three steps in taking action:

- Examining values
- Creating an action plan
- Maintaining momentum.

The appendices contain worksheets that will help to take these actions.

APPENDIX 26.1 Values Worksheet

Values are the things that you would not want to live without: health, family, friends, partner, honesty, courage, freedom, inner harmony, challenge, self-respect, respect for others, and so on.

To formulate ideas about what your values are, the following questions may be helpful.

What is your definition of success?

When you come to the end of your life, what will be the three most important lessons you learnt?

1. ....

....

2. ....

....

3. ....

What qualities do you exhibit when you are at your best?

What do you value most in life?

1 ....

2 ....

3 ....

4 ....

5 ....

6 ....

7 ....

APPENDIX 26.2 Commonly Held Values

Achievement	Fast-paced work	Physical challenge
Advancement and promotion	Financial gain	Pleasure
Adventure	Freedom	Power and authority
Affection (love and caring)	Friendships	Privacy
Arts	Growth	Public service
Being around people who are open and honest	Health	Purity
Challenging problems	Helping other people	Quality of what I take part in
Change and variety	Helping society	Quality relationships
Close relationships	Honesty	Recognition (respect from others, status)
Community	Independence	Religion
Competence	Influencing others	Reputation
Competition	Inner harmony	Responsibility and accountability
Cooperation	Integrity	Security
Country	Intellectual status	Self-respect
Creativity	Involvement	Serenity
Decisiveness	Job satisfaction	Sophistication
Democracy	Job tranquillity	Stability
Ecological awareness	Knowledge	Status
Economic security	Leadership	Supervising others
Effectiveness	Location	Time freedom
Efficiency	Loyalty	Truth
Ethical practice	Market position	Wealth
Excellence	Meaningful work	Wisdom
Excitement	Merit	Work under pressure
Expertise	Money	Work with others
Fairness	Nature	Working alone
Fame	Order (tranquillity, stability, conformity)	
Family	Personal development (living up to one's fullest potential)	
Fast living		

APPENDIX 26.3 Action Plan

Name:

Date:

What is your goal?

What are the steps that will lead to this goal?
Create a timeline, finishing with when you will assess whether you have reached your goal, and what new action plan may be needed:

Action to be taken	Deadline	Completed on:
Reassessment		

How will you overcome likely obstacles?

Who will help you?

How will you overcome excuses?

APPENDIX 26.4 Personal Action Plan for Energy and Vitality

Name: ....

Date: ....

What are your current energy drainers?

1. ....
2. ....
3. ....

What are your current sources of energy?

1. ....
2. ....
3. ....

What further habits will you develop to increase/sustain your:

Physical energy

1. ....
2. ....
3. ....

Mental energy

1. ....
2. ....
3. ....

Emotional energy

1. ....
2. ....
3. ....

Spiritual energy

1. ....
2. ....
3. ....

Now plot these habits into a typical week, giving due consideration to your work schedule:

	Mon	Tues	Wed	Thurs	Friday	Sat	Sun
Pre-work							
Mid-morning							
Lunch							
Mid-afternoon							
After work							
Evening							

27 Summary of Understanding and Dealing with Stress: an Individual Perspective

Introduction

Part V has looked at stress from an individual perspective, with a view also to helping individuals to understand and help others' stress. This chapter will summarize the key themes in a question and answer format that, it is hoped, will be helpful for readers to review this section of the book, as well as to be a stand-alone source of information and guidance.

Question and Answer Review

What Happens to Individuals When They Become Stressed?

The fight or flight response is triggered, with the following obvious symptoms:

- Tense muscles (for fighting or fleeing)
- Rapid breathing (to increase oxygen intake)
- Tightness in the chest
- Pounding heart (to pump more blood to the muscles)
- Sweating
- Dry mouth
- Butterflies, stomach ache or other digestive problems
- Need to empty bladder or bowels (to be lighter!)
- A panicky feeling.

Other aspects of the initial fight or flight response that individuals may not notice are:

- Increased blood pressure
- All senses hyper-alert (but sometimes tunnel vision)
- Decreased sensitivity to pain
- Pale face

- Pupils dilated
- Blood diverted away from extremities, digestive system and brain cortex (the higher brain responsible for logic, reason and learning) to the major muscle groups (hands and feet may feel cold; dizziness or lack of concentration)
- Increase in clotting ability of blood (hence the association with heart attacks)
- Decreased ability to think logically or creatively
- Decreased energy spent on:
  - — Cell repair
  - — Immune system rejuvenation
  - — Fertility and libido (sex drive).

What Happens When Individuals Have Been Stressed for Some Time?

The body becomes worn down as internal equilibrium and health are neglected for the sake of maintaining the emergency state. There is a wide range of conditions that can result from this lack of physical and mental renewal:

Physically:

- Poor sleep (nervous system speeds up and makes sleep difficult)
- Chronic muscle tension, typically in neck, back, and shoulders
- Headache and migraine
- Skin conditions such as eczema, psoriasis, and impetigo
- Appetite loss or increase, therefore weight loss or gain
- Digestive disorders such as indigestion, ulcers, and irritable bowel syndrome
- Decrease in fertility or libido
- Chronic high blood pressure
- Poor circulation (due to blood being diverted from extremities and retained in major muscle groups)
- Numbness or tingling in extremities or different parts of the body
- Trembling or shaking
- Heart disease (due to arterial damage from high blood pressure)
- Stroke (again, due to arterial damage)
- Cancer (possibly due to reduced immune system response).

Psychologically:

- Severe anxiety
- Severe frustration
- A feeling of dread
- Feeling out of control
- Judgment and memory impairment
- Increased number of mistakes
- Decreased concentration
- Panic attacks (an extreme fight or flight response)

- Frequent crying (brain is operating out of its emotional centre, the limbic system)
- Irritability, anger, and aggression (again, the reaction from the limbic system)
- Depression (mental and physical exhaustion makes this more likely).

People do not think reasonably or logically when stressed because stress increases activity in the amygdala (the part of the brain responsible for emotions and the fight or flight response. That is why they can easily become irritable and aggressive or tearful.

HOW CAN INDIVIDUALS KNOW HOW STRESSED THEY ARE?

- It can be unhelpful to "test" whether an individual is stressed, because it is so difficult to devise a questionnaire that is completely valid for everyone.
- It is far better to increase self-awareness by asking one's self a number of questions, such as those listed in Chapter 22.
- It can also be helpful to assess what coping strategies are being used to minimize the impact of pressure, rather than focus too much on the sources of pressure and their impact – see section on coping strategies below.

WHOSE RESPONSIBILITY IS STRESS?

- Since no one can understand a person's state of mind like the individual themself, it is largely up to that individual to notice it and try to influence it positively.
- It is particularly important to develop an early-warning system for stress, so that measures can be taken, or help sought, before mental or physical illness results.

WHAT KINDS OF COPING STRATEGIES ARE THERE FOR STRESS?

- Health and well-being
- Relaxation
- Recreation and hobbies
- Relationships and emotional support; social life
- Humor and fun
- Self-awareness; knowing one's strengths and weaknesses
- Assertiveness and communication, influencing others in a positive way
- Personal organization and time management
- Mind management; attitude and outlook to develop a feeling of being in control, and of self-worth and competency.

WHAT ARE THE KEY HEALTH AND WELL-BEING HABITS?

- Regular aerobic exercise and stretching, a diet low in refined sugar and fat, adequate sleep, and regular (meaningful) relaxation
- Regular recreation and fun to give the sort of mental break that increases concentration and creativity when back at work

These things can be considered a "life sentence" of tough routines and no fun, or they can be considered nurturing one's self in the only lifetime one has.

HOW CAN ONE DEVELOP SELF-AWARENESS?

- Take short mental pauses to assess emotions and gut feelings
- Take note of personal body language and facial expression. What messages are they conveying?
- Set aside time alone for reflection or meditation
- Look for personal "blind spots" such as ambition, driving others, unrealistic goals, perfectionism, needing approval, preoccupation with appearances, or self-doubt
- Gain the courage to live personal values and speak up for beliefs. Appendix 26.1 is an exercise for understanding personal values.

HOW DOES ONE DEVELOP ASSERTIVENESS AND INFLUENCE ON OTHERS?

- Influencing others in a smart way rather than a manipulative one (such as invoking sympathy, using others' weaknesses, or being aggressive) is a positive way of moving toward goals, and reducing stress levels.
- Always seek to understand the other person's point of view. Listen well and acknowledge that view.
- Build rapport and consensus.
- State a personal preference or feelings calmly and clearly without reference to anything personal about the individual (example: "It makes me upset when you do this because this project is important to me", rather than "You make me angry when you do that and you obviously don't care about my feelings.")
- Seek to create win/win situations.
- Build self-esteem by developing a deeper understanding of personal values, beliefs, and goals (see above).

HOW CAN ONE FEEL IN CONTROL?

- Developing a feeling of being in control is a particularly important part of stress management, but one must remember that there is no absolute control over other people or events. If this is fully accepted, then the benefits of control over self can be explored.

- The feeling of "too much to do and too little time" is a result of overcommitment, lack of managing expectations, or lack of negotiating workloads and deadlines.
- When people focus on fewer things, the really important things, there is a much greater sense of achievement, direction, and control.

HOW CAN ONE FEEL COMPETENT?

- A feeling of inadequacy causing stress can potentially be remedied through the use of "affirmations."
- Affirmations are statements that bring mental focus on a particular belief, value, or goal. They take focus away from negative thought patterns, and create a new habit of more positive thought. Examples can be found in Chapter 23.

HOW CAN ONE BE POSITIVE IN THE MIDST OF STRESS?

Choosing a positive response when a negative one would be more automatic is a habit that must be practiced. The following questions might help:

- Could I "reframe" this issue? Could it be a "challenge" or "opportunity" instead of a "problem" or "disaster"?
- Could I let go of this negative emotion (anger, sadness, resentment, guilt)?
- If not now, could I let go of it in the future? When?
- What would it feel like to let go of the negative emotion?
- What positive emotion could replace it (forgiveness, hope, peace, determination)?

Then, imagine feeling this emotion until it becomes easier and easier actually to feel it. If this seems impossible, it is probably necessary to go back to the first question.

HOW CAN ONE BUILD RELATIONSHIPS AND MANAGE OTHERS' EMOTIONS?

- There is nothing very complicated about this. But it is a way of thinking and behaving that needs to be practiced. The simple steps are:
  1. Notice how others may be perceiving you and seek feedback
  2. Decide on the personal skill to be improved (listening, motivating, praising), to achieve the results you want
  3. Focus on that skill or habit daily.

- Remember that it is impossible to change other people. The only things that can be done are:
  - Change one's self so the reaction may be different
  - Find a way to make someone want to do something.
- The following is a good list of tips for dealing with "difficult" people, bearing in mind that "difficult" is a perception:
  - Remain calm, or find a way to take a short break in order to calm down
  - Adapt behavior
  - Listen
  - Seek to understand the person
  - Find a way in to their way of thinking
  - Find common ground
  - Sympathize/empathize
  - Mirror body language, but not if aggressive
  - Make the person feel heard and valued
  - Emphasize positive traits or behaviors – praise something about the person
  - Stay solution-focused
  - Summarize and get agreement for future actions and behavior
  - Keep it specific and in the present – don't dredge up old arguments except to use specific examples
  - Don't personalize – talk about what you observe of someone's behaviour, not what kind of person he/she is
  - Keep a perspective
  - Keep a sense of humor.

HOW CAN ONE BUILD RESILIENCE?

(The ability to restore energy and equilibrium after setbacks and pressures)

- Consider personal perception of events and how others might see them.
- Make a conscious decision about how to restore balance and vitality
  - Persist and recommit every time it is needed: everyone benefits from this
  - Ensure that all four "energies" are restored every day.
- Grow personal wisdom
  - Make a habit of seeing the bigger picture of life and stay focused on what is really important
  - Learn to accept that some aspects of life are negative and will probably not change.

HOW CAN ONE COMMIT TO ACTION?

- Recognize excuses for what they are. People always have time for the things that are most important to them. It may take the realization of what is truly important, such as family or health, to make a shift in behavior.

- Time spent on an action plan is seldom wasted! The elements of a good action plan are:
  - Specific, measurable goals.
  - A specific series of actions to arrive at the goal, to include real dates and times on which the actions will take place.
  - Contingency plans for overcoming obstacles and excuses.
- Two action plan worksheets can be found in Appendices 26.3 and 26.4.

PART VI

Conclusions

28 The Way Forward

This chapter sets out the authors' view of what organizations should be focusing on during the remainder of this decade in order to:

- Meet their requirements in law, which are increasingly stringent
- Minimize stress and increase employee health and well-being
- Remain competitive by having happy, creative employees and becoming an employer of choice.

The chapter is divided into four, easy-reference sections aimed at organizational leaders, HR personnel, OH personnel, and managers.

Leaders

- Begin with the end in mind: what is the long-term vision for the organization?
- Consider sustainable workloads as a part of the vision of the organization. In the short term it may seem a cost saving if one person does the job of two or three people. However, in the long term, if people have unsustainable workloads they will leave, get ill, or litigate (or all three)
- Think about the organizational culture, the emotional and creative climate that would help the business grow. Visualize what the organization would be like with the best, brightest, happiest, and most creative people: then take steps toward realizing that vision
- Consider any other reasons for employee stress. Consider the HSE Management Standards and work towards fulfilling them: there is nothing in them that organizations should not already be doing
- Commitment at the top is essential for any staff well-being program. Employees must see management (and in particular, senior management) living the culture that they are espousing. Remember that attitudes and behaviors cascade down
- Stress management initiatives do not have to be associated with high cost; there is so much that can be done on a small budget. When considering more expenditure on stress management or well-being programs, ensure that savings are measured. If there is no measure of absence, productivity, customer satisfaction, or reasons for staff turnover, then there will be no way of showing that initiatives have proved a cost benefit
- It is essential to get to the root causes of stress, rather than let HR and OH treat symptoms. Organizational leaders hold the power to make that happen.

HR Personnel

- Ensure that the organization has policies that cover organizational stress and procedures that guide managers and employees about what actions to take should it arise. It is then essential to communicate these to all staff on a regular basis
- Create communication channels between employees, OH, managers and HR. Create protocols for all interested parties having a say; this is particularly important when employees are ill, or when there are disputes
- Communicate to management that they must take responsibility for managing the stress of their teams, with HR as a support and backup
- Make information about employment law updates available and readable for management. HR needs to encourage the early use of employment law specialists, help managers to know what records to keep and remind people of policies and procedures
- Make a business case to get stress management at the top of the agenda
- Work with OH to ensure an integrated approach to employee well-being and health. If there is no in-house OH service, establish a relationship with an external provider that can meet organizational needs.

OH Personnel

- Be proactive and vocal in the organization about potential interventions for stress. Rather than just treating individually stressed employees, influence the organization as much as possible to tackle the causes of stress
- Communicate with everyone in the organization, not just the ill and injured
- Educate employees about the symptoms of stress and potential solutions, putting the emphasis on personal responsibility
- Manage absence and return to work after stress-related illness proactively
- Help HR to create a solid business case for stress management interventions.

Managers

- Do not shy away from conversations about stress. Pretending it is not there does not reduce it, and will increase the likelihood that the organization will be sued for breach of duty of care
- Create a culture where it is acceptable to say no, negotiate workloads, ways of working and deadlines. Given good management and mentoring, most people can work well and sustain pressure
- Do not let relationships break down so far they are irretrievable. This is an essential job of management
- Get training in recognizing signs of stress and mental illness, and counseling skills
- Without taking away others' personal responsibility for their own stress, help to manage the stress of others and support them where possible

- Be a good role model by managing your own stress levels and observe a good work–life balance
- Know the HSE Management Standards for stress and work towards them.

Conclusion

In the 21st century organizations and individuals are more aware than ever about stress – its causes, its effects, and ways of dealing with it. This awareness has developed through changing views about organizational and individual responsibilities – often as a result of legal or medical interventions.

There is no doubt that we all have a responsibility – to ourselves, to others around us, and to the organization in which we work – for ensuring that we do as much as possible to identify, control, and optimize stress levels.

Organizations have a legal duty, and a moral one, to manage stress positively. So much more can be done in the majority of organizations to assess risk, promote healthy habits, encourage communication about stress, increase work–life balance, manage stress-related illness, and be innovative about stress management interventions. This need not cost an unreasonable amount of money and will certainly bring cost benefits. It is surprising how few organizations measure stress, but doing so is surely a better way forward than acting out of the fear of litigation.

The one, overarching message that this book seeks to give is: "Grasp the nettle." Managing stress well may seem like an impossible task: it is not. We do not live in a perfect world, so no solution will ever be perfect. However, the more organizations attempt assessment, development of interventions, and support, the better the solutions will become.

29 Further Reading and Websites

This chapter lists those books that readers may find useful for further study of the topics covered in this book. It is categorized by topic, some of which apply to occupational health and human resources professionals and others to individuals, managers and team leaders. The recommended websites are a range of helpful business and health organizations, some of which have phone numbers. They are listed alphabetically for ease of reference.

Reading

General Stress Management – Professional/Academic

Managing Workplace Stress, a best practice blueprint, Stephen Williams and Lesley Cooper, John Wiley & Sons ISBN: 0-470-84287-3

One-Stop Guide to Managing Stress, Dr. Joe Jordan and Prof. Cary Cooper, Reed Business Information, Personnel Today Management Resources

Stress Management 1: nature, cause and effects of stress and *Stress Management 2: effectiveness of interventions,* Bob Briner, *Employee Health Bulletin,* No 18, December 2000 pp. 9–11, 12–17 (in IRS Employment Trends No 717)

Stress Management, Incomes Data Services (IDS Study 732) ISSN: 0308-9339

Strategic Stress Management – an organizational approach, Valerie J. Sutherland and Cary Cooper, Macmillan Business – now Palgrave Macmillan ISBN: 0-333-77487-6

Tackling Work-related Stress: a managers' guide to improving and maintaining employee health and well-being, Health & Safety Executive, HSE Books (HSG218) ISBN: 0-7176-2050-6

Taking the Strain: a survey of managers and workplace stress, Ruth Wheatley, Institute of Management ISBN: 0-8594-6313-3

General Stress Management – Lay Reader

Don't Sweat the Small Stuff at Work, Richard Carson, Hodder & Stoughton ISBN: 0-340-74873-7

Conquer Your Stress, Cary Cooper and Stephen Palmer, IPD ISBN: 085292853X

Stress Free Living, Dr. Trevor Powell, Dorling Kindersley ISBN: 0-7513-0838-2

Thrive on Stress, Jan Sutton, How To Books ISBN: 1-85703-554-2

Work–Life Balance

Balancing Work and Life, Ben Renshaw and Robert Holden, Dorling Kindersley ISBN: 0-7513-3365-4

First Things First, Stephen R. Covey and A. Roger Merrill, Simon & Schuster ISBN: 0-671-71283-7

Relaxation

Calm at Work, Paul Wilson, Penguin Books ISBN: 0-14-026064-1
Calm for Life, Paul Wilson, Penguin Books ISBN: 0-14-028070-7
The Complete Guide to Relaxation Techniques, Jenny Sutcliffe, Headline ISBN 0-7472-0443-8

Resilience – Physical

The Exercise Bible: The Definitive Guide to Total Body Health and Well-Being, Joanna Hall, The Lyons Press ISBN 1-5922-8023-4
Fitness for Life Manual, Matt Roberts, Dorling Kindersley ISBN: 0-7513-3866-4
High Energy Habits, Bill Ford, Pocket Books ISBN: 0-7434-2894-3
On Form, Jim Loehr and Tony Schwartz, Nicholas Brealey ISBN: 1-85788-325-X
Office Yoga: At-your-desk exercises, Diana Fairechild, Flyana Rhyme ISBN: 1-89299740-1
Office Yoga, Darrin Zeer, Chronicle Books ISBN: 0-8118-2685-6

Resilience – Nutrition

Eating Well for Optimum Health, Dr. Andrew Weil, Little, Brown ISBN: 0-316-85479-4
The Food Bible, Judith Wills, Quadrille ISBN: 1-902757-36-X
Jane Clarke's Body Foods for Busy People, Jane Clarke, Quadrille ISBN: 1-84400-085-0

Resilience – Mental

Notes from a Friend, Anthony Robbins, Pocket Books ISBN: 0-7434-0937-X
Change Your Life in Seven Days, Paul McKenna, Bantam Press ISBN: 0-593-05055-X
How High Can You Bounce?, Roger Crawford, Vermillion ISBN: 0-09-181719-6
Shift Happens, Robert Holden, Hodder & Stoughton ISBN: 0-3407-1688-66
Unleash your True Potential (a CD which includes relaxation techniques), Glenn Harrold, Diviniti ISBN: 1-901923-38-X

Personal Understanding and Management

Body Language, Allan Pease, Sheldon Press ISBN: 0-85969-782-7
Feel the Fear and Do It Anyway, Susan Jeffers, Arrow Books ISBN: 0-09-974100-8
How to Win Friends and Influence People, Dale Carnegie, Pocket Books ISBN: 0-671-72365-0
Now, Discover Your Strengths, Marcus Buckingham and Donald O. Clifton, Simon & Schuster ISBN: 0-7432-0766-1
The 7 Habits of Highly Effective People, Stephen R. Covey, Simon & Schuster ISBN: 0-68485839-8
Working With Emotional Intelligence, Daniel Goleman, Bloomsbury ISBN: 0-7475-4384-4

Perspective and Inspiration

If This is a Man, Primo Levi, Abacus, Time Warner Books ISBN: 0-349-10013-6
Man's Search for Meaning, Viktor Frankl, Pocket Books ISBN: 0-671-02337-3
Successful But Something Missing, Ben Renshaw, Vermillion Books ISBN: 0-7126-7053-X
Together But Something Missing, Ben Renshaw, Vermillion Books ISBN: 0-0918 5593-4

Specific Stressors

Difficult Conversations, Douglas Stone, Bruce Patton and Sheila Heen, Penguin Books ISBN: 0-14-028852-X
Getting to Yes (2nd edn), Roger Fisher, William Ury and Bruce Patton, Random House, Penguin Books ISBN: 0-09-924842-5
How to Cope with Difficult People, Alan Houel, Sheldon Press ISBN: 0-85969-682-0

Websites

Whilst not exhaustive, this list provides a number of links and routes for finding out more about stress, health, and related business issues. Some of the sites will be useful to individual employees with health or personal difficulties; others are aimed at HR or OH professionals.

http://www.aa-uk.org.uk
Alcoholics Anonymous is a non-profit fellowship of recovering alcoholics who meet for mutual support. It utilizes a 12-step program to sobriety (tel: 0845 769 7555)

http://www.acas.org.uk
Advisory, Conciliation and Arbitration Service (ACAS) – for information on employment law, good management practices, and bullying and harassment at work

http://www.bacp.co.uk
The British Association for Counselling lists all trained and qualified counselors throughout the UK (tel: 0870 443 5252)

http://www.babcp.org.uk
The British Association for Behavioural and Cognitive Psychotherapies lists qualified psychotherapists throughout the UK (tel: 01254 875277)

http://www.thecalmzone.net/Home/index.php
CALM was set up to tackle stress and depression in young men, but anyone can use their confidential counseling helpline between 5 pm and 3 am (tel: 0800 58 58 58)

http://www.cancerbacup.org.uk
CancerBACUP provides cancer information, practical advice and support for cancer patients, their families and carers (tel: 0808 800 1234)

http://www.cipd.co.uk
Chartered Institute of Personnel and Development – a leading UK professional body in the field of personnel, training and development; it provides guidance on best practice and funding research.

http://www.crusebereavementcare.org.uk
Cruse Bereavement Care for anyone affected by bereavement (tel: 0870 167 1677)

http://www.direct.gov.uk/Homepage/fs/en
Directgov for practical information on death and bereavement

http://www.hse.gov.uk
Britain's Health and Safety Executive (HSE) – together with the Health and

Safety Commission – are responsible for the regulation of almost all risks to health and safety arising from work activity in Britain. Links to a myriad of information on managing stress at work and the Management Standards for stress

http://www.informationcommissioner.gov.uk
The information commissioner is an independent official appointed by the Crown to oversee the Data Protection Act 1998 and the Freedom of Information Act 2000. The Data Protection Act can be accessed in full from this website, and a simple factsheet can also be downloaded (helpline: 01625 545 745)

http://www.isma.org.uk
The International Stress Management Association UK is a registered charity with a multidisciplinary professional membership. It promotes sound knowledge and best practice in the prevention and reduction of human stress. It sets professional standards for the benefit of individuals and organizations using the services of its members

http://www.laughlab.co.uk
Laughlab is an online experiment to discover the world's funniest joke. Each month it releases the latest results, along with the best and worst jokes submitted so far

http://www.londonhealth.co.uk/cancerlink.asp
Cancer Link provides emotional support and information to cancer patients, their families and carers. It also produces a range of publications on cancer (tel: 0800 132 905)

http://www.mind.org.uk
MIND mental health charity information line (tel: 0845 766 0163)

http://www.mrdynamics.com
MR Dynamics has an online survey that will give people insight into how they approach the world and how to reduce stress. The 25-question, online survey can be accessed free of charge

http://www.ukna.org
Narcotics anonymous is a non-profit fellowship of recovering addicts who meet for mutual help. The core of the program is the 12 steps adapted from Alcoholics Anonymous (tel: 020 7730 0009)

http://www.nationaldebtline.org.uk
National Debt Line is a free, confidential telephone helpline for people with debt problems in England, Wales, and Scotland (tel: 0800 074 6918)

http://www.parentlineplus.org.uk
Parentline Plus offers support to anyone parenting a child (tel: 0808 800 2222)

http://www.quit.org.uk
Quitline for help with smoking cessation (tel: 0800 002 200)

http://www.relate.org.uk
Relate relationship counseling, courses and workshops (tel: 0845 130 4016)

http://www.sane.org.uk
Saneline offers information and advice on all aspects of mental health for individuals, family or friends (tel: 08457 678 000)

http://www.samaritans.org.uk
Samaritans – free, confidential counseling organization (tel: 08457 90 90 90)

http://www.TUC.org.uk
Trades Union Congress – for information on trade union representation, employee rights, bullying and harassment at work

http://www.DFEE.gov.uk/work-lifebalance
Work–life Balance Team, Department for Education and Employment – for downloadable documents on work–life balance, flexible working, mobile working, and virtual team working

References

Ballard, D. (2003) "Employers should not wait for victims of bullying to complain," *Financial Times*, 5 August, 16.

BBC News, (2004) "Police staff 'face high stress'," http://news.bbc.co.uk/go/pr/fr/-/1/hi/england/kent/3714943.stm, London, 14 May, accessed 21 August 2004.

Burton W.N., Conti D.J., Chin-Yu C. et al. (1999) "The role of the health risk factors and disease on worker productivity," *Journal of Occupational and Environmental Medicine* **41**(10): 863–77.

Businesshealth 2002 *A Direct Line to Action* – Businesshealth, www.BHGplc.com/BHweb/constructasp?mainurl=CaseStudies/intro.asp&L1=18.

Carnegie, D. (1982) *How to Win Friends and Influence People* (New York: Pocket Books).

Caulkin, S. (2003) "How to move beyond the pale: Companies are beginning to see that diversity pays," The *Observer*, 14 September, p. 9.

CCSU/Cabinet Office (2004) *Work Stress and Health: the Whitehall II Study* (London: Public and Commercial Services Union).

CIPD (2003) "Managing the Psychological Contract," CIPD Fact Sheet, May, www.cipd.co.uk/subjects/empreltns/psycontr.htm?, accessed 3 June 2004.

Collins, A. (2004) "Where they lead we will follow, The *Sunday Times* 100 Best Companies to Work For 2004," *Sunday Times*, 7 March.

Cooper, C.L. (2001) "What about the workers," *Sunday Times*, 29 April, pp. B2, E4.

Cooper, C.L., Cooper, R. and Eaker, L. (1988) *Living with Stress* (London: Penguin Books).

Covey, S.R. (1989) *The 7 Habits of Highly Effective People* (New York: Simon & Schuster).

Covey, S.R. (1992) *Principle-Centered Leadership* (London: Simon & Schuster) p. 122.

Department of Social Security (1998) *Stress-related Illness*, Report for Medical Policy Group, February.

Department of Social Security Corporate Medical Group (1998) Report for Medical Policy Group, February http://www.dwp.gov.uk/medical/sreport1.pdf.

Department of Work and Pensions (2004) "Job Retention and Rehabilitation Pilot: Employers' management of long-term sickness absence" (Corporate Document Services, Research Report 227, November).

Doke, D. (2004) "Happy Talking," *Occupational Health*, April, **56**(4): 14.

Earnshaw, J., and Cooper, C.L. (2001) *Stress and Employer Liability*, 2nd edn (London: CIPD).

Farmer, D. (1999) "Flow & Mihaly Csikszentmihalyi," 18 March www.austega.com/education/articles/flow.htm accessed August 2004.

Frankl, V.E. (1959) *Man's Search for Meaning* (New York: Simon & Schuster).

Friedman, M. and Ulmer, D. (1985) *Treating Type A Behaviour and Your Heart* (London: Michael Joseph).

Gardner, H. (1983) *Frames of Mind: The Theory of Multiple Intelligences* (New York: Basic Books).

Gardner, H. (2003) "Multiple Intelligences after Twenty Years," paper presented at the American Educational Research Association, Chicago Illinois, 21 April, pp. 4–5.

Gibb, F. (2002) "Curb on claims for job stress damages," *The Times*, 6 February, p. 6.

Goldman, J. and Lewis, J. (2003) "Stressful crimes," *Occupational Health*, October, **55**(10): 10.

Goleman, D. (1996) *Emotional Intelligence* (London: Bloomsbury).

Goleman, D. (1999) *Working With Emotional Intelligence* (London: Bloomsbury).

Great Place to Work Institute Inc. (2004a), "What do Employees Say?," www.greatplacetowork.com/great/employees.php.

Great Place to Work Institute UK (2004b), "Enhancing the Workplace Brings in Results," 2004. www.greatplacetowork.co.uk/great/results.php accessed 6 November.

Great Place to Work Institute Inc. (2004c), "Our Model," www.greatplacetowork.com/great/model.php, accessed 6 November.

Great Place to Work Institute Inc. 2004(d), "100 Best Companies to Work for in America," www.greatplacetowork.com/best/list-bestusa.htm, accessed 6 November.

Great Place to Work Institute Europe (2004e), "Flexible Working Hours Improve Among Europe's 100 Best Workplaces," http://resources.greatplacetowork.com/news/pdf/press_release_280404.pdf, accessed 5 November.

Hammonds, "Occupational health and stress," www.cipd.co.uk/EmploymentLaw/FAQ/_OHS/OHS.htm?, accessed 3 June 2004.

Health and Safety Executive (1995) *Stress at Work: A Guide for Employers* (Sudbury: HSE Books).

Health and Safety Executive (2001) *Tackling Work-related Stress: Manager's Guide to Improving & Maintaining Employee Health and Well-Being* (Sudbury: HSE Books).

Health and Safety Executive (2004) *Management Standards for Tackling Work-related Stress*, www.hse.gov.uk/stress/standards, accessed 6 November 2004.

Hoel H. and Cooper C.L. (2000) Destructive conflict and bullying at work, UMIST April www.le.ac.uk/unions/aut/umist1.pdf. accessed 24 March, 05.

Holman, D. (2003) "Phoning in sick? An overview of employee stress in call centres," *Leadership & Organization Development Journal*, **24**(3): 123.

Holmes, T.H. and Rahe, R.H. (1967) "The social readjustment rating scale," *Journal of Psychosomatic Research*, **11**: 213–18.

Hymowitz, C. and Silverman, R. (2001) "Stressed Out: Can Workplace Stress Get Worse?," *Wall Street Journal* (Eastern edition). New York 16 January, p. B.1.

Incomes Data Services (2002) *Stress Management*, IDS Study 732, July 2002.

International Labour Organization (2003) *Draft code of practice on violence and stress at work in services: A threat to productivity and decent work*. (Geneva: Geneva International Labour Organization.

Jaggi, R. (2004) "Work-related stress costs £7bn a year," *Financial Times*, 2 November, p. 2.

James, W. (1998) "Motivating People," in Humphries, J. *Managing Through People* (Oxford: How to Books), p. 37.

Kent, S. (2004) "When is enough, enough?," *Personnel Today*, 15 June, pp. 17–18.

Keogh, O. (2003) "Juggle work and life for greater profits," *Sunday Times*, 19 October, p. 16.

Kodz, J., Davis, S., Lain, D. et al. (2003) "Working Long Hours: a Review of the Evidence: Volume 1 – Main Report," *Institute for Employment Studies* online, www.employment-studies.co.uk/summary/summary.php?id=errs16, accessed 2 April 2004.

Kodz, J., Harper, H., Dench, S. (2002) "Work–Life Balance, Beyond the Rhetoric," IES Report 384, *Institute for Employment Studies* online, www.employment-studies.co.uk/summary/summary.php?id=384, accessed 2 April 2004.

Mail on Sunday (2004) "Teachers in claims for £50m over stress," *Mail on Sunday*, 29 August.

Management Today (2002) "Balancing Acts," *Management Today*, 30 September, p. 52.

McClelland, D. (1961) *The Achieving Society* (New Jersey: Van Nostrand).

Melhuish, A. (1978) *Executive Health* (London: Business Books).

Millar, M. (2004) "Paramedics are the most stressed out," *Personnel Today*, 15 June, p. 2.

MindTools 1 (2004) "What Stress is – Definitions," www.mindtools.com/stress/UnderstandingStress, accessed 28 July.

MindTools 2 (2004) "What Stress is – The Underlying Mechanisms …," www.mindtools.com/stress/UnderstandingStress/StressMechanisms.htm, accessed 28 July.

Mordue, C. (2002) "Guide to stress management policy," *Personnel Today*, 9 July.

Occupational Safety and Health Service (2003) *Healthy Work: Managing Stress in the Workplace* (Wellington, New Zealand: Department of Labour).

Paton, N. (2003) "Stressing the Positive," *Personnel Today*, 21 October, p. 57.

Paton, N. (2004) "Getting Back to Business," *Occupational Health*, **56**(7): 16.

Personnel Today (2003) "Special Report: working time opt-out," 21 January.

Personnel Today and HSE (2003) "Stress in the UK Workplace," October.

Pettit, L. (2003) "Who's the most stressed of all?," *Personnel Today*, 21 October.

Pollard, J. (2000) "Work: 'Please sir, you're a bully.' More than half of our teachers want to leave the job – that's hardly surprising when one in six has been bullied," *Observer*, 2 April, p. 20.

Pollock, E.J. (1998) "Getting Ahead: It's getting STRESSFUL!!! on the Job," *Wall Street Journal* (Eastern edition), 20 October, p. B1.

Rajan, A. (2003) "Harnessing Workforce Diversity to Raise the Bottom Line," www.create-research.co.uk.

Reade, Q. (2004) "New technology causing stress among office staff," *Personnel Today*, 15 June, p. 9.

Robertson, I. and Cooper, C.L. (2004) "Premiership of pressure – Britain's most stressful jobs," Robertson Cooper Limited, www.robertsoncooper.com/pdf/stressfuljobs, accessed June 2004.

Rubens, P. (2004) "When the work–life balance becomes a see-saw," *BBC News Magazine,* http:/newsvote.bbc.co.uk/mpapps/pagetools/print/news.bbc.co.uk/1/hi/magazine/370, accessed 11 May 2004.

Schabracq, M. and Cooper, C.L. (2000) "The changing nature of work and stress," *Journal of Managerial Psychology,* **15**(3): 227.

Seward, K. and Faby, S. (2003) "Stress surprises," *Occupational Health*, September, **55**(9): 12.

Skolnik, A. (2004) "Politics of Family Structure," Markala Center for Applied Ethics, www.scu.edu/ethics/publications/other/lawreview/familystructure.html.

Sparks, K. and Cooper, C.L. (1999) "Occupational differences in the work-strain relationships: Towards the use of situation-specific models," *Journal of Occupational & Organizational Psychology,* June, **72**(2): 2.

Sumner, S. (2004) http://www.hse.gov.uk/press/2004/c04046.htm, HSC press release C046:04 – 3 November 2004.

Sunday Times (2004) "100 Best Companies to Work For 2004," *Sunday Times,* 7 March.

Sutherland, V.J. and Cooper, C.L. (2000) *Strategic Stress Management: an Organisational Approach* (Basingstoke: Macmillan – now Palgrave Macmillan).

Thomson, L., Neathey, F. and Rick, J. (2003) "Best practice in rehabilitating employees following absence due to work-related stress," www.hse.gov.uk/research/rrpdf/rr138.pdf.

Trapp, R. (2004) "A life's work," *People Management*, **10**(9): 38–9.

Trigaux, R. (2002) "In weak economy, stress strong," *St Petersburg Times Online*, 30 October, www.sptimes.com, accessed 26 July 2004.

UCL, *Managing Stress at Work*, University College London, www.ucl.ac.uk/hr/docs/stress.php, accessed 23 July 2004.

Verret, C. (2000) "Generation Y: Motivating and Training a New Generation of Employees," www.hotel-online.com/Trends/CaroleVerret/GenerationY-Nov2000 accessed 6 November, 2004.

Warner, J. (2002) "Mental Stress, Physical Illness, Ready to Blow?," *WebMD Medical News*, 12 August, http://content.health.msn.com, accessed 10 January 2005.

Weymes, E. (2003) "Relationships not leadership sustain successful organisations," *Journal of Change Management,* London, May, **3**(4): 319.

Wigham, R. (2003a) "HSE launches new guidelines on managing stress among workers," *Personnel Today,* 4 November.

Wigham, R. (2003b) "Met to launch stress audit among 10,000 employees," *Personnel Today,* 21 October.

Williams, S. and Cooper, L. (2002) *Managing Workplace Stress* (Chichester: John Wiley & Sons, CBI), p. xiv.

Williamson, M. (1996) *A Return to Love* (London: Thorsons).

Woolf, M. (2004) "Stressed out? Try being a fortysomething female nurse or teacher (with a male boss)," The *Independent*, 11 August.

Woolnough, R. (2004) "The New Space Age," *Personnel Today*, 20 January, pp. 18–19.

Wray, R. (2004) "MCA Awards 2004: Highlighting Best Practice in Management Consultancy: Operational Performance Bronze Award PA Consulting Group: Client GCHQ," *Guardian*, 19 February, p. 13.

Index